Patent Strategy

FOR RESEARCHERS AND
RESEARCH MANAGERS

Second Edition

Patent Strategy

FOR RESEARCHERS AND RESEARCH MANAGERS

Second Edition

H. Jackson Knight
E. I. du Pont de Nemours & Company, Inc.
Virginia, USA

JOHN WILEY & SONS, LTD

Chichester · New York · Weinheim · Brisbane · Singapore · Toronto

Email (for orders and customer service enquiries): cs-books@wiley.co.uk
Visit our Home Page www.wileyeurope.com or www.wiley.com

Reprinted December 2001, August 2002, February 2004

Other Wiley Editorial Offices

John Wiley & Sons Inc., 111 River Street, Hoboken, NJ 07030, USA

Jossey-Bass, 989 Market Street, San Francisco, CA 94103-1741, USA

Wiley-VCH Verlag GmbH, Boschstr. 12, D-69469 Weinheim, Germany

John Wiley & Sons Australia Ltd, 33 Park Road, Milton, Queensland 4064, Australia

John Wiley & Sons (Asia) Pte Ltd, 2 Clementi Loop #02-01, Jin Xing Distripark, Singapore 129809

John Wiley & Sons (Canada) Ltd, 22 Worcester Road, Etobicoke, Ontario M9W 1L1

Wiley also publishes its books in a variety of electronic formats. Some content that appears in print may not be available in electronic books.

Library of Congress Cataloging-in-Publication Data

Knight, H. Jackson.
 Patent strategy for researchers and research managers / H. Jackson Knight. – 2nd ed.
  p. cm.
 Includes bibliographical references and index.
 ISBN 0–471–49260–4 (alk. paper) – ISBN 0–471–49261–2 (pbk. : alk. paper)
  1. Patent laws and legislation–United States–Popular works. I. Title.
 KF3120.Z9 K58 2001
 346.7304´86–dc21

                                                                00–067213

British Library Cataloguing in Publication Data

A catalogue record for this book is available from the British Library

ISBN 0–471–49260–4 (cloth)
   0–471–49261–2 (paper)

Typeset in 10/12pt Times by Acorn Bookwork, Salisbury, Wilts
Printed and bound in Great Britain by Biddles Ltd, King's Lynn, Norfolk
This book is printed on acid-free paper responsibly manufactured from sustainable forestation, for which at least two trees are planted for each one used for paper production.

To Joy...

whose love and patience make all things possible

Contents

Preface

Since the first publication of this book, the world of intellectual property has taken center stage around the world as countries realize the value of having consistent and enforceable patent systems and as companies and inventors attempt to obtain patents globally which are vital to their business. There have been changes throughout the spectrum of the intellectual property world. The harmonization of patent laws and practices has continued. Countries have had to deal with patent issues concerning such things as software and biotechnology, two fields where much was previously unpatentable. The internet has made the acquisition of technology and copies of patent publications a simple matter; both are available to the most remote and independent type of inventor. Much has been written on maximizing the return from the patents a company owns. Emphasis has been placed on making sure one audits the patents they have, licensing any patents which can provide additional revenue, and finally making sure that one obtains some type of patent protection on their business methods which utilize computers.

Regardless of the technology, all potential inventors need a good foundation of understanding of the patenting system, and this is what this book attempts to provide. This book is not meant to be an advanced text of all the possible strategies available to an inventor or a company. It remains a basic guide for the inventor; a source of information to read and then keep for further reference. College students should find this information very valuable because rarely are they exposed to patents until they have earned their degree. Patent agents and attorneys may find some new ideas in this book, however, the primary use for this book is as a guidebook for their clients.

One issue that was perhaps underemphasized in the first edition was that the information contained in this book applies to all types of inventors. Much of the information will be readily applicable to inventors in corporate technical organizations. Despite the fact that the author also has a background in a corporate technical organization, independent inventors and academic inventors will also obtain benefit from a study of the information in this book. The concepts expressed here are applicable widely across many different types of products and patent types.

My intent with the first edition of this book was to write a book which needed very little updating, and in many respects that was accomplished. However, there has been a constant flux in the patent law over the past few years so some changes are now necessary. The book still retains its general tone; this is not an in-depth guide of all of the quirks of the latest patent law changes, but rather an overview of tools one can use while working with a patent attorney or agent.

Chapter 1 on Basic Intellectual Property Concepts has been updated to include some of the major new changes in patent laws and additional clarifying information on basic concepts and international treaties. New concepts have been added on the informational value of patents in Chapter 2 on The Value of Patents. Some additional strategy techniques have been added to Chapter 3 on Developing a Strategy.

From a book construction standpoint, a major change in this book is a reorganization and streamlining of the remaining chapters to eliminate duplication that was present in the original book. New sections were added throughout these chapters also. Chapter 4 on Researching with Intellectual Property in Mind has been expanded to include more information on how proficient inventors get ideas and invent. A new Chapter 5 on Infringement and Freedom to Operate adds important information to better help one understand this important facet of intellectual property. The remaining chapters were also updated and clarified throughout. Additional information was included in the Reference sections at the end of the book along with a new index.

I have many new friends because of this book, and I am grateful for the many kind words that have been said. I want to thank my supervisor Paul Pearlman for his support of this second edition. I remain indebted to all the attorneys I have worked with throughout my career, and I believe I have learned something from all of them. However, I want especially to thank Robert Shafer for his help and advice with all types of intellectual property matters. I wish him the best as he starts his well-deserved retirement later this year.

H. J. Knight
Midlothian, Virginia
October 1, 2000

Preface to the First Edition

When I told a friend of mine, a patent lawyer, that I wanted to write a book on patent strategy, he gave me a quizzical look and said, 'That's quite a task. You could write several volumes and still not cover it all.' And right he was. From a legal standpoint, each patent application is different, so the strategy developed for each application is different. So, any book on patent strategy must both limit and focus the content for a particular audience.

The purpose of this book is to introduce the technical professional to strategic thinking as applied to patent applications and patent portfolios. An additional purpose is to introduce intellectual property concepts to the researcher to enable the researcher to work successfully with attorneys in the development of patent applications. This book will help both researchers and research managers understand how better patents can be obtained for inventions, and how to develop an entire portfolio of patents to protect intellectual properties.

My goal is to present these ideas and techniques in a straightforward manner with as little 'legalese' as possible. However, patents are legal documents, and you can never remove all of the legal terms and concepts from a discussion of patents. I will also attempt to provide global patent information which will be useful to the average researcher, while not attempting to provide all the details a researcher may need in dealing with patents. To do so would be an impossible task.

Since I was once a researcher and I work with researchers every day, I realize that 'working on patents' is not what most researchers want to do. Typically, it requires a fair amount of writing, performing experiments only for the sake of the patent application, and working with attorneys and 'legalese', none of which sound appealing to a researcher. Still, patents can provide a business with a competitive advantage and can help improve the professional standing of the inventor. While most researchers feel confident with the technical content of patents, most successful researchers at some point in their career must also deal with the much less comfortable legal aspects of patents.

Whether you are in academia or industry, this book will help you understand patents and the patenting process from a different perspective than 'patent law' books. This book deals less with the specifics of the law, and instead attempts to lead the researchers to a higher conceptual plane to review some of the philosophical and practical concepts which result because of the patent laws. In so doing, I hope to help you understand how attorneys and intellectual property professionals tend to look at patents, and help you understand such things as why your invention ends up being described the way it is in a patent application.

Another purpose of this book is to identify how to develop a strategy for preparing the best possible patent applications, obtaining the best possible patents, and generating the best possible patent portfolio for your business. As you will see in the following chapters, a strategy can be developed either very narrowly, such as to address the very specific issues in a single patent application, or can be developed broadly for an entire business.

If you are employed by a large industrial company which has both intellectual property specialists, or patent liaisons, in addition to patent attorneys or agents, you can also benefit from this book. These specialists are normally technically trained professionals, employed to work with both inventors and the patent attorneys to coordinate the filing of patent applications. While their role can vary with differing organizations, intellectual property specialists typically provide information to help determine whether or not researchers have made patentable inventions and make sure the business implications of patents are being adequately addressed in the preparation of patent applications. Although most intellectual property specialists and patent liaisons should already be familiar with the concepts in this book, they will never understand an invention as well as the inventor. If inventors can learn just a few concepts of basic patent strategy, they can dramatically impact the patents which are filed on their inventions. Unfortunately, because most researchers and research managers do not work with patents on a routine basis, they normally don't have an opportunity to develop an expertise in patent strategy and many times major mistakes are made, resulting in a company obtaining far less legal protection than could have been obtained.

If you do not have the benefit of company patent specialists, then you will need to take on more responsibility and play an even more important role in the patenting process. This book will provide you with the basic concepts of patent strategy to help you obtain the best possible protection for your intellectual property.

Chapter 1 deals with basic concepts of intellectual property. While this book is not a patent law book, the researcher does need to know certain basic concepts in order to fully use this book. This chapter is designed to provide a foundation on basic patent law concepts on which to build the rest of the book. Since this is not a patent law book, the topics are covered fairly briefly; I encourage the reader to obtain some of the other references listed at the end of the book which will provide more detailed patent law information.

Chapter 2 discusses the reasons to obtain patents and introduces strategic thinking as applied to patents. Chapter 3 continues this process by defining what is meant by the word strategy and outlining the issues one should consider in developing a strategy for a business or a particular patent application. Chapter 4 extends the strategic thinking process, introducing global patent issues which should be considered by researchers and research managers.

Chapter 5 discusses how inventors invent and how the researcher can approach his research to obtain the best possible patent. Chapter 6 reviews what researchers should expect when working with attorneys, agents, and other patent professionals, and what responsibilities the researcher has with respect to the preparation of the patent application.

The last two chapters deal with issues that arise after the research is complete. If your invention isn't patentable, you must decide whether to disclose the work you have completed, or keep it secret. Chapter 7 reviews issues to consider when making these decisions. Also, during the patent examining process in the patent office, the legal description of your invention can change, therefore perhaps changing the value of your patent. Chapter 8 discusses the responsibilities of the researcher after patent applications have been filed and the role the researcher can play in the maintenance of a global patent estate. Finally, the references used in the preparation of this book and references for further reading are included at the end of the book.

A few formalities should be mentioned. While masculine pronouns are used throughout, this is done only out of convenience and no slight is intended toward women in any way whatsoever; also, the generic term patent agent has been used throughout, recognizing a patent agent may or may not be an attorney of law. In those cases where a patent attorney is truly needed, I have tried to point that out; otherwise, for the purposes of this book the terms agent and attorney should be interchangeable. Finally, while I have tried to present the concepts in a complete manner, I find there is always an exception when one discusses anything dealing with law. Therefore, any description of the concepts will be lacking in some manner or may not hold under some circumstance. The concepts included here are to help focus the thoughts of a researcher in an area the researcher has not normally considered; in so doing, some concepts have been simplified. While this book will be helpful in introducing new concepts, in the final analysis, the researcher or research manager should rely on their own patent attorney or agent for advice in their particular situation. This book is not a substitute for professional patent and intellectual property help.

My own troubles in developing patent strategy as an intellectual property professional led to this book. As a patent specialist, I wanted a guidebook to help me establish patent strategy, but I found little in the open literature.

I also wanted to help educate researchers, because I found most researchers were interested, but they lacked sufficient knowledge to establish a strategy themselves. My thoughts are contained in this book. As a chemical engineer, they pertain to, in general, the chemical industry, however, they should have value in other industries. I hope you find them useful.

I am greatly indebted to my wife Joy for her support during the writing of this book. She sacrificed her time and activities to tend to our family on many a weekend and weeknight so that I could barricade myself in front of my computer. I thank her from the bottom of my heart.

I would also like to thank my current supervisor at E.I. du Pont de Nemours & Company, Inc., Roger Hailstone; and my former supervisor, Bob DiLuccio, for their support of me and my efforts in the writing of this book. In addition, I'd like to specifically thank my co-worker Bob Shellenbarger for his help in proofreading the document.

In addition, I have been fortunate to work with many outstanding people that I wish to thank. These include the current and former members of the DuPont Fibers' Intellectual Property Management Group, especially my mentor Carl Bostic, now retired, who helped me to get started in intellectual property work. I would also like to thank company attorney Bob Shafer for his legal advice and help in all sorts of patent matters, and his attempts to help me understand the true value of patents; I also thank him for his comments in proofreading the document.

H.J. Knight
Midlothian, Virginia
April 29, 1995

About the Author

H. Jackson Knight is a Patent Associate with the E.I. DuPont de Nemours & Company, Inc., where he has experience in many different phases of technology development, including process engineering and operation, research and development, and applications research. He has been working in patent matters for over fifteen years and is registered to practice before the United States Patent and Trademark Office. He received a Bachelor of Science degree in Chemical Engineering from Auburn University in 1982 and a Masters of Engineering degree in Chemical Engineering from the University of Virginia in 1994. Currently he is the Intellectual Property Group Team Leader responsible for managing intellectual property for Dupont's Advanced Fibers Systems and DuPont Personal Protection businesses.

1 Basic Intellectual Property Concepts

INTRODUCTION

To develop a patent strategy, a researcher or a research manager must be familiar with certain intellectual property concepts, and this chapter is designed to provide that intellectual property foundation. As stated in the preface, this book is not a 'patent law' book. There are many 'patent law' books on the market and many continuing education courses which teach patent law fundamentals. This book will attempt to provide the researcher or research manager with the minimum information required to help develop an intellectual property or patent strategy with a patent professional. Patent professionals – patent attorneys and patent agents, which prepare, file, and prosecute patent applications; patent liaisons, which coordinate patent filings in larger companies; and information specialists, which search the prior art – all play an important part in the development of the overall strategy of a business. The researcher's exact involvement with these professionals will depend in great part on whether or not the inventor is a private researcher or an employee of a large corporation.

In any case, this chapter on basic intellectual property concepts is not complete, and the researcher will still need to rely on professionals for help with patent law matters. There are three reasons for this. First of all, it is impossible to cover all aspects of global patent law in one chapter. The second reason is that, while one can develop and implement a patent strategy, should there be a need to interpret patents legally, the best person to provide guidance in patent law and negotiate the legal realm is a good patent attorney. Finally, laws are not like fundamental scientific principles; they are at the mercy of governments and laws change, sometimes dramatically. Again, a patent agent or attorney should be able to keep up with these changes and advise how they impact research work. There are no better examples of the need for the help of a knowledgeable patent attorney or agent than the recent developments in high growth areas like biotechnology, software, business methods, and the internet. Change is occurring in these areas at a high rate, not only in the generation of inventions, but also in the methods by which these inventions are protected. Over the last few years countries around the world have had a constant flow of new laws affecting the patentability of inventions in these areas. Patent offices have also had a steady stream of new guidelines, rules, and regulations affecting patent applications in these same areas. Only a patent attorney or agent can possibly keep up with all of these changes. A researcher can get an idea of the extent of the changes by looking to the internet. A quick check of intellectual property pages will reveal the massive number of new issues involved in these technology areas. It is hoped that the information presented here will be of a basic nature, so that it will not appreciably change in the near future. Where possible, potential changes in the patent law will be pointed out so that the researcher will be able to anticipate and ask a patent professional about them.

BASIC PATENT LAW CONCEPTS

A patent is a legal grant by a government. Governments establish patent systems and grant patents to encourage innovation, technical development, and ultimately economic prosperity. The terms of the grant are quite simple; in return for disclosing an invention publicly so that others can learn from it, and paying the processing fees, the government of the country will grant the inventor of the invention the right to exclude others from making, using, or selling the invention for a limited period of time.

The first and most fundamental concept to learn about patents is that patents do not give the patent owner the right to practice the invention claimed in the patent, but only to exclude others from practicing this invention. The patent owner may only practice his invention as long as it, or any part of it, is not covered in a valid patent by someone else.

For example, say a researcher hears about a new ceramic material which has been developed, and for illustration purposes, let's say the ceramic material has the chemical name of 'X'. Further, let's say the researcher's commercial interest in this ceramic is in coffee mugs, because when a coffee mug is made from 'X', the coffee can be kept hot indefinitely. The researcher obtains a patent in many different countries having the following claim:

1. A container for keeping hot liquids hot, comprised of the ceramic 'X'.

The practical result of the research obtaining this claim is that in those countries where he has obtained a patent, he can theoretically stop another person or company from making or selling any kind of container made from 'X'. (The word 'theoretically' is used, because the researcher will have to enforce his patent by taking the infringer to court; the court will determine whether or not the patent is valid and infringed.) The claim, however, does not give the researcher the right to make or sell containers containing 'X'. The researcher can legally make or sell containers containing 'X' only if in so doing he doesn't infringe a patent held by another. If the inventor of the ceramic 'X' has a patent, say with claims like:

1. A ceramic comprised of 'X'.

The researcher will infringe the ceramic inventor's patent if the researcher makes his own ceramic when he makes his coffee mugs. The inventor's patent is said to dominate the researcher's patent, and if the researcher wants to make coffee mugs using the ceramic, he will need to work out some arrangement with the inventor of the ceramic.

The second basic concept to understand is that a patent is only effective in the country of issue, and legal concepts and questions about 'What is patentable?' and 'What constitutes a valid patent?' can be interpreted differently in different countries. Since patents are grants from the governments of countries and all countries are different, then it follows that patent laws will be different in every country around the world. However, countries have realized that cooperative treaties which allow inventors to file patents easily are beneficial in that they provide additional revenue in the form of patent fees, and strong cooperative intellectual property laws provide incentive for businesses to invest in these countries. These cooperative treaties have harmonized some of the basic procedures and requirements for obtaining patents from country to country, although substantial differences still remain from country to country in the actual patent law.

PATENT OFFICE OPERATIONS

Countries set up patent offices to handle the processing of patent applications and the granting of patents. As one might expect, each patent office will have its own rules, regulations, and procedures. While some disputes may be resolved within the individual patent offices, in general, any unresolved dispute will ultimately be settled in the court system of the country.

Although the patent offices of different countries have different procedures, the basic steps taken to obtain a patent are fairly uniform. Assuming a researcher has made an invention, the researcher has a patent agent prepare a patent application and send the patent application to a patent office (that is, 'file' the patent application), along with any required filing fees. Depending on the country, the patent office will take one of three actions. The patent office will either (1) start immediately to process the application for patentability, for example, start the examination of the application; or (2) essentially hold the application and wait for the applicant to tell the patent office to examine the application; or (3) register the application without examination. In this last group of 'registration' countries, there is no examination of applications; the validity of the patent remains undecided until the patent owner attempts to exert the patent against another, at which time a court will decide whether or not the patent is valid and infringed. For now, let's assume the country in which the application is filed is in an examination country and examination is either automatic or the researcher's agent has asked for examination.

The examination is made by a patent examiner, which is typically a technically trained individual with knowledge of what has been patented in a particular area of technology and the formal governmental requirements for obtaining a patent. The patent examiner will look to see whether or not the application complies with all of the formal regulations and procedures and meets the requirements for the patent grant. If the application meets these requirements, the examiner will allow the application, that is, send the agent a notice stating that the patent may be granted if the applicant is willing to pay the issue fee. However, if the examiner is not convinced he will send the agent a rejection notice – a written response called an office action. The office action will state why the application has been rejected, and the examiner may make suggestions as to what is required to correct the flaws in the patent application.

The applicant or his agent then has a period of time to respond to the office action, and put forward either (1) changes in how the invention is claimed, which will address the concerns of the examiner in the form of amendments to the application; or (2) reasons why the examiner has erred and has not considered or interpreted the application properly, or (3) additions or corrections to address formal problems in the application, that is, problems not associated with the patentability of the invention, but the patent application itself, such as appropriate drawings. The applicant's response may or may not convince the examiner, and several office actions and responses may be exchanged between the applicant and the examiner before the patent is allowed.

The applicant may eventually receive a 'final rejection' from the examiner, which means that the examiner does not think the invention is patentable and intends to close prosecution on the application. Normally, the applicant has one final shot at convincing the examiner after a final rejection. If the applicant does not succeed in convincing the examiner, the applicant can either give up, refile the application with changes which improve the patentability of the invention, or appeal the examiner's ruling to a higher authority in either the patent office or the country courts. If an appeal is made, this essentially starts another round of negotiations with a new set of governmental eyes.

If the patent application is allowed during any of these stages, the applicant will be required to pay a fee to have the patent issue; however, the procedure to actually grant or issue the patent will vary from country to country. The patent can issue without public review as in the United States; or the patent may be provisionally granted pending a public review period, as is done in the European Patent Office and Japan. If a public review period is offered, a copy of the patent application and the allowed claims are made available to the public, and those that do not think the invention claimed is patentable can oppose the patent grant. This is typically done by filing, within the review period, an opposition document which contains reasons as to why the patent should not issue. If an opposition to the grant is filed, then the patent applicant is given a period of time to answer the assertions of the opposer, and an appeal is usually possible if the opposer prevails and the patent is not granted. Depending on the strength of the opposition, the patent may not issue, may issue with modified claims, or may issue with the original claims.

After the issuance fee is paid and the patent has issued, the applicant will normally be required to make additional payments, called maintenance fees, to the country's government. These fees are paid during the term of the patent to maintain the patent in force. If the fees are not paid, the patent will lapse in that country and the technology claimed will be in the public domain, which means that anyone can now use that invention in that country. Governments, for the sake of economic development, want as much technology in the public domain as possible, so they encourage the abandonment of patents by increasing the amount of the maintenance fees as time goes by. In many countries, the maintenance fee amount due is also dependent on the number of claims that have been granted. A patent having 40 claims would be much more expensive throughout its life than a patent having just three claims. As a result, maintenance fees in the last few years of the patent term can be very costly because of the combination of the fee increase based on the age of the patent and the multiplier based on the number of claims.

To disseminate information about new inventions, most countries require filed patent applications to be published automatically, regardless of the patentability of the invention, 18 months after the first filing of the application. Until just recently, the United States was the most notable country which did not publish filed applications; it only published granted patents.

This meant a patent application filed in the United States which was deemed not patentable did not ever need to be disclosed publicly. The applicant had the choice as to whether or not to keep the invention secret. It also resulted in what were called 'submarine' patents – patents which issued on applications that took many years to examine. These patent applications were called this because the content of the application would remain secret, lurking in the patent office for a number of years, only for the patent to issue without a warning like a submarine rising out of the water. If the time from the filing to the issuance for a patent was a significant period, say 10 to 20 years or more, others without any knowledge of the patent application might independently develop similar technology during the examination period. Many found that after the issuance of a submarine patent, they had to license their independently developed technology from the submarine patent holder or change to a different technology.

The impact of submarine patents has been lessened by changes to the laws in the United States. The first law change took effect in 1995. It changed the rules concerning patent term and refiled applications, which meant that now the applicant has a major disadvantage in purposely delaying a patent application in the patent office. This is more fully discussed later in this chapter (See The Term of a Patent). The second new law to impact submarine patents provides for the publication of US applications. Beginning in late 2000, all patent applications filed in the United States which will also be filed in a foreign country will have to be published 18 months after the priority filing. Publication of the application is not required, however, if the application will only be filed in the United States and will not be filed in a foreign country. The new law also gives the patent applicant the opportunity to have the patent application published early if either the publication of the application or provisional protection is wanted.

REQUIREMENTS FOR OBTAINING A PATENT

The first requirement to obtain a patent is that the invention be 'new'. 'New' is interpreted differently in different countries, but there are some general guidelines which are useful. As one might think, 'new' means the invention has not been known before. In most cases, this means there has been no written public record of the invention, and no public disclosure of the invention. Many countries in the world are 'absolute novelty' countries, the word 'new' and 'novel' being used interchangeably. That is, any public disclosure, written or otherwise, before the filing of the patent application will prevent an inventor from obtaining a valid patent on his invention. Note that the inventor may still be able to obtain a patent on the invention, but the patent might be shown to be invalid if ever challenged in court. If an invention is disclosed at a trade show and then a patent application on the invention is filed the next day, a patent may issue. However, if someone saw the invention at the trade show, this knowledge could be used to invalidate the patent in an absolute novelty country. Some countries require 'absolute novelty' only within their borders. That is, a simple disclosure of the invention (but generally not a publication) outside the country may not hurt the novelty of the invention.

There are ways to avoid forfeiting rights to a valid patent. In most countries of the world, if the inventor wants to show his invention to another company or individual, the inventor can get the other party to sign a non-disclosure or confidentially agreement, which enables the inventor to continue to operate in secret and retain patent rights. The United States is different from most countries in that the applicant is given a grace period to determine whether the invention is of value. The applicant can disclose his invention publicly, and then has one year to file a patent application on the invention. However, note that by disclosing the invention publicly, the inventor loses patent rights in most of the other 'absolute novelty' countries of the world. Therefore, even inventors in the United States utilize non-disclosure agreements to retain patent rights.

The second requirement to obtain a patent is that the invention be useful. In some countries this usefulness is a requirement that the invention have some sort of industrial utility. At one time, patent applications were rarely rejected because the inventions were not useful. Almost anything was useful, and normally the things examiners rejected for usefulness were inventions which did not seem as though they would perform as stated in the application. Perpetual motion machines were commonly cited inventions which were not 'useful' because perpetual motion is not possible.

However, in many countries the invention must have what is called industrial utility. That is, it must have some industrial use or value. In the United States, recent court rulings have raised the bar for usefulness. The words used by some to describe this higher standard are 'substantial utility' or 'practical utility'.

This has most recently been applied to patents dealing with advances in genetic technology; the whole issue of utility has taken on what appears to be even more stringent requirements in this area. Many patent offices worldwide now require that patents on certain genetic material have 'real-world' utility, a clearly expressed use. From a practical standpoint, this means that one is better off if, in the patent application, an example is included which actually illustrates the utility of the invention. This helps avoid being saddled with what many call an alleged use or 'throw-away' utility which may happen if one simply lists some possible uses for a genetic invention.

The third requirement to obtain a patent is that the invention must not be, in the opinion of the examiner, an obvious extension of previous inventions or technology. In some countries, the invention is required to be a 'technical advance' over the prior art. This third requirement is the most hotly debated requirement in the prosecution of a patent application. The examiner will consider whether what is claimed as the invention is suggested by prior patents or whether an individual skilled in the technology area would logically develop the invention based on reading the closest prior art. The examiner might also consider the invention as a normal optimization of some other technology. Many times the issuance of a patent hinges on the applicant's response to an 'obviousness' rejection by the patent examiner. The formulation of this response is where patent agents quickly earn their fees, since in many cases, it can be very difficult to generate a response which convinces the examiner an invention is not obvious.

A fourth requirement to obtain a patent is a patent application must be prepared that has a specific form and specific sections. While each country has its own requirements, normally the patent application will have (1) a list of claims which legally describe the invention for which a patent is desired; (2) supporting information for the invention, normally called a specification, including written examples if needed; (3) drawings of the invention, if these are required for someone to understand the invention; and (4) some declaration of ownership of the invention. Some countries require the actual inventors be identified, others require that only the patent owner, or patent assignee, be identified. Some countries, like the United States, require disclosure to the patent office of the closest prior art known to the applicant, and any pertinent information relating to disclosures which might impact the validity of the patent. Most countries do not have this disclosure requirement.

A fifth requirement is that the applicant must pay fees. This is becoming a very important consideration, because countries have figured out that they can increase their revenue by increasing the amount and the type of required patent fees. Normally, a fee is required to file the application, and a fee is required to have the patent issue. In addition, in most countries of the world, maintenance fees are required on a regular basis throughout the term of the patent or patent application to keep the patent in force or the application pending. While the fees for one country may not be prohibitively expensive, if the application is filed globally, a single invention can quickly generate a tremendous patent bill even before the cost of special patent agents, translations, and other ancillary requirements are added.

Other Requirements

In addition to these requirements, each individual country may have other requirements. One of the more important requirements in the United States is a commercial use bar; that is, an inventor has a one year grace period to file a patent application after a product is on sale, regardless of any confidentiality agreements. Note the commercial use bar starts at the offer for sale, not the actual sale; it would apply if an offer for sale occurred and no sale was made. The bar also applies to processes and machines used to make that product. So, if an offer for sale is made and more than a year passes, the inventor is barred from obtaining a valid patent on either the product or the process used to manufacture that product, or a machine used in that process. Clearly, the idea is that no one should be able delay the patenting of their commercial invention past a reasonable length of time. Most other countries do not have such a commercial use bar, however, many of them have more stringent novelty requirements such as absolute novelty or shorter periods of time the invention can be in the public domain before the patent application is filed.

TYPES OF PATENTS

Utility Patents

When most people talk about patents, they are referring to utility patents, and in this book, we will concentrate on utility patents. These have been traditionally viewed as patents on new machines, new compositions of matter, new manufactures, or new methods or processes of making machines, compositions of matter or manufactures. A 'machine' is normally thought of as a mechanical invention having moving parts, while a 'manufacture' is normally considered a mechanical invention having no moving parts, such as a hammer or screwdriver. 'Compositions of matter' are normally new chemicals, polymers, and the like.

In addition to these traditional types of patents, computers and advanced electronics have ushered in patents on the measurement and control of processes where the software is a major element in the invention. While copyrights have been used in an attempt to protect computer code in Europe and the United States, patents offer greater protection in that they cover the concept expressed in the code, not just the code itself. While the validity of these inventions is being debated, some countries have established some criteria that computer-oriented inventions must pass.

For many years in the United States the official position was that a procedure for solving a mathematical problem, or an algorithm, could not be patented. However, a process having several steps which used an algorithm as one step might be patentable if the process recited a statutory process if viewed without the algorithm. Recently however, an important ruling *(State Street Bank & Trust v. Signature Financial Group, Inc.)* by the Federal Circuit Court of Appeals (CAFC) determined that the practical application of a mathematical algorithm to make a tangible and concrete result, even if it involved the abstract transformation of data as in monetary transactions, is patentable subject matter in the United States. The same ruling eliminated a general restriction on software patents related to a business method. Previously, such business method inventions were not patentable. The result of the decision is that many types of software inventions are patentable and worthy of protection.

The number of applications filed and patents granted on software-related inventions has increased enormously, and clearly numerous court challenges have been and will continue to be initiated to determine validity of these patents. Even so, when some computer companies have been faced with the prospect of infringing a large number of another's computer patents, they have in many cases turned to licensing and cross-licensing agreements versus challenging the validity of the patents in court. The reason is the sheer number of patents being obtained by these companies means the legal fees alone in proving or disproving validity could be staggering. Therefore, when a large number of patents are involved, paying license fees may be more economically attractive than trying to prove invalidity through multiple lawsuits which could tie up resources for several years.

Likewise, advances in biotechnology have created questions over what can be patented. The area of biotechnology is large and growing. It includes many different technologies in the medical, agricultural, and food processing industries, along with a wide range of other applications. Some of the most widely debated issues in biotechnology deal with genetic engineering to modify organisms, and what inventions in genetic engineering are truly patentable.

Any item that can be found in nature cannot be patented. However, one of the questions in the forefront of the patent debate is 'how close to nature can one come and still have a patentable invention?' Patent offices around the world have issued and continue to issue new guidelines around patenting such inventions, such as the 'real-world' utility requirement discussed in the previous section. The validity of patents on this type of technology will continue to be debated and challenged in court and one should anticipate that the rules and guidelines will continue to evolve for this embryonic technology.

Utility Model

Some countries, for example, Japan, Germany, and Korea, allow utility model patents, which can be thought of as small, more specific utility patents. Utility models typically have a shorter life than a utility patent, and were originally intended to provide some quick, inexpensive legal protection for the small inventor. From a practical standpoint, utility models are normally very narrowly claimed, or very specific to a particular product or machine. Utility model patents are sometimes called utility model registrations, because they are not typically examined rigorously by a patent examiner, if they are examined at all, and some systems require the applicant to assert the invention is worthy of a utility model patent. In countries where the time required to obtain regular utility patents is long, utility models can provide some limited protection for the inventor almost immediately. Most countries that have utility model patents also have provisions for converting utility applications to utility model registrations.

Design Patents

Design patents are used to protect new, original ornamental designs for an article of manufacture. The subject matter of a design patent can relate to the configuration or shape of an object, to the surface ornamentation on an object, or both. Normally design patents consist of a drawing of the ornamental design and a simple claim to the design, which is illustrated in the patent.

Plant Patents

Normally, plant patents refer to asexually reproduced, new and distinct varieties of plant. The word plant is normally used in its ordinary sense, so that things that might be plants, strictly from a scientific sense, such as bacteria, are not accepted as plant patents. The types of plants eligible for patent protection normally include cultivated sports, mutants, hybrids, and new seedlings, other than tuber propagated plants or those found in an uncultivated state. In some countries, the plant must be capable of industrial application. Other countries do not provide for plant patents.

PARTS OF A PATENT

A patent application has traditionally been the collection of papers the applicant files in the patent office. However, the idea of 'a collection of papers' needs to be rethought because many patent offices, like the Japanese Patent Office, have accepted the necessity and inevitability of the filing of paperless applications. Each country specifies what an applicant needs to include in the patent application. Normally, this consists of a written explanation of the invention in the form of a specification and drawings (if needed to explain the invention), and formal documents such as oaths or declarations as to the owner(s) and inventor(s) of the application. Normally the application is not complete unless it is accompanied by a filing fee. Some countries require the inventors to be designated.

    The specification is the written description making up most of the patent application, and this is what is loosely called the 'patent application'. The specification is constructed in a manner to help explain to the examiner why an invention is patentable. There are some commonly used sections in the application, which all become part of the resulting issued patent; these are:

(1) a title;
(2) a cross-reference to other related patent applications which have already been filed;
(3) a section describing the background and general technical area of the invention, which will sometimes include reasons why prior inventions are lacking;
(4) a summary of the invention;
(5) a description of the contents in any drawings;
(6) a detailed description of the invention, and if needed, the preferred embodiment of the invention;
(7) a series of examples used to illustrate how the invention is made, used, or is different from the prior art;
(8) a listing of desired claims; and,
(9) an abstract describing the invention in a general way so that the invention can be easily searched.

The title is descriptive of the invention, and the cross-reference section, when included, allows the reader of the patent to understand the pedigree of the patent application. The cross-reference section also indicates whether or not the application claims an earlier priority date from another country.

While not required, patent applications normally have a background section at the very beginning which describes the general status of technology in the field of the invention, and more importantly describes where the current technology fails to perform or is lacking in some manner. Patent agents use this section to list why previous attempts to solve a certain problem have not been satisfactory and to put forth reasons why a new invention would be of value. The background, along with the summary of the invention and the detailed description of the invention, may or may not be set out in clear sections of the patent application, but most applications follow this form.

The patent agent attempts to describe the problem, and then concisely describes the solution – which is the invention – in the summary of the invention section of patent application. A detailed description of the invention then follows, which normally defines any new concepts or any unfamiliar terms in the patent application and describes what the inventor believes is his invention. Normally, many of the embodiments of the invention are listed in the detailed description of the invention. Included in this detail is normally some discussion of any figures or drawings included in the patent application.

In many patent applications, there is a section containing examples. Examples are used to show specifically how the invention is made or used, or may be used to illustrate the differences between the new invention and inventions which were previously known to exist. Examples are almost always present when the patent application is for a chemical process or for a new composition of matter. The examples provide additional detail so that others can duplicate the claimed process or compound.

The listing of claims in a patent application is the legal description of the intellectual property owned, if the claim is in a granted patent; or of the property the applicant wishes to own, if the claim is in a patent application. Claims in published patent applications may change before the application issues as a patent. There are two major types of claims. There are independent claims, which stand alone as a legal description of the owned property. The second type of claim is a dependent claim, which depends on another claim.

For example, the following listing of claims might be in a patent application.

1. A molded part containing 80 to 60 weight percent polymeric resin and 20 to 40 weight percent reinforcing fiber.
2. The molded part of Claim 1, wherein the reinforcing fiber is an inorganic fiber.
3. The molded part of Claim 2, wherein the inorganic fiber is a glass fiber.

Claim 1 is an independent claim, while Claims 2 and 3 are dependent. Note how the dependent claims describe a more specific invention than the independent claims. Dependent claims either restrict the breadth of independent claims, add new elements to independent claims, or do both. The reason dependent claims exist is because if the main independent claim is found for some reason to be invalid, the dependent claims may not, and still provide the patent owner with a measure of protection. For example, if there was a prior disclosure of a molded part having an *organic* fiber as a reinforcing fiber, the main claim would not be valid. However, the second and third claims would still be valid, and the patent owner would still be able to exclude others from these types of molded parts.

The claims are normally either at the very end of the patent publication, as is the case for European patents and United States patents, or they are at the very beginning of the publication, as they are in Japanese patents. Patents approved by the European Patent Office are published in one language, either French, German, or English; the claims section, however, has three sets of claims, one in each language. Therefore, the claims can normally be understood, even if you don't know the language of the application.

The formal abstract is the part of the patent specification which summarizes what the invention is about, and is placed in the application so that the general content of the patent application can be determined quickly by future patent searchers. This is required because if a patent is granted on an application, the patent office will want to use the information contained in the application in the review of other applications. The researcher will come in contact with two types of abstracts in working with patents, the first one being the formal abstract included in the patent application by the applicant. The second type are those generated by on-line computer abstracting services which provide patent abstracts for a fee to the general public. The inventor will normally see these during the drafting of the application when the patent agent is preparing a prior art search. These two abstracts are normally not the same, but both are used to give the reader or the searcher a general idea about what is contained in the patent specification.

Patent offices around the world have recognized the need for a uniform method of identifying certain information in patents, and making this information accessible even though the reader might not know the language used in the application. The front or first page of patent publications typically contain a great deal of important bibliographic information, so, on the first page(s) of patents and published patent applications, most patent offices print this important information using the 'Internationally agreed Numbers for the Identification of Data' codes, or INID codes.

The most useful INID codes for the researcher are:

10 series – Document Identification

(11) The Patent Number or Patent Publication Number of the Document
(12) The Language Used in the Document

20 Series – Domestic Filing Data

(21) The Application Number(s)
(22) The Filing Date(s) of the Application(s)
(23) Other Date(s) Including Date of Filing of Completed Application
(24) The Date From Which Industrial Property Rights May Have Effect
(25) The Language in Which the Published Application was Originally Filed
(26) The Language in Which the Application is Published

30 Series – Priority Data

(31) The Number(s) Assigned to the Priority Application(s)
(32) The Date(s) of Filing of the Priority Application(s)

40 Series – Date(s) Patent Publications Were Made Available to the Public

(41) The Date Made Publicly Available of an Unexamined Document on Which no Patent Grant has Taken Place on or before the Said Date

(42) The Date Made Publicly Available of an Examined Document on Which no Patent Grant has Taken Place on or Before the Said Date

(43) The Date of Publication of an Unexamined Document on Which no Patent Grant has Taken Place on or Before the Said Date

(44) The Date of Publication of an Examined Document on Which no Patent Grant has Taken Place on or Before the Said Date

(45) The Date of Publication of a Document on Which Grant has Taken Place on or Before the Said Date

(46) The Date of Publication of Only the Claim(s) of the Document

(47) The Date Made Publicly Available of a Document on Which Grant has Taken Place on or Before the Said Date

50 Series – Technical Patent Office Identification and Classification Information

(51) The International Patent Classification
(52) The National Classification
(53) The Universal Decimal Classification
(54) The Title of the Invention
(55) Keywords Used for Searching
(56) List of Prior Act Documents Not Included in Descriptive Text
(57) The Abstract or Claim
(58) The Field of Search

60 Series – References to Legally Related Domestic Patent Documents (Including Unpublished Applications)

(61) The Number/Filing Date of an Earlier Application to Which the Present Document is an Addition

(62) The Number/Filing Date of an Earlier Application from Which the Present Document has been Divided

(63) The Number/Filing Date of an Earlier Application of Which the Present Document is a Continuation

(64) The Number of an Earlier Publication which is 'reissued'

(65) The Number of a Previously Published Patent Document Concerning the Same Application

70 Series – Identification of Parties Associated with the Patent Document

(71) The Applicant(s)
(72) The Inventor(s)
(73) The Grantee(s)
(74) The Attorney(s) or Agent(s)

(75) Any Inventor(s) who is(are) also Applicant(s)
(76) Any Inventor(s) who is(are) also Applicant(s) and Grantee(s)

80 Series – Identification of Dates Related to International Conventions other than the Paris Convention

(81) Designated State(s) According to the PCT
(83) Information Concerning the Deposit of Micro-organisms
(84) Designated Contracting States Under Regional Patent Conventions
(85) Date of Fulfillment of Requirements of Article 22 and/or 39 of the PCT for Introducing the National Procedure According to PCT
(86) Filing Date of the Regional or PCT Application
(87) Publication Data of the Regional or PCT Application
(88) Date of Deferred Publication of the Search Report
(89) Document Number, Date of Filing, and Country of Origin of the Original Document According to the CMEA Agreement on Mutual Recognition of Inventor's Certificates and Other Documents of Protection for Inventions.

A researcher can look for the INID numbers in parentheses and ascertain certain information, regardless of the language of the patent. For example, the priority data for the application will always appear beside a number in the (30)s, and the applicant will always be identified by a number in the (70)s. These numbers can be helpful in sorting out the dates and other information quickly and easily.

THE TERM OF A PATENT

Defining the 'term' of a patent can be somewhat confusing unless one understands the word can be used in many ways. Term can mean the amount of time a patent is in force after the patent issues assuming maintenance fees continue to be paid. Term can also mean the amount of time a patent application and resulting patent is active, and includes both the examination time plus the time the patent is in force. Most countries use this second definition when they say their patents have a 20-year term.

In return for disclosing a patentable invention to the patent office, an inventor receives a patent grant for a specific period of time. The length of time can vary from country to country, but the patent grant in many countries is now based on 20 years from the day the application was filed. Since the time period starts when the patent is filed, the actual enforceable patent grant is something less than 20 years because all patent offices need some time to examine the application. Normally, if a patent takes two years to

PCT WORLD INTELLECTUAL PROPERTY ORGANIZATION
International Bureau

INTERNATIONAL APPLICATION PUBLISHED UNDER THE PATENT COOPERATION TREATY (PCT)

(51) International Patent Classification ^{5} : G01N 33/28	A1	(11) International Publication Number: WO 91/15762
		(43) International Publication Date: 17 October 1991 (17.10.91)

(21) International Application Number: PCT/US91/01635

(22) International Filing Date: 5 March 1991 (05.03.91)

(30) Priority data:
506,391   9 April 1990 (09.04.90)   US

(71) Applicant: ASHLAND OIL, INC. [US/US]; P.O. Box 391, BL2, Ashland, KY 41114 (US).

(72) Inventor: MAGGARD, Steven, M. ; 106 Broadmoor Drive, Huntington, WV 25705 (US).

(74) Agents: WILLSON, Richard, C., Jr.; P.O. Box 391, BL2, Ashland, KY 41114 (US) et al.

(81) Designated States: AT, AT (European patent), AU, BB, BE (European patent), BF (OAPI patent), BG, BJ (OAPI patent), BR, CA, CF (OAPI patent), CG (OAPI patent), CH, CH (European patent), CM (OAPI patent), DE, DE (European patent), DK, DK (European patent), ES, ES (European patent), FI, FR (European patent), GA (OAPI patent), GB, GB (European patent), GR (European patent), HU, IT (European patent), JP, KP, KR, LK, LU, LU (European patent), MC, MG, ML (OAPI patent), MR (OAPI patent), MW, NL, NL (European patent), NO, PL, RO, SD, SE, SE (European patent), SN (OAPI patent), SU, TD (OAPI patent), TG (OAPI patent).

Published
With international search report.
With amended claims.

(54) Title: PROCESS AND APPARATUS FOR ANALYSIS OF HYDROCARBONS BY NEAR-INFRARED SPECTROSCOPY

(57) Abstract

Certain selected wavelengths in the near infrared spectra permit analysis of weight percent, volume percent, or even mole percent of each component, e.g. PIANO (paraffin, isoparaffin, aromatic, naphtenes, and olefins), octane (preferably research, motor or pump), and percent of various hydrocarbons, e.g. alpha olefins. Analysis can be nearly continuous anlysis on-line or at-line, as well as batch analysis, e.g. in a quality control laboratory. Preferably the NIR data is converted to a second derivative of the spectra and multiple linear regression performed to model the individual PIANO concentrations, and to predict physical properties of fuel blending components, e.g. research octane of reformate, etc.

Figure 1.1 The Front Page of a Published PCT Patent Application

United States Patent [19]

Lombardi

[11] Patent Number: 5,188,061

US005188061A

[45] Date of Patent: Feb. 23, 1993

[54] PET AND ANIMAL NURSER

[76] Inventor: Diane F. Lombardi, 171 Hichborn St.,
                 Revere, Mass. 02151

[21] Appl. No.: 659,224

[22] Filed: Feb. 22, 1991

[51] Int. Cl.⁵ A01K 9/00
[52] U.S. Cl. 119/71
[58] Field of Search 119/71

[56]   References Cited

         U.S. PATENT DOCUMENTS

    2,106,562 1/1938 Bucci .... 119/71 X
    2,577,849 12/1951 Henry 119/71
    3,122,130 2/1964 Brown et al. 119/71

       FOREIGN PATENT DOCUMENTS

    109121 3/1899 Fed. Rep. of Germany 119/71

    874535 8/1961 United Kingdom 119/71

Primary Examiner—Gene Mancene
Assistant Examiner—Thomas Price

[57]   ABSTRACT

A new and improved pet and animal feeder which provides small pets and animals with nursing means within
a surrounding soft material. The present invention provides a container with a plurality of nippled, hollow
protuberances simulating the teats depending from a
mother. The container is positioned in a cavity within a
stuffed cushion having an external shape similar to the
adult version of the mammal for which the invention is
being used. The nippled protuberances protrude from
the cushion, through apertures in the cushion, and are
available for suckling by the newborns.

6 Claims, 2 Drawing Sheets

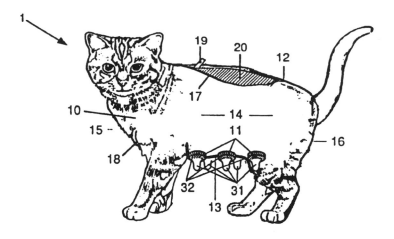

Figure 1.2 The Front Page of an Issued United States Patent

issue, the patent will be in force 18 years; if it takes 10 years to issue, the
patent will be in force for only 10 more years. Of course, most countries
require the patent holder to pay fees during the lifetime of the patent to
maintain the patent in force. If the patent holder does not pay these maintenance fees, the patent lapses and the technology is put in the public
domain.

From 1861 until 1995, the length of time a patent was in force in the United States was 17 years from the date of issue. The filing date had no impact on the length of time the patent was in force. Therefore, if it took several years for the patent to issue the inventor profited because the patent grant was delayed but the enforceable time was not reduced. The inventor got the benefit of the invention during the years the application was being examined plus the limited monopoly granted after examination. As discussed in an earlier section, this allowed some people to manipulate the system in the form of submarine patents, the issue of which would be intentionally delayed in the patent office by the patent applicants. In 1995, however, US law was changed to bring the US system more in line with systems in Europe and Japan, and now patent rights expire 20 years after the first filing of the application. Applications pending or patents in force at the time of the changeover get the longer of 20 years from the first filing date or 17 years from issuance.

Also, if an application in the United States is divided or refiled, the 20 year period starts at the first filing of the patent family. For example, if you file a patent application in the year 2000, any patents that result from that application will be be in force until 2020, assuming you pay the associated maintenance fees. If that application has both a product invention and a process invention, the patent office will probably want to divide the application and prosecute the claims separately. This will mean you will have to refile the divided claims sometime after the year 2000, say in 2002. Any patents that result from this divided application will also be in force only until the year 2020 because it results from an application originally filed in 2000. Prior to the law change, applicants could obtain additional years of enforceable life by delaying the filing of divisional applications, because the key was to delay the issuance of the patent as far into the future as possible so that you could obtain 17 years from the date of issuance. These types of maneuverings are all but eliminated under the new law.

One of the new provisions in a law enacted in the United States in 1999 was the extension of patent rights due to Patent Office delays. The new law extends the expiration date of a patent if the patent office fails to take action on an application within a specified number of months or if delays in the patent office prevent a patent from issuing within three years from filing. Delays in prosecution caused by the applicant reduce these extensions, so applicants will have a major incentive to respond to the patent office within the time set by the examiner. Another part of the law extends the expiration date for delays in other types of office activities like appeals and secrecy orders. The overall aim of this law is to ensure inventors are not negatively impacted by the 20 year term; they now have the opportunity to retain the equivalent of a grant of 17 years from the date of issue as was the case in the old patent law.

Provisional Protection

Most countries that publish patent applications 18 months after the priority date also provide for provisional protection. That is, the applicant can obtain damages from a perceived infringer for actions prior to the issuance of the patent. A provisional patent system relies on the publication of the patent application so that the application for invention is on record. As with many patent matters, the exact rules pertaining to provisional protection can vary from country to country. However, a person that practices another invention may have to pay a reasonable royalty for any use of that invention prior to patent being issued, and may not be allowed to practice that invention once the patent is issued.

A part of the new law in the United States providing for publication of applications was the addition of provisional protection. One may be due a reasonable royalty from an infringer if the infringer is given notice and the infringed claims in the granted patent are substantially identical to those in the published application.

DEFINITIONS OF COMMONLY USED TERMS

There are some terms used frequently by patent agents and professionals which may be new to the researcher. Here are a few of the most common terms the researcher will be exposed to:

Prior Art

While this term is normally used to identify any published references which disclose information which would impact the patentability of an invention, prior art is also known engineering practice or things that are 'known in the art'. A previously published patent can be recognized as prior art if it discloses information which comes close to describing an invention; it does not have to specifically claim the same invention. Patent agents will normally use the 'closest prior art' in preparing the patent application. The closest prior art are those references which come closest to disclosing an invention, whether used individually or in combination. The closest prior art will impact the way the patent application is written, for if there is very close prior art, the invention claims in the new patent application may be very specific and narrow, and the inventor may have to have examples showing how this new invention is different from prior inventions. On the other hand, if there is very little prior art, there is a very good possibility the patent will have broad claims, and the patent application could be written to emphasize and exemplify whatever features are most important to the inventor.

Priority Date

This is the date a patent application was first filed in any country which is a signatory to a co-operative filing treaty (see the Paris Convention, below). The priority date is the effective filing date for most countries, regardless of the actual filing date in any subsequent country. The priority date is normally the most important date when considering the impact of prior art.

Filing Date

This is the date a patent application was actually filed in a particular country. If the country is a signatory to an international treaty, then the applicant may be afforded the opportunity to use the priority date for examination purposes. The filing date may vary from country to country for the same patentable invention, because international treaties allow for this without the applicant losing any patent rights.

Prosecution

In the patent world, this term is used to describe the efforts by an applicant or patent agent to obtain a patent. While an applicant's patent application is being considered in the patent office, the application is said to be 'under prosecution' in the patent office.

Office Action

This term refers to the written communication sent by the Patent Office patent examiner to the applicant during prosecution of the patent application. The office action will normally consist of standard forms and written text explaining the examiner's position on the patentability of the invention. The office action will normally require a written communication, or 'response', from the applicant or the applicant's agent to continue prosecution of the application.

Rejection

If the examiner does not think the invention is patentable, the applicant will receive an office action from the examiner called a rejection. This type of office action lists specifically why the application is being rejected, and may include suggestions as to what the applicant can do, or how the applicant can amend the application to make the invention patentable.

Objection

If the examiner thinks the applicant's application is incomplete or is in the wrong form, or some formal requirement is not met, the examiner may 'object' to some part of the application. Normally, objections can be easily overcome by the patent agent, since they typically deal with the form of the application.

Amendment

During prosecution, the applicant may want or need to change the scope of the claims, add new claims, or in some way amend the application. If this is the case, the applicant will make these changes in the form of an amendment, which is normally included in the response to an office action.

Final Rejection

If the applicant's arguments are not persuasive, the examiner may issue a final rejection. This indicates to the applicant that the examiner intends to close prosecution on the case, and normally the applicant can submit one final argument for patentability, which may or may not be sufficient to overcome the rejection.

Patent Pending

After a patent application has been filed, it is said the patent is pending and active in the patent office. 'Patent pending' is placed on inventions to make sure the public understands a patent has been filed on the invention; this warning has legal implications should a competitor knowingly duplicate the invention before the patent issues. The identification of 'patent pending' serves as a notice to others that damages may be taken from the first day the patent on the invention issues. However, the labelling of 'patent pending' on a device does not mean a patent will actually issue on the device; it just means a patent is pending in the patent office.

Publication

In most countries of the world, the patent laws require the patent application to be published after filing, regardless of the ultimate status of the application. In addition, the patent application can be published again after examination if the patent is either granted or is slated to be granted. Therefore, there are numerous patent 'publications', some of which are not patents. The status of these publications at the time of printing will either be available on the front page of the publication, or can be inferred from the publication number.

Laid-open

This term is used to describe the process of publishing patent applications, and is normally associated with Japanese patent applications. The term comes from the thought that the application is 'laid open' for public inspection, which serves notice that the patent application is pending in the patent office. Laid-open patent applications are not issued patents, but rather encourage the development of technology by the rapid dissemination of information.

Published for Opposition

In many countries, when patents are granted they undergo a period of public scrutiny. It is said these applications are 'published for opposition'. In the European Patent Office the public has a period of nine months after the publication of the patent application with its allowed claims to oppose the grant. In Japan, someone concerned with the issuance of a patent has six months to lodge an opposition in the the Japanese Patent Office.

The opposition filing initiates an entire new round of negotiations and communications with the patent office by both the opposer and the patent applicant. The role of the opposer in these communications varies depending on the particular rules of the patent office in question. Sometimes, as in the European Patent Office, both the opposer and applicant play major parts in determining the merit of the opposition by having the opportunity to request an oral hearing to debate their position. Other patent offices, like the Japanese Patent Office, take the opposition documents filed by the opposer and work directly with the applicant to determine whether a mistake was made in granting the patent.

While there is no specific provision for a published-for-opposition period or opposition system in the United States, there is a re-examination procedure which allows the patent office to review the appropriateness of the granted claims of a particular patent in view of specific prior art which was not seen by the examiner during prosecution of the patent application. Re-examination, unlike the opposition procedures in other countries, can be initiated in the United States Patent and Trademark Office at any time during the life of the patent. Up until recently, a person or third party requesting the re-examination of another's patent simply provided the references that had been missed; this person played no part in the final determination of what were appropriate claims. With the passage of a new law in 1999, third parties are now able to read and comment on the re-examination correspondence between the applicant and the patent office. It is not out of the question that these re-examination laws will change again to help arrive at a system somewhat similar to the European system.

Appeal

Should the examiner not think an invention is patentable, or should the applicant lose in an opposition procedure, the applicant can appeal either decision by filing additional fees and briefs, which in essence keeps the question of patentability alive and under review in the patent office. Should the applicant lose all appeals in the patent offices, in some countries the applicant can further appeal the case in the judicial system of the country. Obviously, appeals take a lot of time and money to resolve.

Infringement

Whenever one makes, uses, or sells a patented invention without permission from the patent owner, that person is said to infringe the patent. Infringement is a very serious issue and the penalties for infringement can be very severe. For example, if it is very clear a patent is being infringed by another the patent owner may be able to get the courts to issue a summary judgment to stop the infringing activity immediately. This can mean a business that is operating one day is immediately shut down the next. Also, one willfully infringing a patent in the United States could be forced to pay the patent owner three times the damages caused by the infringement. To avoid infringement, normally a patent search is made to determine whether any other patents will be infringed if a new invention is commercially introduced. (See also Chapter 5.)

Prior User Rights

Some countries allow for prior user rights, or the ability for one to continue to use a secret process one has been using commercially if another party independently obtains a patent on that process. These rights vary from country to country and can be quite complicated and restrictive on how one may continue to operate in the face of the patent. In the United States, a law protecting prior user rights for business methods was passed in 1999. Many business methods were at one time not patentable subject matter. This new law allows one to continue to use a business method, if it has been in use for at least a year, even if another receives a patent on that method. So, this law attempts to avoid penalizing those still using business methods developed at a time when they were not patentable.

INTERNATIONAL TREATIES

An overview of patent law would not be complete without providing information about global treaties which have made the global acquisition of intellectual property protection easier and more uniform. While there have been a number of agreements, and revisions to those agreements, the researcher needs to be familiar with only the major provisions.

In general, these treaties are used to make the filing of patent applications easier for the applicant. Although the actual filing should be handled by a patent agent, it is helpful for the researcher to understand how the various systems work, since it is likely the researcher will be asked to help respond to office actions from around the world.

THE PARIS CONVENTION

The Paris Convention for the Protection of Industrial Property, commonly shortened and called the 'Paris Convention', is a multilateral treaty which originated in 1883, and has been revised several times since. Over 100 countries have become signatories to this treaty, which is administered by the World Intellectual Property Organization (WIPO) located in Geneva, Switzerland. This treaty essentially allows an applicant a year's grace period after filing an application in a signatory country to file the application in other signatory countries while still retaining the original filing date, or priority date. The convention applies to patent applications, utility model applications, design patent applications and trademark applications, although the timing for patents and utility models is twelve months, and the timing for designs and trademarks is six months. Most countries have signed this treaty; a notable exception is at the time of this writing Taiwan, although Taiwan has negotiated separate treaties with many countries.

The Paris Convention helps the applicant in two ways. First, it gives the applicant the freedom to openly publicize his invention after filing his first patent application, while still retaining his patent rights in most countries. Since a public disclosure of an invention prior to the filing of a patent application would make a patent issued for that invention invalid in many countries of the world, if the Paris Convention was not in place, an inventor would have to keep his invention secret while he frantically filed patent applications worldwide. However, because the treaty is in place for most countries, an inventor can file his original patent application in his home country and then leisurely file the same application in other countries up to one year later, claiming the original priority date in all countries. It is as if he magically filed patent applications in all of the countries on the same day.

The second advantage the Paris Convention provides is it provides the applicant a year's time after the initial filing of his patent application to get some feedback on his invention before he must make his final decision on where in the world to apply for patent protection. Few inventions are true commercial successes. Inventions which seem wonderful in the laboratory may have some flaw, hidden to the inventor's eyes, which makes the invention entirely unworkable. By allowing the inventor to get initial feedback on his invention, the inventor can better decide whether or not he has a hit

Table 1.1   Paris Convention Countries

Albania	Equatorial Guinea	Mauritius
Algeria	Estonia	Mexico
Antigua and Barbuda	Finland	Monaco
Argentina	France	Mongolia
Armenia	Gabon	Morocco
Australia	Gambia	Mozambique
Austria	Georgia	Netherlands
Azerbaijan	Germany	New Zealand
Bahamas	Ghana	Nicaragua
Bahrain	Greece	Niger
Bangladesh	Grenada	Nigeria
Barbados	Guatemala	Norway
Belarus	Guinea	Oman
Belgium	Guinea-Bissau	Panama
Belize	Guyana	Papua
Benin	Haiti	Paraguay
Bhutan	Holy See	Peru
Bolivia	Honduras	Philippines
Bosnia and Herzegovina	Hungary	Poland
Botswana	Iceland	Portugal
Brazil	India	Qatar
Bulgaria	Indonesia	Republic of Korea
Burkina Faso	Iran	Republic of Moldova
Burundi	Iraq	Romania
Cambodia	Ireland	Russian Federation
Cameroon	Israel	Rwanda
Canada	Italy	Saint Kitts and Nevis
Central African Republic	Jamaica	Saint Lucia
Chad	Japan	Saint Vincent and
Chile	Jordan	the Grenadines
China	Kazakhstan	San Marino
Colombia	Kenya	Sao Tome and Principe
Congo	Kyrgyzstan	Senegal
Costa Rica	Lao People's	Sierra Leone
Cote d'Ivoire	Democratic Republic	Singapore
Croatia	Latvia	Slovakia
Cuba	Lebanon	Slovenia
Cyprus	Lesotho	South Africa
Czech Republic	Liberia	Spain
Democratic People's	Libyan Arab Jamahiriya	Sri Lanka
Republic of Korea	Liechtenstein	Sudan
Democratic Republic	Lithuania	Suriname
of the Congo	Luxembourg	Swaziland
Denmark	Madagascar	Sweden
Dominica	Malawi	Switzerland
Dominican Republic	Malaysia	Syrian Arab Republic
Ecuador	Mali	Tajikistan
Egypt	Malta	The former Yugoslav
El Salvador	Mauritania	Republic of Macedonia

Table 1.1 Paris Convention Countries (*continued*)

Togo	Ukraine	Uzbekistan
Trinidad and Tobago	United Arab Emirates	Venezuela
Tunisia	United Kingdom	Viet Nam
Turkey	United Republic of Tanzania	Yugoslavia
Turkmenistan	United States of America	Zambia
Uganda	Uruguay	Zimbabwe

invention or a dud. In some cases, the inventor may receive only limited feedback during the year's grace period, so the inventor may still have to use his best judgment for the global filing. However, in most cases, inventions with major flaws will be apparent almost immediately after a new set of eyes has viewed them. The Paris Convention helps the inventor save money and patent examiners save time when additional applications are not filed on worthless inventions.

Some countries have not signed the treaty. In order to obtain valid patent protection in these countries, the inventor must maintain secrecy until the application is filed in these countries. This inconvenience can be compounded if the country in which the invention was made requires a license to file patent applications in other countries on this technology. For example, if one invents something in the United States, a country which requires a foreign filing license, and the invention is not associated with some sensitive national security issue, one can publicize the invention immediately after the filing of the patent application and will automatically receive a foreign filing license six months after the filing of the application. The inventor will then have another six months to file any additional patent applications using the Paris Convention, but one will have the opportunity to sell the invention for almost a year before the filing process is actually completed in countries worldwide. However, if one wants to file in a non-Paris Convention country, and still wants to publicize the invention as soon as possible after patent rights have been reserved, one must first file the application in the United States, immediately request a foreign filing license, and then file the application in the other country as soon as the license is received. If a country has not signed the Paris Convention, not only does one have to make an extra effort to file as soon as possible after making the invention, but the secrecy of the invention must also be maintained to retain patent rights.

INTER-AMERICAN CONVENTION

Individual countries and groups of countries have also enacted separate agreements which act in essence like the Paris Convention and provide

Table 1.2 Inter-American Convention Countries

Bolivia	Haiti
Brazil	Honduras
Costa Rica	Nicaragua
Cuba	Paraguay
Dominican Republic	United States
Ecuador	Uruguay
Guatemala	

reciprocal rights to applicants. An example of one of these agreements is the Inter-American Convention relating to Inventions, Patents, Designs, and Industrial Models, signed in 1910. The members of this Convention at the time of this writing are given in Table 1.2.

THE PATENT COOPERATION TREATY

The Patent Cooperation Treaty, commonly referred to as the PCT, dates from 1970 and has become a major method by which patent applications are filed internationally. The PCT is also administered by WIPO.

The most obvious advantage of the PCT is that it provides a convenient mechanism for filing patent applications for the same invention in many different countries at one time. The application can be filed in any of the signatories of the treaty by filing essentially one set of papers in any one of several receiving offices worldwide. The application can also usually be filed in the applicant's native language, although a translation may later be required during the prosecution of the application.

The PCT provides an additional advantage in that applicants have the opportunity to defer the payment of filing, translation, and other fees for up to 30 months after the priority date of the application. This can provide the applicant extra time to determine whether or not the invention is worth the money and effort to obtain patents globally. Applications filed via PCT are published 18 months after the priority date. The PCT procedure also provides provisional protection in those countries which provide for such protection, which means an inventor could be able to claim damages for infringement as early as the publication date.

An application filed using the PCT has an international search provided by one of the international search offices. This search is completed within three months of receipt of the application, or nine months after the priority date, whichever is longer, and the search indicates how pertinent the cited references are to the application.

In addition to the international search, many countries have agreed to additional treaty provisions, called Chapter II, which allow for a preliminary examination of the application, which is essentially an opinion of patentability. Regardless of the preliminary examination, all countries have their own procedures for examining the application, although a favorable preliminary examination is a good indicator of the patentability. The Chapter II provision also provides the 30 month delay mentioned earlier; if the country is not a signatory of Chapter II, then the delay is only 20 months. Member states of the PCT at the time of this writing are shown in Table 1.3, along with the accepted country codes or abbreviations.

It is not unusual for an inventor to file a patent application using both the Paris Convention and the PCT; the Paris Convention is used to establish the priority date for the application, while the PCT is the actual filing mechanism for most of the global applications. In this case, the inventor first files in his home country, and then files the PCT application within a year of that filing date. This allows for the home country to start examination of the application and some additional time to understand the value of the invention before paying the fee for filing the PCT application. Of course, one can file directly in the PCT first, however, this will delay the start of the examination. When one files a patent application through the PCT, one is adding an additional step, for convenience, to the process of obtaining patents in countries. One's application must first follow and satisfy all of the PCT procedures and requirements, and then the application is sent to the patent offices of the various countries for final prosecution.

The PCT provides the applicant with other advantages:

• The individual payments of the national filing, translation, and other fees are delayed for 20 months (or 30 months if the country is a signatory of Chapter II), after the priority date of the application. This provides the applicant extra time to determine whether the invention will be a commercial success and worth the money and effort to obtain patents globally.

Table 1.3 Patent Cooperation Treaty Countries and Country Codes

Country	Code	Country	Code
Albania	AL	Belarus	BY
Algeria	DZ	Belgium	BE
Antigua and Barbuda	AG	Belize	BZ
Armenia	AM	Benin	BJ
Australia	AU	Bosnia and Herzegovina	BA
Austria	AT	Brazil	BR
Azerbaijan	AZ	Bulgaria	BG
Barbados	BB	Burkina Faso	BF

Table 1.3 Patent Cooperation Treaty Countries and Country Codes (*continued*)

Country	Code	Country	Code
Cameroon	CM	Mali	ML
Canada	CA	Mauritania	MR
Central African Republic	CF	Mexico	MX
Chad	TD	Monaco	MC
China	CN	Mongolia	MN
Congo	CG	Morocco	MA
Costa Rica	CR	Mozambique	MZ
Cote d'Ivoire	CI	Netherlands	NL
Croatia	HR	New Zealand	NZ
Cuba	CU	Niger	NE
Cyprus	CY	Norway	NO
Czech Republic	CZ	Poland	PL
Democratic People's	KP	Portugal	PT
Republic of Korea		Republic of Korea	KR
Denmark	DK	Republic of Moldova	MD
Dominica	DM	Romania	RO
Estonia	EE	Russian Federation	RU
Finland	FI	Saint Lucia	LC
France	FR	Senegal	SN
Gabon	GA	Sierra Leone	SL
Gambia	GM	Singapore	SG
Georgia	GE	Slovakia	SK
Germany	DE	Slovenia	SI
Ghana	GH	South Africa	ZA
Greece	GR	Spain	ES
Grenada	GD	Sri Lanka	LK
Guinea	GN	Sudan	SD
Guinea-Bissau	GW	Swaziland	SZ
Hungary	HU	Sweden	SE
Iceland	IS	Switzerland	CH
India	IN	Tajikistan	TJ
Indonesia	ID	The former Yugoslav	
Ireland	IE	Republic of Macedonia	MK
Israel	IL	Togo	TG
Italy	IT	Trinidad and Tobago	TT
Japan	JP	Turkey	TR
Kazakhstan	KZ	Turkmenistan	TM
Kenya	KE	Uganda	UG
Kyrgyzstan	KG	Ukraine	UA
Latvia	LV	United Arab Emirates	AE
Lesotho	LS	United Kingdom	GB
Liberia	LR	United Republic of Tanzania	TZ
Liechtenstein	LI	United States of America	US
Lithuania	LT	Uzbekistan	UZ
Luxembourg	LU	Viet Nam	VN
Madagascar	MG	Yugoslavia	YU
Malawi	MW	Zimbabwe	ZW

- The applicant can initially file in almost all countries of the world for one fee, and reduce the number of countries at a later date without incurring additional fees. This provides the applicant extra time to determine where in the world a patent will be useful. Since the payment of most fees are delayed, the applicant can keep his options open for a long time after filing. This flexibility can be most welcome if it is unclear whether or not an invention will be successful.
- Applications filed via PCT are published 18 months after the priority date. Publication of the application also serves as a disclosure of the invention claimed, which should prevent another from patenting the same invention.

There are some negatives to the PCT:

- Using the PCT to file patent applications can increase the total global filing bill, especially if one only files in a few countries. The PCT is essentially an additional step in the global filing process; one must still prosecute the application in the individual examining identities as before. The extra cost is for the convenience in getting the application filed and obtaining a preliminary examination.
- The application is not examined for at least 20 months; this delay may not be prudent if one is trying to stop an infringer of the invention. However, if the applicant knows about the infringer at the time of filing, he still can have the possibility of combining the national and PCT filings to try to get an expedited examination in the country where infringement is occurring. So, those in fast moving technology areas where patents are more valuable near-term than longer term have to carefully weigh how and when they will use PCT.
- The PCT invites indecision. Since there are so many options, the tendency is to put off deciding where to file the application. The deadlines in the PCT procedures are firm; one normally can't correct being late by paying a fee. Therefore, if faced with the decision, but with limited time, the tendency is to retain too many countries because of inadequate attention to the decision. It is far better to decide before filing where patents are really desired. One can still 'file' in all of the countries and then restrict later, and if a list of key countries is already known, the final decision will be whether or not to add to that original list. This is a much easier task to accomplish than to consider all countries of the world and try to restrict to only a few.

As is the case with the Paris Convention, there are some countries that have not signed the PCT. To file in the countries that have not signed the PCT normally requires translating the application into the accepted language for the country and filing the application using an agent in the country. If the country has also not signed the Paris Convention, then one normally must also keep the invention totally secret until the patent application is filed. Over the past few years, more countries have signed the PCT, and most industrial countries are now signatories. At the time of this writing, the most notable country which has not signed the PCT is Taiwan.

THE EUROPEAN PATENT CONVENTION

Since establishment of the Convention on the Grant of European Patents (EPC) in 1973 in Munich, many countries have signed on to establish a uniform patent system in Europe. The aim of the Convention is to make the protection of inventions easier, more reliable, and less expensive in the member states. The patent system, which has a centralized searching and examination authority, is administered by the European Patent Organization (EPO) for the member countries. The headquarters of the EPO is in Munich, with a branch in The Hague and offices in Berlin and Vienna.

The EPC provides a single grant process for all of the EPC contracting states. Under the EPC, applicants that are successful in prosecution receive a 'European Patent'. This European Patent however, is not automatically effective in all contracting states, but in only the EPC countries that the applicant has designated. It is therefore similar to obtaining a bundle of national patents in Europe. Applicants can still file applications separately in each country. However, if one were to file separately in each country one would have to not only deal with separate applications and the higher cost if many of the European countries were selected, but also some countries do not examine patent applications but only provide a registration system. Therefore, if one uses the EPO, the applicant knows that their granted patent has undergone a substantive examination procedure which should mean the patent is probably more valuable.

The term of a European patent is 20 years from the filing date of the application, and the patent confers the same rights in each country as would be conferred by a national patent in that country. However, any patent infringement is dealt with by national law, and efforts have been made to uniformize the treatment in all the contracting states.

Member states of the EPC at the time of this writing are shown in Table 1.4, along with the extension states. These countries have signed agreements with the European Patent Organization; European patents and patent applications can be extended to these countries. Eight states are slated to accede to the EPC in 2002; they are Bulgaria, Czech Republic, Estonia, Hungary, Poland, Romania, Slovakia, and Slovenia.

Table 1.4   European Patent Convention Countries

	Member States	
Austria	Greece	Netherlands
Belgium	Ireland	Portugal
Cyprus	Italy	Spain
Denmark	Liechtenstein	Sweden
Finland	Luxembourg	Switzerland
France	Monaco	United Kingdom
Germany		

	Extension States	
Albania	Latvia	Romania
Lithuania	Former Yugoslav Republic of Macedonia	Slovenia

There has also been an ongoing effort to establish a regional patent in Europe. The Community Patent Convention was first signed in 1975 and would establish a European Community Patent which would be in force in all the European Union countries. Negotiations have continued, however the Community Patent is not a reality as of the time of this writing.

THE AFRICAN INTELLECTUAL PROPERTY ORGANIZATION

The African Intellectual Property Organization, known as OAPI after the French 'Organisation Africain de la Propriete Intellectuelle', provides protection for inventions, trademarks, and designs for those states that have signed the Bangui Agreement, which dates from 1982. (The organization is also known by AIPO.) The Bangui Agreement is effective in 15 countries of the OAPI, and all adhere to the Paris Convention. Unlike the EPC or ARIPO (see below), patents issued by the OAPI office automatically cover all 15 member states at once, without registration or designation. The one exception to this is that patents obtained via the PCT designating the OAPI extend to only those states which are actually members of the PCT as well as the OAPI. There is a single patent law which extends to all member states. Both French and English are generally accepted by the patent office. The term of the patent is 10 years from the filing date of the application. This can be extended for two additional five year periods if the patent holder can show that the patent is being worked in a member state or there are legitimate reasons for no working. The OAPI patent office is located in Yaounde, Cameroon. The member countries are shown in Table 1.5

Table 1.5   African Intellectual Property Organization (OAPI) Countries

Benin	Cote d'Ivoire	Mali
Burkina Faso	Congo	Mauritania
Cameroon	Gabon	Niger
Central Africa	Guinea	Senegal
Chad	Guinea Bissau	Togo

THE AFRICAN REGIONAL INDUSTRIAL PROPERTY ORGANIZATION

The African Regional Industrial Property Organization, known as ARIPO, is empowered to grant patents and to register industrial designs, through one office, for those states which have signed the Harare Protocol on patents and industrial designs. It has evolved from an organization that resulted from a diplomatic conference involving the English-speaking African countries in 1976 and was for a period of time called ESARIPO (English-Speaking African Regional Industrial Property Organization). Although the name has now changed, even now non-English documents submitted to ARIPO must be accompanied by an English translation. Membership is open to members of the United Nations Economic Commission for Africa or the Organization of African Unity. The headquarters for ARIPO were established in Harare, Zimbabwe, in 1981; the 15 member countries at the time of this writing are shown in Table 1.6. (Many other African countries are potentially member states and have observer status in ARIPO meetings.)

The Harare Protocol provides for a simplified procedure where an applicant can obtain protection in several designated states with a single patent application. The amount of fees paid for an ARIPO application is dependent on the number of member states designated. Also, ARIPO is a member of the Paris Convention and any applicant filing a PCT application can designate ARIPO for any member of the ARIPO that is also a member of the PCT. Countries at the time of this writing that are also members of the PCT are The Gambia, Ghana, Kenya, Lesotho, Malawi, Sierra Leone, Sudan, Swaziland, Tanzania, Uganda, and Zimbabwe.

Once an application is filed, the application is examined by ARIPO who decides if a patent grant is appropriate. The patents then granted under this system can be designated or registered as patents in the individual contracting states. However, member states have the right to refuse to grant a patent if it conflicts with their national law. An applicant can also get independent

Table 1.6   African Regional Industrial Property Organization (ARIPO) Countries

Botswana	Malawi	Swaziland
The Gambia	Mozambique	Tanzania
Ghana	Sierra Leone	Uganda
Kenya	Somalia	Zambia
Lesotho	Sudan	Zimbabwe

patents in many of the member states, separate from the procedures of the ARIPO. In most of the member states the patent term is 20 years from the filing date, although some countries have shorter terms and some have the provision for patent extensions.

EURASIAN PATENT CONVENTION

In late 1991, the patent office of the USSR ceased to function due to the collapse of the state apparatus. Over the next few years many of the countries of the Commonwealth of Independent States worked to develop a new patent system. In September 1994, the heads of nine CIS countries signed the Eurasian Patent Convention in Moscow. These countries were the Russian Federation, the Azerbaijan Republic, the Republic of Belarus, the Republic of Georgia, the Republic of Kazakhstan, the Kyrgyz Republic, the Republic of Moldova, the Republic of Tajikistan, and Ukraine. The purpose of the Convention was to create a system for obtaining legal protection based on the issuance of a single patent valid in all Contracting States. The Convention would become effective when it had been ratified by three states. Soon thereafter Turkmenistan joined the other countries in signing the Convention and then became the first state to ratify the treaty. When Belarus and Tajikistan ratified the Convention, it entered into force on August 12, 1995.

At the time of this writing, there are nine Contracting States to the Convention, and these are listed in Table 1.7. The Eurasian Patent Organization (EAPO) has been established to handle the administration of the patent system. The official language is Russian, and presently all searches for the EAPO are done by the Russian Patent Office. Membership in the Convention is open for any member of the United Nations that is also bound by the Paris Convention and the Patent Cooperation Treaty.

The term of the Eurasian patent is 20 years from the filing date; from the date of its publication the Eurasian patent is valid in all Contracting States. The requirements for a patent is that the invention be new, involve an inventive step, and be industrially applicable. The World Intellectual

Table 1.7   Eurasian Patent Convention Countries

Armenia	Kazakhstan	Russian Federation
Azerbaijan	Kyrgyz Republic	Tajikistan
Belarus	Moldova	Turkmenistan

Property Organization (WIPO) has permanent advisory status in the Administrative Council of the Convention, and it also has the role of mediator among the member states in case of possible disputes concerning the Convention.

COPYRIGHTS, TRADEMARKS, AND TRADE SECRETS

Intellectual property is not restricted to patents, but also includes copyrights, trademarks, and trade secrets. It is important the researcher understand and not be confused about what these are and how they differ. The last part of this chapter will briefly review these concepts.

COPYRIGHTS

Patents protect inventions. Inventions are ideas that have been reduced to practice. By reduced to practice it is meant an idea must be put in tangible form before it can be patented. In any case, just like patents protect ideas which have been reduced to practice, copyrights protect the expression of ideas. Note that copyrights cannot protect the idea itself, but the way the idea is fixed in a tangible medium like a book or another type of expressive work.

Copyrights are used to protect many types of authorship, including literature, drama, music, and computer software, and other expressions of ideas such as choreographic works, pictorial works, and architectural works. While patents prevent others from practicing an invention, and this protection can be extended to reasonable facsimiles of the invention, copyrights prevent others from strictly copying a work.

In many countries, the copyright lasts for the life of the author plus 50 years. In the United States, the copyright term is now the life of the author plus 70 years; however, if the work was made for hire or was anonymously authored, the duration is the shorter of 95 years from the date of publication or 120 years from the creation date. Clearly copyrights are very valuable long term properties. The Berne Convention for the Protection of Literary and Artistic Works and the Universal Copyright Convention are multilateral treaties created for the protection of copyrights worldwide.

TRADEMARKS

Trademarks are names used by manufacturers to identify their products. They are based on the concept that some manufacturers made better products than other manufacturers and therefore wanted to make sure that they differentiated themselves to potential customers. Trademarks are also used to maintain the reputation of a manufacturer, preventing others from simply copying the product or making a lower quality product and using the other manufacturer's name to pass the product off as being authentic.

Essentially any word or symbol can be used by a manufacturer, assuming there is no conflict with another trademark and the word or symbol meets the guidelines for the country involved. Trademarks are not necessarily descriptive of the product, but only associate a product with its manufacturer. Service marks are similar to trademarks, differing only in that trademarks generally protect goods while service marks protect services.

Trademarks are tremendously valuable to companies, in fact they can be among a company's most valuable assets. Many marks are recognizable worldwide; for example, there are many soft drinks sold worldwide, but almost everyone knows of the specific soft drink called 'Coca-Cola'. When a trademark becomes recognizable, its licensing value increases. Let's say, for example, that you make a very popular additive for polymers which you have trademarked and the trademark is widely known and associated with high quality products. Your customers, who use your additive in their polymers, may want to advertise that their polymers not only contain the additive but have your particular trademarked additive. You can then license the use of your trademark to your customers for use with their products, and you can control how your trademark is used. If for some reason you do not want your trademark associated with that product because it will somehow detract from your mark's reputation, you can also prevent your customers from using your trademark in association with their product.

Trademarks, like patents, must be obtained from individual countries, and fees are required from most countries in order to register and maintain the trademark. However, unlike patents, if the trademark owner continues to pay the associated fees to maintain the mark, trademarks can be kept indefinitely. Therefore businesses should take care that trademark management is a major part of their intellectual property management.

TRADE SECRETS

A trade secret is critical information and know-how of a business that is kept out of the public domain. Trade secrets can at times be more effective than patents in slowing competition, however, the owner of the trade secret must take extra precautions to maintain the security of the trade secret. Since trade secrets are kept with the organization, they can hold their value indefinitely. However, once a trade secret is disclosed publicly, its value can quickly diminish because there is essentially no way to protect the secret once it is publicly disclosed.

Trade secrets can be lost in many different ways. They may be inadvertently disclosed in company literature or technical papers. They can be lost when an individual leaves the company. However, much sensitive information is lost through the use of confidentiality or secrecy agreements. This is because of several factors. First, with many agreements the time for which the receiving party is obligated to maintain information as confidential is clearly spelled out, and may only be a few years. After that time the receiving party may be free to disclose that information. Second, the receiving party may inadvertently disclose the confidential information. It is difficult for others to have the same sensitivity to one's own secrets. Finally, once an agreement is in place, most people tend to disclose more confidential information to the second party than is required. One must be very careful to only disclose the information necessary to achieve the desired goal of the agreement.

Many times it is useful to outline what information in a business is deemed especially critical and a trade secret so that everyone is sensitive to the fact that information should not be disclosed outside the company. When working with other companies under a confidentiality agreement, it is useful to have special meetings within a business to discuss what information will have to be disclosed and what information will not. If especially sensitive information must be disclosed, perhaps special provisions for maintaining the secrecy of that information can be included in the agreement, or the secrecy provision can be extended for a longer period of time.

Trade secrets play a major part in the development of a patent strategy, because patents will disclose information known only to the inventor's company. One critical question which must be answered when considering the filing of a patent application is whether or not the disclosure of the secret information in the patent application will be worth the legal protection obtained by the patent.

OTHER RESOURCES

Researchers interested in learning more about patents, intellectual property, inventors, innovation, and strategy can refer to the last two sections of this book. The 'References' section contains information about references used in the writing of this book. The 'For Further Reading' section contains additional information on a wide variety of intellectual property topics. These two listings are not meant to be complete, but they will direct the interested reader to those periodicals which routinely cover intellectual topics and to books that have been written, which in turn will have additional references. The reader should remember, however, that patent law changes from year to year, and should endeavor to obtain the most recent edition of any book on intellectual property.

2 The Value of Patents

EXCLUSIVITY – THE DESIRED GOAL

Patent systems are set up by governments to encourage innovation. In general, patent systems have a central theme; in return for disclosing technical innovations and developments, a government grants the patentee the right to exclude others from practicing these innovations and developments for a certain amount of time. Governments hope other inventors will learn from these technical developments, these patents, and use this learning as the basis for more innovation, therefore improving the economic health of the country and the standard of living.

Patents help enable the creation of economic wealth by providing exclusivity to the inventor. In a sense, the patent system grants a legal monopoly to the inventor. However, this monopoly is not a license to practice an invention, but only the right to prevent others from practicing an invention without permission of the patent owner. For example, an inventor may be able to patent an improvement on a previously patented process. That inventor can exclude anyone else from practicing the improvement; however, if the previous process patent, the one the inventor built on, is still in force, he in turn cannot practice the improvement because the early patent is said to dominate his patent. However, the exclusivity granted by the improvement patent can open the door to cross-licensing of both patents, if the original patentee values the inventor's improvement.

Therefore, the concept of exclusivity is the most important issue when considering the patenting of a potential technology. Exclusivity, or the degree of exclusivity which an be obtained, is impacted by the nature of the invention itself, the actions the inventor takes to preserve patent rights, and the decisions the inventor makes in developing the invention. An invention may be patentable, but having a patent may not provide the patent owner with an exclusive position if the inventor thinks too narrowly about the invention during his research. So the degree of exclusivity which can be obtained is dependent on many things, including:

- What features of the invention are already known 'in the art?'
- What function does the invention perform, and can this be accomplished in a different manner?

- Have patent rights been preserved?
- How broadly will alternative technology and modifications be examined?
- When must the product be commercialized?
- How much is the exclusivity going to buy?

Let's examine each of these questions in turn.

What features of the invention are known?

One of the requirements of a patent is that the invention claimed in the patent must be novel, or in other words, 'new'. Patent examiners are paid to determine whether an invention as claimed in a patent application is new. In most cases, this means determining whether or not someone else has already publicly done or disclosed what is claimed. If the invention is not known, or someone has previously made the invention secretly without telling anyone, the chances for a patent are improved immensely. This is a necessary starting point for achieving exclusivity.

Even if in a strict sense an invention is new, it was no doubt developed using teachings from previous patents and other technical information known to other inventors. Most patent offices require an invention to be a 'significant' advance over previous patents. However, the definition of 'significant' can change from country to country, and can vary somewhat from examiner to examiner in the same patent office. If someone has already patented an invention which is close in nature to an invention claimed in a new patent application, a patent examiner, say from the United States, may claim that 'one of ordinary skill' could take one or more previous patents, add known skills, and come up with the same invention. An examiner in the European patent office might suggest the invention is not a 'technical advance' over previous patents. Both are essentially saying the same thing, that is, the invention is obvious in view of the prior art. It is in dealing with questions of obviousness that patent agents really earn their fees, for in many cases the question of patentability comes down to whether or not the response that an invention is not obvious is persuasive to an examiner.

Obviousness is not always interpreted broadly. In some countries this has always been the case, however, recently many patent offices seem to grant patents based only on the fact that the invention claimed has not been specifically disclosed in detail in a prior publication. That is, unless there was a literal disclosure of the invention in the published art, there has been an increasing trend that one could expect to obtain a patent, seemingly regardless of the obviousness of the invention. The most commonly mentioned patent system supposedly adhering to this literal interpretation is Japan's. In fact, recent publicity has given the impression there is no obviousness standard in Japan. This is simply not true; however, the interpretation of prior art is more literal in Japan than in some Western countries. This interpretation is not nearly as literal as some would have the researchers believe; many Western countries have also become much more literal in their interpretation, but without the fanfare that Japan has attracted. This trend toward a literal interpretation has not gone undetected, because now there are rumblings and the beginning of movements in patent offices, especially in the United States Patent Office, to make sure obvious inventions are not patented.

Since one of the keys to exclusivity is the extent to which a new invention is suggested by prior inventions, then in a very general sense, the degree of exclusivity a patent can provide is inversely proportional to the number of prior inventions previously disclosed in the technology area. This is because, as more information is generated in the technology area, the chances increase that someone will describe some feature of the invention. As a result, either the invention will need to be narrow, and not obtain broad exclusive claims, or the degree of exclusivity may be lessened because the prior disclosures will act as a collection of knowledge for competitors to use in devising alternate inventions which will have a similar result without infringing the patent.

Patents in other technology areas can also impact the patentability of an invention. The closest prior art to an invention docs not always have to be in the technology area with which the invention is most commonly associated. Sometimes a disclosure in one area can impact a patent application in a totally different technology area, causing the invention claimed in the patent to be significantly narrowed.

While timing is always important, if there is a lot of activity in a particular technology area, the speed in developing inventions and filing patent applications becomes a definite asset and may become the deciding factor in obtaining real exclusivity. However, it must be recognized that rapid development and filing may compromise some part of the patent, which is normally the broadness of the claimed invention, unless an effort is made to closely coordinate those involved with the development and filing. Even if the effort is coordinated, eventually a decision will have to be made as to where the experimentation stops and the patent filing begins. It must also be recognized that this decision also dictates the maximum extent of exclusivity the patent will have. For one business, the goal may be to stop all types of in-kind and functional competition, which will require broad patents. Another business may only require a narrow patent to protect the least costly route of manufacture. In any case, the exclusivity desired from the patent should match the needs of the business, and if in the haste to file a patent application the business implications are not fully considered, the resulting patent will probably not provide the exclusivity which is really needed.

What function does the invention perform, and can this be accomplished in a different manner?

The degree of a patent's exclusivity will depend on how easy it is to duplicate the function of the invention. A patent may be obtained on a machine or apparatus, or a particular process for making a product, which will provide the owner with an exclusive position for the tangible embodiments claimed or embraced by the claims. However, this exclusivity is of less value if a competitor can perform an equivalent function or generate an equivalent product or service through the use of an entirely different method that is not embraced by the claims of the patent. The one exception to this is when one patents the lowest cost process; obviously, patenting the lowest cost process gives the owner a better position than his competitors. To determine how exclusive a process or apparatus might be, analyze the proposed claims of the patent application the way a competitor might. Look at the end result of the invention and then consider how one might accomplish the same result a different way. If this analysis can be done during the development of the invention, the inventor can provide the patent agent with additional information and examples which will better support and broaden the invention description so it will potentially embrace more competitive developments.

Have patent rights been preserved?

The degree of exclusivity obtained will be dependent on the efforts the inventor takes to preserve his patent rights. The patent offices of the world have definite requirements for secrecy in patent matters. In most countries, premature public disclosure of an invention, that is, before a patent application is filed, can be used to invalidate a subsequent patent on that invention. If maximum exclusivity is desired, the invention must have been developed with adequate secrecy not only to withstand stated patent office requirements, but also tests of validity in court. Thus, the maximum amount of exclusivity can be obtained only if there are no gray areas around the secrecy of the invention. From a practical standpoint, this means the fewer people involved with the invention before the patent filing, therefore the better the secrecy around the invention, the more likely one is to maintain patent rights and thus exclusivity. This is the case regardless of whether or not the inventor is working within his own company or with other companies. Even though one may emphasize within his company the need for secrecy, the possibility of an undesired, premature disclosure increases as the number of people involved with the invention increases. Even though confidentiality agreements may be signed with other companies which should provide some measure of secrecy, the possibility for a premature disclosure increases as the number of companies and people involved with the invention increases. Also, agreements are sometimes signed by the manager of a company and the workers are not informed of the details of the agreement. Agreements are also sometimes forgotten with time, meaning any new people which join a development may not know how critical secrecy is to the invention.

How broadly will alternative technology and modifications be examined?

Earlier, exclusivity was said to be dependent on how easy it was to duplicate the function of an invention, and it was said an analysis could be made of how a competitor might engineer around any patents which might be received. In some cases, a researcher can use his technical training and experience to mentally picture various alternatives, or to advise the patent agent on wording to include in the patent that would better cover various alternative embodiments of the invention. However, in many cases, the researcher will have to perform additional experiments to confirm whether or not these alternative embodiments truly can be claimed in the patent. Even if the researcher is convinced enough information has been generated for the patent application filing, he must also ask himself whether or not the invention is important enough to continue to develop this invention, that is, work on improvements on the basic invention.

It is very important that these implications be considered, because the amount of exclusivity a business will experience can be dependent on the amount of effort and money expended to examine variations and extensions of the inventions of the business. If there is only a limited exclusionary opportunity, or the invention is not that critical to the business, then there is little need to spend additional effort to broaden the patent application or to work on developing improvements. On the other hand, if there is a good chance for a substantial exclusionary position, or that the technology is critical to the business, then a decision must be made as to whether or not the business has the desire and the resources to fully exploit this opportunity. Most businesses have the desire but not the resources. In this case, the researcher or research manager will have to decide what will be the essential work needed to achieve a modest but acceptable exclusionary position. If there are still no resources to develop even this position, and this is very commonly the case, then action should be taken to guarantee the business will at least continue to have freedom to operate.

When must the product be commercialized?

One must weigh the possible negative business impact of delaying product introduction to prepare and file a patent application versus the exclusionary value a patent may bring. A saleable product form may be developed fairly quickly with the desire to get the product to the marketplace as rapidly as possible. However, if a broad, exclusionary patent is to be obtained, not only will the optimum form of the product have to be identified, but also the ranges under which the product will perform or can be produced. Developing this information will take time and the urge will be to commercialize the product without completion of all the experimentation. By recognizing this possibility exists early in the development of the invention, it is possible to put additional resources on the development in an effort to speed both the experimentation and the product introduction.

Also, while not a strict requirement, if the researcher truly understands the invention and its application, the chances of obtaining a good degree of exclusivity are dramatically increased. It might be surprising that many inventors never truly understand how their invention works. Many know little more than if they add component A to component B, a new component C results which has very useful characteristics. A patent agent will ask what other components can be substituted for A and B. If the inventor truly understands the invention, he will be able to provide the agent with an answer. However, if the inventor does not understand the invention, the development of the alternative components may require empirically testing many more components, meaning the time to develop an adequate description of the invention is dramatically increased. Not fully understanding an invention is more likely if the inventor is working in a new technology area, or has discovered a surprising synergy or result.

If the inventor can take the time to understand an invention fully, he will be more likely to know what are the critical parts of the invention. This in turn, will save time in the eventual preparation of the application and improve exclusivity. It will allow the inventor both to run the minimum number of useful experiments to illustrate the full range of these critical elements and to advise the patent agent so that the patent application can be written to cover the critical components.

Also, if time is spent to fully understand an invention, alternative technologies can be better developed to improve the exclusionary position, probably through other patents. However, this time could reduce the speed at which the invention is introduced in the marketplace. So, it is best to decide how much time is reasonable for the development of the technical understanding of an invention and how much time the business is willing to delay product introduction. If these two times do not agree, it may be preferable to put more manpower on the project to obtain the desired information at a faster rate, and therefore meet both desires for exclusivity and product introduction.

How much is the exclusivity going to buy?

John Gilman, in an article in the journal *Physics Today*, found that when the patents of a large corporation were studied, only about 1 out of 10 patents were actually commercially significant. So, this means many of the patents that are issued are really not worth the paper on which they are printed, and the fact that an exclusive position is obtained is of no worth. But if so many patents are worthless, why do people continue to file applications?

One reason people file patents is for professional recognition. If a researcher obtains a patent, then he can truly refer to himself as an inventor, and his marketability as a researcher may be increased. If a researcher has several patents, the implication is that the researcher is truly a creative and driven individual, capable of developing new things. The inventor may be accorded this respect even if none of the patents have proven to be of any value in the marketplace. Therefore, some people file patents just to improve their professional image.

A common reason many patents end up being worthless is that the patent claims that are issued are much different than the claims which were filed. In other words, the scope of the patent was severely narrowed in patent prosecution. Claims are narrowed for many reasons, but perhaps the most common reason is that the patent examiner has found a close prior art reference that was not found by the applicant's agent in the preparation of the application. The ultimate result can be a substantial narrowing of patent claims so that anyone can essentially practice the invention but not infringe the patent.

Perhaps the most common reason worthless patents are filed is that sometimes it is difficult to determine the true commercial value of an invention at the time of the patent filing. It seems obvious that before filing a patent application, which one hopes will eventually become a patent and which will exclude someone else from an invention, one should establish in their own mind that someone would actually want to practice the invention; that is, produce the product, run the process, or make and sell the apparatus. However, the true value of an invention may only become apparent several years after the patent is filed. In many cases, inventors decide that filing a patent application is fairly cheap insurance for protecting their technology. Still, attempting to analyze who would want to use the invention can be a very useful technique in identifying the limits of exclusivity of a patent application or invention. If, after such an analysis, the invention has only limited value, then one should question whether or not a patent is really necessary for business success, or whether or not there are other drivers, such as the inventor's professional reputation, which are pushing for a patent on the technology.

Another issue to consider is whether or not the disclosure made in the application may impact subsequent work. Researchers certainly do not want to 'foul their own nest' by disclosing technology in a worthless patent which might make other, more important developments more obvious. The disclosure in patents is always valuable; the actual claimed invention may not be.

If a patent application is filed with the licensing of the issued patent in mind, it is all the more important to perform an analysis of value to another company. If the exclusive qualities of the patent are weak, the best one can hope for is that some uninformed company may be willing to license the patent.

THE MECHANICS OF ACHIEVING EXCLUSIVITY IN A TECHNOLOGY AREA

Exclusivity in a technology area can be achieved by one or more 'broad' patents or a number of 'narrow' patents. A 'broad patent' is a subjective descriptor of a patent that typically has claim language that excludes others, or could be interpreted to exclude others, from a large chunk of a technology area. Because of this claim language, broad patents are said to have broad claims. Broad patents will normally disclose many different embodiments of the invention and perhaps will have new test methods or will disclose new techniques or concepts. Typically, they claim a new composition of matter, a new product, a new process, or perhaps even a special machine which performs a special function. It is not uncommon for broad patents to have a long listing of independent and dependent claims, claiming any number of different embodiments of the invention, and hoping to extend the coverage of the patent to other embodiments not specifically disclosed in the patent application.

The other subjective descriptor, 'narrow patent', is typically used to describe a patent that has claim language that excludes others from a more specific piece of a technology area. A narrow patent is said to have narrow claims because these claims try to exclude others from only a few embodiments of an invention, a specific operating range, or a specific improvement to a previously disclosed invention. Narrow patents tend to be shorter in length and very specific in application, and while they may introduce new concepts, they typically build on and extend previously patterned inventions. Because of the specificity, it is not uncommon for narrow patents to have only a few claims.

Since by our definition, broad patents exclude a chunk of technology, a single broad patent can provide exclusivity in a technology area, similarly to a fence around the technology area, as in Figure 2.1.

It is possible to obtain a somewhat similar exclusive position using narrow patents, however, one must obtain a number of narrow patents. The effect is more like erecting a maze, as in Figure 2.2.

One might be tempted to assume this means that broad patents are more

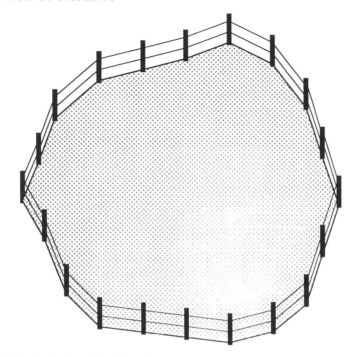

Figure 2.1 A single, broadly-claimed patent

valuable than narrow patents, since entire businesses have been based on broad patents. However, broad patents by their nature try to extend coverage to all embodiments, which is, in a practical sense, difficult to do. Referring back to our fence analogy, this means that the fence may have some holes caused by the applicant trying to extend the coverage of the patent too broadly, as in Figure 2.3. Competitors may be able to use these holes to their advantage. A competitor might also be able to patent an improvement invention that is dominated by the broad patent; if this improvement is of high value, both the patent owner and the competitor may decide to cross-license in order to operate.

Erecting a maze of narrow patents is not without its own problems. Clearly, there will be advantageous routes through the maze; in developing an exclusive position the key issue is to attempt to block the least costly or least prohibitive route. To obtain adequate coverage, a number of patents will probably have to be individually filed and prosecuted, so the chances for not obtaining a vital piece of the maze is always present. Narrow patents are in some cases the only practical way of developing a position if the technology area already has a large amount of prior art. Narrow patents can

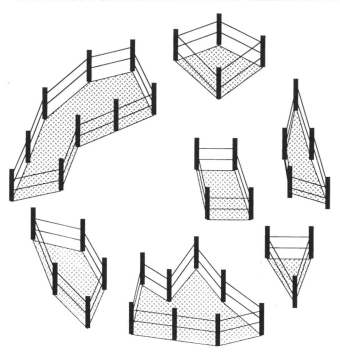

Figure 2.2 Several narrowly-claimed patents provide a maze

also serve as short term roadblocks in a technology area where competition is growing at a rapid rate. Narrow patents can also be used by one company to induce another company into cross-licensing patents so that both can utilize the technology. This type of strategy, along with the concept of 'patent flooding' where all improvements to a particular invention are investigated and patented, has been associated with patents in Japan.

It is obvious from a review of patents filed that many Japanese patent practitioners have opted to try to obtain narrow patents in Japan. This stems from a more literal reading or interpretation of the prior art in Japan, which has in turn encouraged the patent applications to be more specifically focused. In a literal interpretation system, a patent that claims a very narrow invention will provide very good exclusivity for that specific invention. Patents for other embodiments of the invention can also be constructed. In this manner, a portfolio of patents can be generated which when combined together can provide exclusivity. If at a later date, a disclosure is found that invalidates one of these patents, the patent owner still has a chance of maintaining an exclusive position because not all the other patents are harmed. On the other hand, if a broad patent is obtained, which might

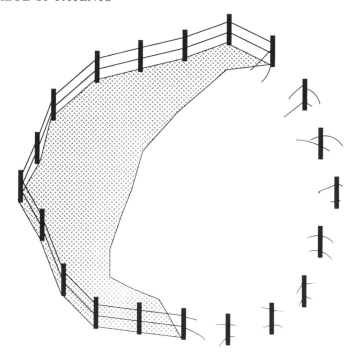

Figure 2.3 Broad patents which attempt to extend coverage too broadly may be effectively narrowed because of holes in the protective fence of claims

actually describe all of the embodiments represented in this previously mentioned portfolio of narrow patents, and the same disclosure is found, the entire exclusive position could be jeopardized because the entire patent or a large part of it could be judged invalid. The more literal interpretation of the patent art means that the broad patent covers essentially only the embodiment specifically disclosed; therefore, when the examiner is using a literal interpretation standard there may be more good reasons to file narrow patents than to file broad patents.

To say that Japanese practitioners always file narrow patents would not be correct, however. It has been publicized that practitioners in the United States and Europe have tried to obtain broad patents wherever they filed, but particularly in the United States and Europe. However, a review of patent filings indicates it is quite common for Japanese practitioners also to combine several Japanese patent filings into one larger international application, that is, to combine several specific inventions into one broadly claimed invention, and file this broader application in the United States and Europe. As a rule, all patent practitioners, regardless of the country, normally attempt to obtain the best possible claims for their clients, and in most cases this means the broadest claims possible, while at the same time accounting for the specific characteristics of the national patent offices.

In practice, exclusivity in a technology area is achieved by developing a portfolio of patents, some broad and some narrow, that effectively restrict the options competitors have in a technology area. There are some useful analogies that can help illustrate how this is accomplished. As mentioned before, companies have been said to use a technique of patent 'flooding' or 'blanketing' a technology area. This type of strategy can be thought of as being composed of a series of individual fences, very quickly erected around a technology area, with each fenced-in area being a separate patent application enclosing a separate invention, as shown in Figure 2.4. The object of blanketing a technology area is either to patent, or if unsuccessful with the patent, to disclose as much of the technology area as possible in an attempt to have an exclusive position, or in the worst case, freedom to operate. Blanketing an area of technology is normally the result of a deliberate effort to examine each and every facet of a technology are. To accomplish this,

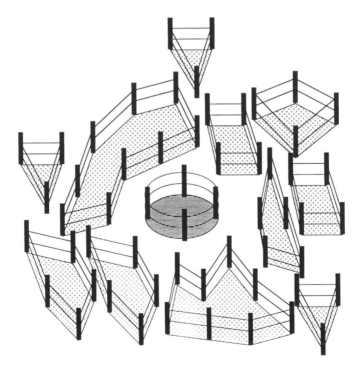

Figure 2.4 Patent flooding or blanketing around an original patent of another inventor – the ability of the original inventor to expand invention is effectively blocked

normally a team of researchers is required. The result of a blanketing strategy is an in-depth group of patent applications filed over a few months which suddenly appear in the patent literature. In other words, most of the fences are developed and erected concurrently, so that when the patent applications are published, the result is that the fence around the technology area is put in place without a lot of warning to competitors.

Blanketing has two difficulties. It is difficult to achieve without a great deal of resources, and the natural development of a commercial enterprise is seldom as planned or coordinated as one might design. Blanketing has been used to force companies into joint ventures. The typical scenario is that a new technology is patented by a first company, a second company reads the patent and sees a lot of potential in this technology. However, because of the pioneering patent by the first company, the second company cannot practice. The second company, however, can immediately begin work to patent improvements on the pioneering invention, and if the stakes are high enough, can assign enough resources literally to blanket all of the potential improvements to the invention by filing patents on these improvements. The first company is then essentially forced into some type of cross-licensing agreement if they want their business to grow.

An alternate strategy that is useful for specific parts of a technology area, and which assumes the researchers of the first company are just as aggressive as their competitors, is the 'wall' strategy. In the wall strategy, the first company assumes some of the patents they obtain will eventually be bypassed by competitors, and that the true value for the patent is the time delay caused by the need for extra work by a determined competitor who wants to 'get around' the 'wall' of the patent. A competitor must first locate, read, and understand the patent, and then must develop a true understanding of the technology in the patent through experimentation, all of which takes time. A company wishing to implement the wall strategy files one or more patents on a technology or a part of the desired technology. After the filing of the patent(s), research by the company continues at a high rate, with the goal of filing additional patents on the technology area before the first patent(s) have published. This cycle is continued as long as the company wishes. The result of this strategy is that by the time the original patent applications have been published and digested by competitors, additional patents have been filed that build on the original patents. The original patent filer has already developed new technology that will make the old technology obsolete. The effect is the same as that of constructing small walls in a technology area as shown in Figure 2.5. The competitor, once he understands the technology, may be able to engineer around the patent. However, by the time this is accomplished, the originator has erected several new walls to be scaled. In this manner, the competitor is always behind the originator and at least theoretically a company's patent monopoly can be continued indefinitely.

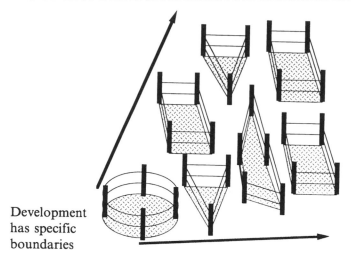

Development
has specific
boundaries

Figure 2.5 The wall strategy is more focused in one direction for impact

TRAPS AND MISCONCEPTIONS – WHAT PATENTS CAN'T DO

Unless a researcher deals with patents on a regular basis, there are a few common errors in logic or understanding which frequently happen. Try to avoid the following traps and misconceptions.

The 'Value' Trap

The value of patents can be overstated. Remember, patent systems are established to help disseminate inventions and innovations so that others can learn and continue inventing and innovating; the dissemination process is achieved by the patent application, where the inventor conveniently summarizes the major concepts and teaches the reader how to make the invention. The loss of secrecy because of the disclosure must be weighed against the limited monopoly that may be granted to the patent applicant. In some cases, it is better to keep an invention secret rather than attempt to obtain a patent.

The 'Protection' Trap

A basic tenet of patent law is that a patent does not give the patent owner the right to practice his invention, but only gives him the right to exclude others. Therefore, there are times when two different patent holders, holding similar patents, cannot practice their inventions, and must negotiate cross licenses. By 'protecting' an invention through patents, one is assuming that these inventions are valuable and there is a business reason not to want anyone else practicing these inventions. Protecting an invention, however, does not mean guaranteeing the inventor's right to practice the invention.

The idea that every invention must be protected must be weighed versus the cost of filing many applications. The bottom line should always be that those applications which describe inventions that increase the competitive position of a business should be filed, while applications on lesser attractive inventions should not. In either case there will be mistakes. Things which should have been patented will not be, and money will be spent on lousy inventions. However, if the business has a patent strategy, the number of these mistakes should be reduced.

The 'Patent at All Cost' Trap

Just because a business obtains a patent does not make its competitive position better. If the claims of a patent application are severely restricted during prosecution, the value of the application may be reduced to such an extent that it is no longer worth the issuance and maintenance cost (see Figure 2.6). Holding onto a worthless patent is the same as holding onto a worthless business. Both will suck funds from the items that have value and reduce the overall profitability of the business.

The 'Uniform Treatment' Misconception

While attempts are ongoing to harmonize patent laws and the filing of global applications has become easier, this should not be interpreted as making the treatment of patents more uniform around the world. A patent is still a grant from an individual country and the prosecution of patent applications in patent offices and the treatment of patents in judicial systems will differ from country to country. A good example of this non-uniform treatment is in prior-user right laws. In the United States, the granting of a patent to one company can prevent a second company from practicing the invention, regardless of when the second company started practicing the invention, if the second company has been practicing the invention in secret. Many countries have prior user rights laws, which in general, would allow this second company to continue to practice an invention if they were practicing the invention before a patent was filed on that same invention by another. Now, prior user rights for business model patents were passed into law in the United States in 1999. However, the actual legal issues involved with prior user rights can be quite complicated, and sorting out these issues requires a competent patent attorney in the

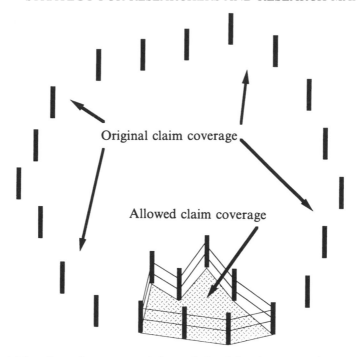

Figure 2.6 The effect of severe restrictions of the claims in prosecution may make a patent worthless

country in question. While the person first utilizing the invention may have a prior user right, he may also be restricted in how he can change or use this invention in the future.

The interpretation of patents, patent applications, and patent laws can vary from country to country, and the best source of information is an agent in the country in question. Since interpretation can be fluid, it helps to have an up-to-date contact. One should not assume that a patent application or a patent will be treated the same way in many different countries.

The 'Idea' Misconception

Finally, patents are essentially legally granted monopolies on an embodiment of an idea in tangible form. Ideas are the lifeblood of the patent system, because they generate inventions, but it is the invention, the tangible form, which must be patented; an idea cannot be patented. Therefore, patents can grant the holder the right to a legal monopoly of the inventions claimed. Patents cannot give anyone a monopoly over the basic idea contained in the patent.

THE INFORMATIONAL VALUE OF PATENTS

Technical Information

When an inventor obtains a patent, he discloses secrets; so, patents are a great source of technical information. It has been said that 70 to 80 percent of all technology can only be found in patents, because patents contain details which would normally not be disclosed in a sales brochure or even a technical journal. Patents can teach how to perform experiments, can show how to test for results, and may define new concepts which have not previously been disclosed. Patent laws in some countries, such as the United States, require the patent applicant to disclose the most preferred form of the invention in the patent application, so preferred equipment arrangements and operating ranges are disclosed in the patent. If a number of patents are filed pertaining to the same general invention, say a process for manufacturing an item, there may be parameters that are consistent from one patent to the other which disclose important features. For example, if a process is operated at a particular temperature in all of the patents, then this is probably the preferred temperature even though the patent does not specifically state it is.

It is common for patent applications to have a background section near the beginning of the application. This section can provide information on the general technical area of the invention, but more importantly it can describe the failings of previous inventions and why the new invention is needed. It will occasionally also disclose the close art along with some explanation why that art does not apply or is deficient in some manner.

Some patent applications have drawings or process diagrams which show how an invention is put together or how a process operates. Normally in the patent application these drawings are explained in detail. Many times the actual dimensions of parts are given or the application gives the company name and address where certain parts can be bought. One can then better understand the makeup of the invention.

A large part of most patent publications is a section containing detailed information about the critical components of an invention. It will often disclose operating ranges such as concentrations, pressures, and temperatures that are important to the practice of the invention. It should adequately explain the invention so that one could determine if they are infringing the patent. This detailed section will define any ambiguous terms used in the patent, and in some cases will disclose not only how an invention works but why it works the way it does. This section will also disclose alternative forms of the invention that the inventor wanted to obtain coverage for in the original application.

Most applications will have one or more examples illustrating some feature of the invention. Sometimes these examples will contain comparisons showing how the new invention differs from the closest disclosure in the prior art. These examples can also contain recipes for compositions and detailed instructions on how one can make the new invention. From these examples one can learn techniques just like one was studying the inventor's lab notebook.

By combining a number of patent publications from a particular company in a technology area, one can infer certain details by looking for patterns in the disclosure. For example, if all patents disclose a process which operates at 50 degrees Celsius, then it is a good bet the commercial process for that company operates at 50 degrees Celsius. A single patent may disclose many different versions of an invention, and it may be difficult to determine which version of the invention is best. However, subsequent patent publications may use one of the versions of the invention disclosed in a previous patent as a comparison with the new invention. One may infer that the comparison invention was the best version of the invention up until the new invention was made. Since many inventions are somewhat minor improvements over existing inventions, the disclosure of the improvement may also inadvertently point out the best method of using a previous invention.

In addition to the technical information, many patent publications also contain lists of those patents the examiner considered in the prosecution. This list of patents will normally include the closest and most pertinent prior work. This list of patents provides a researcher with a quick initial literature search with which to start developing information on a particular technology area.

Competitive Information

The growth of on-line computer databases has allowed quick and efficient tracking of competitors' patent applications. Although it is not unusual to wait 18 months plus abstracting time after the filing date before the publication of filed global patent applications, a fairly decent snapshot can be developed of a company, a technology area, or of a particular company's interest in a certain technology area. A perspective can be developed of where in the world the company believes its patents will be valuable, and who in their organization has the knowledge of a particular technology area. To develop a general idea of a competitor's technology requires only the name of the competitor, an idea of how many years back in time one wishes to search, and the particular technology area involved. A computer researcher can quickly print out a list of abstracts of patents and published applications from the competitor. The patents can then be obtained and reviewed for the desired information.

Sometimes useful information can be inferred from the inventorship on the patent application. For example, suppose a company has filed many patent applications in a particular technology area over five years. A simple compilation of the filing data from online databases for those applications will reveal whether those patent applications are the result of one inventor's efforts or a number of inventors. If there are many different inventors on numerous patent applications over several years, this would imply that the company has devoted a fair amount of manpower to this technology area, and therefore believes that it is an important part of their future. If on the other hand, all of the applications come from just one inventor, it is clear this company has a prolific inventor in this field. It is much less clear whether or not the patents are truly valuable to the company. If the company is a large one, with many resources, it may be very telling if only one inventor is involved with the technology. It may mean that this inventor has enough status in that company to get his patents filed but that perhaps the company is not overly excited by the technology. Otherwise, more inventors would be involved with the development.

ASSIGNING VALUE TO PATENTS

If patents are used as an information source, a researcher will no doubt wonder which patents are truly valuable, and which are not. If a researcher is monitoring patent abstracts to see what competitors are doing, the researcher will also want to review the actual patents to see on what they are actually obtaining claims and whether they are of value. But how does one evaluate a patent to assign value to it?

First, one must decide whether or not one is interested in what the patent claims; that is, whether or not what is claimed restricts ones operation, and whether or not it is the technical disclosure contained in the patent that is of interest. If there is a concern with the possibility that this patent will affect future operations, one will want first to review the summary of the invention section of the patent and the claims section of the patent. This will give the researcher an idea of the basic invention claimed. The researcher can then use the rest of the patent specification to understand further how terms are defined in the claims, and better understand the invention. If there are any concerns that a company might be an infringer, it is important that a patent attorney be involved with the analysis of the patent. Obviously, a patent attorney has specialized knowledge interpreting claims that can be very beneficial in the analysis of the patent. Also, if the patent looks like a serious infringement concern, the patent attorney may be able to obtain a copy of the prosecution history of the patent application from the patent office. This public record will sometimes give hints to any weakness in the patent application.

If one is interested in the technology disclosed in the patent, the easiest way to assign value is for an expert, that is, someone who has in-depth knowledge and stays up to date in the particular technical field, to review the patent for keys to its worth. In-depth knowledge of an area means this person can review a patent and recognize any new concepts the inventor has used in the development of the invention, and whether the invention itself is a major new development or contribution to the technical field. Often the expert can quickly tell whether or not the invention or disclosure is of much value. Many claims will be restricted to a particular operating range. An expert can sometimes review these ranges and determine whether or not the claimed operating range is a narrowing of the patent or not.

In-depth knowledge of the technical area in question is obviously a great help to the individual who is trying to understand the value of an individual patent. Developing this in-depth knowledge requires detailed study in the basics of a technology area and maintaining a current awareness in the field. While some researchers are able to do this, the current trend toward specialization of the work of researchers means that many will not have this in-depth knowledge, especially if they are looking into a new technology area, or they are trying to evaluate a company's patent portfolio. Therefore, techniques are needed to help evaluate the value of patents that do not rely on the technical knowledge of the individual making the analysis. There are a few techniques which can be used to help generate a picture of the worth of a patent. However, one must realize that these techniques are not an exact science, but simply indicators of value which one can use on a daily basis without a lot of investment time.

The first indicator that a person not skilled in a technology area can use, can be found on computer databases which provide filing information on patent applications, such as the World Patents Index provided by Derwent. Using the data in these databases, one can take a look at where and how broadly the applicant decided to file the application, especially in view of other patents the applicant has filed. This indicator is based on the principle that the applicant has an opinion about the value of an application when it is filed, and the more important the application to the applicant, the more broadly the application will be filed. For example, if an applicant in Japan has filed an application in Japan and has also filed or obtained patents in the United States and Europe on this invention, it is a good bet that this patent has value to that company.

This indicator fails in two common situations. The first is when an individual or company is not concerned about developing a global patent estate, and files all of its applications in its home country; or conversely, it files all of its applications in the same countries. If the patent is assigned to an individual, one must also consider the individual will not have the resources of a larger company, and may not be financially able to file patents globally. In order for this indicator to work, the applicant must make some distinction in the breadth of filing from case to case, which is typical of most companies.

The second place this indicator fails is if the applicant does not understand the true value of a patent application when it is filed. This is a very real problem, because many times an invention is thought to be quite valuable during the preparation and filing of a patent application, and is filed in a large number of countries, only to be found to be quite valueless in the marketplace. If this happens, the patents or applications will probably be abandoned, but to determine the status of the applications is more complicated, normally requiring a check for each patent or application at each patent office where the application was filed. Conversely, the applicant may not know the true value of the application when it is filed, and not file a valuable application broadly.

In any case, a broadly-filed application should be considered appropriately, because when someone is going through the filing decision process there are normally more reasons not to file an application broadly than to do so. Filing broadly requires more money and time, so one does not file broadly unless some value is expected from the patented invention. Further, since the legal community views the enforcement climate for patents to be questionable in many countries, there is a bias to filing patents in only a few countries – normally countries where the legal system values private property. So, if an applicant is willing to take the gamble to spend money to obtain patents in many countries, the applicant normally believes the invention to be very valuable.

Another indicator of value is the length and structure of the claim language itself. In general, the longer the claim, the narrower its coverage. For example, assume a researcher has a polymer with the chemical name 'X', and is the first to make a fiber from this polymer. One might be able to obtain a claim with the wording:

1. An artificial filament comprising X.

Notice how broad this claim is. There are no restrictions, except the filament must be made from polymer X. This claim is easy to police, because if one finds a filament with X in it, and it wasn't made by the owner of the patent, then someone else is infringing the patent.

However, if one was not the first to make a fiber from this polymer, one would not be entitled to such a broad claim. However, if an additive 'Y' is added to the fiber which improved the appearance of the fiber, one might be able to get a claim with the following wording:

1. An artificial filament comprising X and Y.

Notice now the claim has been narrowed. To infringe the claim, someone would have to make a fiber having both polymer X and additive Y. If the claim had been written:

1. An artificial filament of improved appearance comprising 80–95 weight percent X and 20–25 weight percent Y.

Notice now that a fiber having X and Y in a weight ratio of 99:1 might be interpreted as falling outside the claim. Claim interpretation is for patent attorneys; however, the key point to make here is that as the wording in the claim has grown, the claim has been limited each time. Therefore in reviewing patents, be careful to consider the length of the claim. A very long claim will probably have many different elements, and the more elements, the better the chance someone can develop an alternative invention which does not infringe the patent claim.

At this point, it's useful to mention a very widely used type of claim, a Jepson claim. Jepson claims are used for improvement-type inventions, that is, when new elements are added to old inventions to provide a patentable new invention. Jepson claims contain three distinct parts. The first part is a description of the old elements or items. The second is almost always either the phrase 'the improvement comprising' or 'wherein the improvement comprises'. The third part is a description of the new elements. In evaluating a claim of this type, one must realize that the invention is really the new elements that occur after the phrase 'the improvement comprising'. All this may sound confusing, but just remember that Jepson claims, when first read, always seem very broad. However, once the researcher realizes only the improvement is being patented, Jepson claims can then be properly viewed in their restricted form. Since Jepson claims are almost always very long claims, they tend to be more narrow than other types of claims. A Jepson claim for the above invention would be as follows:

1. An artificial filament of improved appearance comprising X and Y, wherein the improvement comprises X and Y being present in a weight ratio of 80:20 to 95:5.

There is another method of obtaining information on the possible value of a patent. Computer databases allow one to check how many times a patent has been cited in other patents. As mentioned previously, cited patents are those patents used in the prosecution of a patent application. This citation searching is based on the premise that the most important patents will initiate additional work, and thus they will be cited as references in subsequent patents. Therefore, the patents with the most citations are the most valuable patents. The rule of thumb is that if a patent is going to be cited, it will be cited within a few years of its first publication. If the patent hasn't been cited after a period of time, say five years after its publication, it probably will never be.

However, conclusions based on citation searching need to be arrived at very carefully. It can be useful in determining how a technology is improved with time. It can show, like a family tree, how different inventions have been developed which built on previous inventions. Assigning value based strictly on the number of citations can be tricky. First of all, an improvement patent may cite another more basic patent, however, the improvement could be easily worth more than the basic patent. Moreover, the idea that a large number of citations means that a patent is important because others are developing technology based on that patent could fall apart if one company is citing the patent over and over and skewing the results. It is more likely that a patent that has many citations has an especially good disclosure of some key part of the technology that must be used in other patents rather than being especially valuable.

LICENSING OF PATENTS

Patents act to exclude, but many companies do not use them in this manner. The owner of a patent can also grant a license to another to practice the invention claimed in the patent, and in return receive a licensing fee on the patent and, in many cases, royalties on the sale of whatever is made using the invention. Licensing of patents can be a very lucrative business because many companies are looking for sources of technology. For these companies, licensing technology is more economical than developing this same technology in-house. In addition, other companies and consortia have been started in which their sole source of revenue is the licensing of technology.

Many companies make a deliberate choice to license the technology in their patents to whoever wishes to do so, and in so doing, generate additional revenue for their company. They, in turn, only exert their patent against a wilful infringer that totally ignores the patent. In licensing their patents, these companies can recoup the cost of obtaining the patent and generate additional monetary support for additional research and business goals. Also, by taking an aggressive stand to license essentially any and all of its patents, a company is acknowledging the monopoly given to them by a patent is a limited one, and that new technology must be developed to replace the old.

Typically, a patent license agreement includes more than the right to use the patent. While the patent license may give the licensee a right to use the technology, many license agreements have provisions for the transfer of know-how in addition to the patent. So, while the patent might be the legal reason to license, the key to true business success may be the acquisition of know-how and trade secrets which allows the licensee to use the information contained in the patent in a practical way.

Licensing fees for a patent can vary widely and it can be difficult to put a monetary value on a patent. Traditionally, is not uncommon for the licensee to pay a royalty of up to 5 percent of the gross sales or up to 25 percent of the net profits of those products that involve the licensed invention. The license may also involve up-front payments that may be in addition to an annual royalty. There are firms that assist in the licensing of patents in return for a portion of the licensing fees. Sometimes this can be as high as a third of the fees recovered by the license.

If patents and knowledge are available on technology areas in which one no longer has a major interest, licensing can be a valuable alternative to either doing nothing or abandoning the patents. Today, unless one pays fees to maintain one's patent in force, the patent grant lapses and the claimed technology becomes publicly available. One may be tempted to abandon patents on technology developed but not commercialized or not critical to the business. One may be able to generate, perhaps with the help of an outside agent, a list of potential licensees. If successful in licensing these patents, one will be able to turn non-productive assets into productive ones.

3 Developing A Strategy

PROFESSIONAL HELP

Unless a researcher has previously filed a patent application, he will have little idea of what a researcher must do to obtain a patent. Almost every researcher develops something he is excited about, and since patents are known to provide competitive advantage and prestige, researchers need to know what is involved in obtaining one.

The first decision that must be made is whether or not professional help will be hired to prepare and prosecute the patent application. There are a fair amount of specific tasks, so this decision should not be made lightly. In Chapters 1 and 2, we discussed the value of patents, and gave an idea of the type of information that may be included in the patent application. At a minimum, a patent application will have to be prepared and filed, and someone will have to correspond with the patent office. To improve the chances of obtaining a strong patent, a patent search will need to be performed before the patent application is drafted. While it is possible for the inventor to handle the prosecution of a patent application in his home country, it is much more difficult for an untrained individual to succeed in obtaining strong global patent rights. Countries have different laws, and although progress has been made in making filings uniform across the world, there are still many complexities; for this reason most patent offices recommend inventors use authorized patent attorneys and agents. Unless the researcher has some special experience or training in the development and prosecution of patents, he will want to have an attorney or agent handle the preparation, filing, and prosecuting of the patent application.

Some inventors are very independent and resist the idea of getting any type of patent agent involved in the handling of the patent application, either because of the extra expense involved or because the inventor believes that he can prepare a patent application just as well as an agent. The inventor should resist the urge to 'go-it-alone.' An inventor who is not experienced in the preparation and filing of patent applications has a very limited chance of obtaining a strong, enforceable patent, and without the guidance of a competent patent agent can very easily forfeit some of his patent rights.

A patent agent will assist the inventor in determining patentability, writing the patent application, and prosecuting the patent application. The agent should endeavour to understand the invention and have a search of the prior art made, either by his office or another patent search firm. The agent should then prepare an application for filing, file the application, and handle the correspondence with the patent office. If a decision is made to file the patent application in other countries, the agent should advise as to how best to do this. If the agent needs specialized guidance in the patent law of another country, he may have to hire an agent in that country to help prosecute the application.

Some companies advertise that they will help file patent applications and market a researcher's invention. While some of these firms may be reputable, some inventors have not been satisfied with their treatment by these firms, and this dissatisfaction has drawn the attention of governmental agencies and other groups. In the United States, the Federal Government – through the Federal Trade Commission, many State Governments – through their state 'Offices of Innovation' or of 'Technical Development', and state inventors' associations may have information on the track record of any particular firm. Other countries have similar governmental innovation offices that may be able to supply information on the experience of inventors in that country with such firms.

Since the personal interaction between a patent agent and an inventor is so important, the inventor should strive to develop a relationship with a relatively local patent agent where it is convenient to meet with the agent in person. The inventor should retain control over his invention and the money spent to patent it; this may not be the case if he deals with an unknown firm in another state or country.

If an inventor decides to contact a large corporation about his invention, the inventor should be prepared for almost any reaction. Depending on how the company views unsolicited inventions, its reaction can range from welcoming the inventor with open arms, to rejecting the invention almost without any consideration of the invention's potential. Most large companies have standard procedures on how to handle inquiries from inventors, and since most of these inquiries turn out to be of very little use, most companies are not the welcoming type. Those companies that are cool to unsolicited inventions are that way in order to avoid potential lawsuits. Should the unsolicited invention be rejected, and later a similar invention is innocently developed by the company (because in large corporations the left hand doesn't always know what the right hand is doing), the spurned inventor may take legal action against the company. While some companies do welcome ideas from independent inventors, the inventor will be in a much better position if a patent application has already been filed before the initial contact is made. By filing the patent application before contacting companies, the inventor helps to guarantee that his rights will be protected if his invention is stolen. The patent filing also shows that the inventor is serious about his invention and the invention is not just a good idea, but an idea that has been developed to some tangible form and is thus something that can be evaluated. The filing of a patent application prior to the initial contact also indicates to the company that the inventor will to feel more comfortable about discussing the invention, since this issue of ownership is settled.

DETERMINING WHETHER OR NOT AN INVENTION IS PATENTABLE

Let's say a researcher has invented a machine, and wishes to have a patent application filed; that is, if the chances are that he will receive a patent. In addition, let's say the researcher has either just made the invention or has taken steps to maintain the secrecy of the invention, and has not done anything to forfeit any patent rights. Since the researcher knows that just because the invention is new to him doesn't necessarily mean it is patentable, he now wants to know what, if anything, about his machine is patentable.

As we indicated in Chapter 1, an invention will have to meet some basic requirements for patentability which apply in most countries; these requirements are that the invention must be new, useful, and non-obvious. The useful requirement is the easiest to meet. Since most inventions have real-world utility, in practice this requirement is not an issue. How well the invention meets the other two requirements can be determined by conducting a search of prior publications for inventions similar to the new invention. The prior art search will normally be provided by the patent agent and will indicate what publications should be reviewed to see to what extent certain features of the invention have already been disclosed. Once a review of these publications has been completed, the agent should have a good idea whether or not the invention is patentable.

It is not unusual for the prior art search to find a reference that discloses some, or even most, of the features of an invention. Sometimes the search will reveal that others have already made the invention and have improved on it, and obtained patents on the improvement. A man once came to me with a new invention he had made – a new type of tomato stake made from a plastic tube, which made the watering of tomato plants easier and more efficient. To water a tomato plant, one only had to fill up the hollow tomato stake; the stake would automatically direct the water to the roots of the tomato plant. A search of the prior art revealed others had thought of the same idea long ago, and patents had issued on this type of tomato stake with improvements such as built-in ties for staking the tomato plant. In this case, the invention the man had made was not patentable in view of the prior art.

But this story illustrates two additional points. The first is that the man, now armed with this knowledge, could go back and design his own new features for the hollow tomato stake, and the combination of these new features and the tomato stake would probably be patentable. By reviewing the prior art, the man now knows what is the state-of-the-art, and he can obtain a patent if he can significantly add to that art.

The second point to the story is that while others had patents on various improvements to the basic invention, none of the prior-art patents prevented this man from selling a stake of his original design. Apparently, the basic idea of a hollow tomato stake had been disclosed some time ago. Patent protection could only be obtained on a hollow tomato stake with 'bells and whistles', and it's not apparent these additions are necessary for commercial success. Since the basic invention, the hollow tomato stake, would probably meet the needs of the marketplace, the value of these improvement patents is very low. The claims in these patents had been restricted so much that one wonders whether or not these improvement patents would ever pay for themselves.

So, perhaps the question that should be asked is not only whether or not an invention is patentable, but how restrictive the claims have to be in order to obtain a patent. In many cases, unless the invention is completely disclosed in a prior publication (as was the tomato stake) a patent agent will be able to construct some claims which will be found to be patentable. But obtaining this patent may not have any impact on anything but the inventor's bank account, because any potential competitors will be able to operate without infringing the claims. One needs to consider how broadly the agent will be able to construct claims, and what effect these claims will have. Even though an invention may be patentable, one may be wise not to file a patent. By approaching the task in this manner, the researcher has, in essence, begun the development of a patent strategy for the invention.

DEFINING STRATEGY

'What is the strategy?' is an often asked question. Answering this question can be difficult, because the word strategy means different things to different people. In many aspects of business and personal life one must develop strategies. In general, if a strategy has been developed, the implication is that one knows where one is going and how one intends to get there. Note, however, that the questions 'Where to go?' and 'How to go?' require two separate analyses. While strategy is really associated with the 'How?' question, one cannot develop a strategy unless it is first decided where one wishes to go or what one wishes to achieve. Therefore, the reason a strategy is highly prized is that in order to develop one, a fair amount of analysis and decision making should have occurred. What is hoped for is that the development of a strategy, as well as the strategy itself, will assist the achievement of some end in an efficient manner.

Webster's Ninth Collegiate Dictionary gives several definitions for the word strategy. Strategy can be (1) the science and art of employing the political, economic, psychological, and military forces of a nation or a group of nations to afford the maximum support to adopted policies in peace and war: (2) the science and art of military command exercise to meet the enemy in combat under advantageous conditions; (3) a careful plan or method: a clever strategem; (4) the art of devising or employing plans or strategems toward a goal. Notice there are three levels of complexity denoted by the first three definitions. Let's look at how we can tailor these definitions to define a patent strategy.

The part of the definition, 'of employing the political, economic, psychological, and military forces of a nation or a group of nations' defines who is recipient of the strategy, who will act differently as a result of the strategy. For a patent strategy, one will be using foremost the intellectual faculties of key personnel, so this part of the definition becomes 'of employing the business, technical, and legal resources of a company.' In the last part of the definition, 'to afford the maximum support to adopted policies in peace and war,' the key phase is 'adopted policies.' The implication is that certain principles or policies are first established, and then a strategy is developed 'to afford the maximum support' to these policies. Finally, 'in peace and war' can be translated to the business-oriented 'with or without competition.' The result is the definition for patent strategy which would pertain to a large business or a large product line with many types of markets:

Patent strategy for a product line is the science and art of employing the business, technical, and legal resources of a company to afford the maximum support to adopted policies with and without competition.

The second definition can be reworded to apply on a smaller scale to a specific technology or market area. The phase 'military command exercise' is much less clear. The implication is the application of military drills to actual practice. What is needed is an analogy to the business and scientific world which can be called on for use in 'action' against the competitor. If we choose scientists and researchers to be the warriors, the most appropriate analogy becomes 'the science and art of managing research.' Simply convert 'the enemy' to 'competitors' and 'combat' to 'the marketplace' and a definition for strategy emerges which could relate to a specific technology or market area:

Patent strategy for a technology area is the science and art of managing research to meet competitors in the marketplace under advantageous conditions.

The third definition, 'a careful plan or method: a clever strategem' requires the examination of the word strategem. The dictionary again provides definitions related to the military: (1) an artifice or trick in war for deceiving and outwitting the enemy; (2) a cleverly contrived trick or scheme for gaining an end; and (3) a skill in ruses or trickery. Combining these definitions, one gets a definition for a strategy for a specific patent application or family of cases:

Patent strategy for an invention is a careful plan for gaining an end, including clever schemes for outwitting a competitor.

This semantic exercise was intended to illustrate why the term 'patent strategy' can mean different things in different situations, and why it is important that a decision be made on what conceptual level a patent strategy will be generated. The definitions at different conceptual levels have some common themes, but each has its own flavor and its own issues. Later we will use the concepts in these definitions to help us ask the right questions in preparing patent strategies.

THE PRINCIPLES BEHIND THE STRATEGY – THE MILITARY MODEL

It is difficult to think about strategy and not consider analogies to the military. The reason the military strategy model is so useful in the development of strategic concepts is that the objective of the strategy is fairly easy to understand: defeat the enemy. Strategy, in a military sense, is the combination of a set of principles in the conduct of a war or of a major campaign. When the principles are combined for a single battle, the term 'tactics' is normally used. When the principles are used for the overall conduct of a war, the term 'grand strategy' is normally used. So the military model also has three conceptual levels for strategy.

Traditionally, in the military strategy model, there are nine fundamental principles:

1. Objective: Identify a decisive, obtainable, objective.
2. Offensive: Seize the initiative and take offensive action.
3. Simplicity: Simplify plans as much as possible.
4. Unity of Command: Unify and coordinate all forces.

5. Mass:	Concentrate maximum available means at the point of decision.
6. Economy of Force:	Employ minimum essential means at points other than that of decision.
7. Maneuver:	Position forces to place the enemy at a relative disadvantage.
8. Surprise:	Strike the enemy in a manner for which he is unprepared.
9. Security:	Deny information to the enemy and preserve freedom of action.

These principles provide a guide for what questions should be asked when developing a strategy. They break down the large task of generating a strategy to generating a set of decisions, policies, or procedures which, when properly thought out can be combined into a comprehensive strategy. We will attempt to do the same in the developing of a patent strategy.

We will state some general patent strategy principles, but in general, we will develop the principles in the form of a series of issues or topics to consider in the establishment of a patent strategy. We will also steal from the journalistic idea of asking the questions of Who? What? Where? When? and How? and use these questions as a device to help in the development of a patent strategy.

DEVELOPING A PATENT STRATEGY MODEL

Using the military model, we will develop a set of principles which will become the model to be adapted for use in many different situations to generate an integrated intellectual property strategy. Once developed, this model can be applied to either an existing or new business, a new product introduction, or an integrated product line. Remember, by generating a strategy, one is more likely to be successful in legally excluding others from a business for a period of time. The principles that should be combined in generating a patent strategy for a business or a company (and their military counterpart) are as follows.

1. Extent of patent coverage desired (objective)

A clear objective for the strategy should be established. This objective may be on a very high conceptual plane, or may be very specific to a single patent application. This objective should be based either on a clear business objective or a clear research objective. The business-related objective should include what advantage is to be gained by obtaining an intellectual property position. The research-related objective should include the technology area where one wishes to target effort in the hope of developing new intellectual property.

The expected use of the intellectual property is the key focus for the business-based objective. In general, one is attempting to restrict competitors by the use of patents, or make money through the licensing of patents. The particular objective might be to obtain strong patents which are broad and will prevent or delay both in-kind and functional competition from obtaining a window of operation. One may decide to patent the lowest cost route for producing some product to obtain a financial advantage over competitors. If a new product is being developed, one may decide to obtain patents on the product, and variations of the product in different end uses, so that control over both the product and the free use of the product in the marketplace can be had.

There are situations, however, where scouting work is done where there is no established business. In these situations, it is the development of intellectual property which is the key, and for this a research-based objective is needed. An objective to develop intellectual property implies that an area has been identified where there may be opportunity to develop a strong proprietary position. While the business implications are never truly out of the picture, this type of objective concentrates on scouting and investigating a technology area in an effort to develop and patent the area so that eventually a business can be developed on the portfolio of patents. For example, the objective might be to develop a portfolio of patents related to the use of an additive in plastics; or, the objective might be to do basic research in a technology area and patent whatever tangible results are developed.

It is important for the conceptual level of the objective to be consistent with what the business or researcher is trying to accomplish. In most cases, a specific objective is more useful than a general one; developing a specific objective also requires more risk taking and decision making, but ultimately more is accomplished when the objective is clearly and specifically stated. If the objective is to obtain a proprietary position in a technology area, one should consider if this proprietary position is in a specific part of a technology area or the entire area. It is one thing to obtain a proprietary position in engines; it is an entirely different thing to obtain a proprietary position in aircraft engines. Patents are specific documents, and if an objective is too broad conceptually, the resulting patent strategy will be unclear and have little meaning.

2. Method of acquiring intellectual property (offensive)

Once the objective has been identified, the next step is to determine how to obtain the intellectual property, and once the property is obtained, how to protect it. This requires making decisions as to what actions one is willing or able to take.

There are several ways to obtain intellectual property. One can develop it, pay someone to develop it, develop it jointly with researchers from another company, or buy it from someone else. By developing the intellectual property in-house, more control is maintained over the developed information and the developer can decide when and how to apply it. However, technical resources must be committed to the development, and normally this will be a major commitment of resources. If this technology area is intended to be a major, long-term part of the business, and there is a want or need to develop a series of inventions, then this will be the preferred method of obtaining intellectual property. Also, if the technical capability is already available in-house, one may decide to keep the development in-house and manage the development to make sure the appropriate personnel have the resources to develop the technology. From a practical standpoint, however, whether or not technology is developed in-house is dependent on the amount of resources that are available to do this work.

If someone is paid to develop technology on a contract basis, one can make confidentiality agreements to attempt to maintain effective control over the developed information, for at least a limited amount of time. However, one will have less control over the information than if the technology was developed in-house, because now the information may be disclosed when the confidentiality agreements expire. Also, the probability that an inadvertent disclosure might occur increases, because the contractor may not be as cognizant of the eventual impact of the disclosure. However, if the expertise to do the technical development is not available in-house, or another company would be more effective in developing this information, contracting the development might be a very smart option. In some cases, contracting the development is more likely to quickly achieve the research objectives, while at the same time keeping the amount of in-house technical resources that must be committed to the contract at a minimum.

Joint developments with other companies can be very similar to simply contracting the work. However, joint developments will require more resources from an organization. Also, in joint developments, usually both companies are free to use the developed information for whatever purpose they choose. In many cases, any patents that issue from the work have joint ownership, which means in some countries either of the joint owners is free to license the patents to anyone. In joint developments, unless specific provisions are included in the joint development agreement, control of the technology is reduced. However, many times other companies will have a certain technical capability, or even a good patent position, that makes them a valuable joint-development partner. Therefore, one may decide the best action is to establish a joint-development arrangement between companies, assuming an appropriate agreement can be developed that both parties will sign.

Licensing is a very common method of obtaining intellectual property when another company has already developed and patented the technology that one wishes to practice. If the other company has already patented the technology, licensing may be the only option to use that intellectual property; also, the owner of the patent must be willing to license the technology and their know how. The resources from the organization that will need to be committed will vary, depending on the situation and the licensing agreements that are developed. Also, in a licensing situation, it is the licenser who controls the amount of disclosure; control over what is disclosed to the licensee will be determined by the licensing agreement.

3. Identifying competitive advantage (simplicity)

A key part of establishing a patent strategy is the recognition of what provides a real competitive advantage, and then attempting to maintain the proprietary nature of this advantage. Therefore, a conscious effort should be made to identify one's competitive advantages, and then be very sensitive to any disclosure that might weaken or destroy this advantage. This advantage may be a particular method of making a piece of equipment, or it may be a technique used in a manufacturing process, or it may be the manufacturing process itself. If the entire competitive advantage is tied up in a single invention, one will want to consider whether or not patents will truly protect the competitive advantage, if not, one may want to keep the invention as a trade secret.

By identifying competitive advantages or considering what competitive advantage is desired, the strategic thinking process is simplified. It focuses thinking on what are the critical components of either the invention or the business, which in turn can help dictate how to go about researching or conducting business. By selecting an objective, one identifies what is to be accomplished; by considering competitive advantages one determines whether or not the objective will be achieved in a manner that will have lasting value.

For example, let's say a researcher wants to develop a new polymer which has certain properties useful in the electronics industry. The researcher has searched the literature, and after combining that information with his own expertise, he sees a way to modify a particular class of polymers and generate a new polymer which will have the properties desired. He also thinks he might be able to develop a proprietary position in this new class of polymers. Therefore, the strategy could include an objective to develop a new polymer and a process to make this polymer and to file patent applications to exclude others from making this polymer. This objective may be achieved; but the polymer might not be a commercial success when it is introduced in the marketplace. The polymer might not have the purity required for the expected end use, or the polymer cost might be higher than the increased value to the customer. In any case, the overall development may not succeed. However, if the requirements for a competitive advantage had been considered at the outset, efforts could have been directed not only to develop the polymer, but also to develop a process which would produce the polymer at the required purity or cost. The chances for a commercial success would be dramatically improved.

Thomas Edison is remembered today as the inventor of the incandescent light bulb, although light bulbs had been made by many others before Thomas Edison. In Ira Flatow's book, *They All Laughed*, Flatow tells the story of how Edison designed a total electrical system, of which the light bulb was just a part. The light bulb is now associated with Edison because he was the first to be commercially successful. He had a clear idea of what competitive advantage he could bring to the marketplace. He would be successful only if he designed a method by which lighting could be brought to an entire city, not just one room. So, he designed not only the bulb, but also the distribution system, and the electric dynamos to produce the electricity.

One small company I know, which is very profitable but does not have many employees, makes a practice of not filing patents on technology developed by their researchers. They realize that their competitive advantage is in the ingenuity of their researchers and their ability to develop and commercialize technology quickly. They also realize that the combination of their small size and their strategy to develop solutions quickly means they will not have the luxury of researching more than just a few possible solutions. They know that any patents they might receive would only lead their competitors to develop alternative solutions which would not be covered by their patent. This company realizes it is not only their technology which makes them successful, but their technology combined with their ability to deliver the technology quickly. By identifying their competitive advantage, their strategic thinking process is not complicated by the need to file patent applications.

4. How will decisions be made? (unity of command)

Making decisions on whether or not to file patent applications is difficult. The issues involved can be complex, and many times there are good reasons both to file and not file an application. So, it is best if one person is responsible for making these and other hard decisions about intellectual property, and for establishing specific procedures for handling intellectual property.

The person making these decisions must be able to stand back from the specific decision in question and see how this decision affects the rest of the organization's goals. He must be able to separate himself from a specific patent application and understand how the patent application fits into the overall patent strategy of the business. He must make sure the patent strategy is aligned with both the business strategy and technical strategy of the business. He should be able to think strategically on a large scale, while at the same time be able to consider small details in the decision-making process.

In many cases, the inventor is too close to his invention to be able to make an independent decision. In some situations, particularly with independent inventors and small companies, the patent agent's involvement includes this decision-making role. In a large corporation with many different business issues, the patent agent normally is less likely to assume this responsibility, normally wanting to provide a service and advice, but not making strategic decisions. In many cases, the research manager is the best choice for decision-maker, because he should understand both the business and technical impact of an invention. Also, while he is a part of the invention in that his researchers are involved, he is not normally too tied to the invention. A business manager might tend to be too far away from the invention and be more short-term oriented, and therefore more quick to abandon an invention that was not clearly an immediate advantage to the business.

Some organizations have patent liaisons, or intellectual property managers, who have the responsibility to manage the acquisition of patents. Such a person, if given sufficient authority by the organization, can be a good choice for the decision maker. There are many smaller decisions that must be made about patent applications that need only a short discussion between the liaison and the agent, and the liaison can easily assume this decision-making responsibility. An experienced patent liaison, because of his training, is almost always capable of making almost all of the decisions affecting the intellectual property for a business. However, the patent liaison must seek out and understand the business and technical strategies of the business.

This decision-making person must also act as part of a patenting team, working both with the patent agent and the inventor, because intimate knowledge of the content and thrust of patent applications in progress is critical to the decision-maker. The decision-maker will also need input from both the patent agent and the inventor on the strengths and weaknesses of the various patents that are considered.

It is best if a procedure, either formal or informal, is established to address certain questions about intellectual property strategies. These procedures might take the form of a yearly, high-level meeting to review the patent strategy of a business for alignment with the business and technical strategy. On a smaller scale, these procedures might outline how an inventor in the organization goes about obtaining a patent; that is, the system(s) the organization has set up to prepare and file patent applications. On an even smaller scale, there might be a procedure set up to decide whether or not to file certain patent applications globally. In any case, any of the decisions that must be made on a routine basis, but require input from several different sources, might benefit from the establishment of a procedure.

5. The focus of efforts (mass)

A key principle to consider in a patent strategy is the allocation of resources to the task at hand, because just having enough resources to accomplish a desired task is a difficult task in itself. However, one should consider from a practical standpoint whether or not the requisite amount of manpower, money, and equipment are available to complete the objective. If adequate resources are not allocated to achieve the objective, something, either the objective or the timing, will suffer. Therefore, it is vitally important to be honest at this point in the strategy development. If the resources are just not available, the objective should be changed to bring it into more alignment with what can be accomplished.

The allocation of sufficient resources really requires one to focus on the desired objective. The more specific the objective, the easier it is to focus and plan, and in turn assign resources. For very large projects with very broad objectives, many times it is best to break the broad objective into several smaller, more specific objectives, on a scale that a single inventor or a small team of researchers could manage and accomplish.

Even after an invention has been made, resources may need to be assigned to the invention to improve the value of the patent application. Once a key finding has been made, for patent purposes it is best to experiment throughout the entire operating range of the invention, and investigate many different embodiments of the invention. This knowledge will increase the breadth and strength of the patent, and will provide one's business with a distinct technological advantage when the invention is introduced in the marketplace. For a considerable length of time after the introduction, the background of developed knowledge will provide the business with an opportunity to further capitalize on the invention. Even though one inventor might have made the invention, and the natural tendency is to let the original inventor develop all of the data required for the patent application. This inventor might not be the right individual to develop the information that will broaden and flesh-out the invention. Some inventors are very intuitive and do not have the temperament to conduct the methodical experiments required to identify how broadly an invention will perform. The interest of these intuitive inventors lies in the development of the new concept, and once developed, they want to move on to other interesting concepts. In many cases, it would be wise to allocate a methodically-minded person to this invention for a period of time to better develop the insight of the other inventor. Even if the inventor is very methodical, the desire to get the invention to the marketplace quickly may be so important that the most prudent thing is to assign a massive, short term effort to the invention in order to complete all of the experimentation quickly. This can be a very good way to get a very important invention not only to the marketplace, but also to the patent office very quickly.

While many great inventions have been developed by focusing on a single objective, do not forget that just as many inventions have been developed or discovered while someone was actually trying to do something else. Flatow, in his book, contrasts the efforts of Thomas Edison and Alexander Graham Bell. Thomas Edison, while developing the light bulb, developed some of the basics of the vacuum tube, but did not pursue the development. He instead concentrated on the development of the light bulb and was very successful. Bell, on the other hand, was trying to develop a better telegraph when he came across the technology which became the telephone. One was very single-minded, the other was very flexible. Both were very successful.

The allocation of resources and the development of objectives shouldn't be so fixed so as to eliminate work on unexpected results which occur. If a new development occurs that doesn't fit with the original objectives, the most practical thing to do is to go ahead and allocate a specific amount of time to the new development to determine whether or not it is something to be considered further, and if an invention with perceived higher value has been developed, initiate a separate project to capitalize on this new invention. Therefore, the setting of objectives and the allocation of resources should not be so rigidly fixed so as to eliminate the possibility of developing the unexpected.

6. Response to competitive patents (economy of force)

When developing a strategy for a business, it is helpful to consider how the business will respond when patents in the technology area are filed by competitors. A methodology for handling these patents should be established. These patents will first of all need to be detected, then they will have to be analyzed, and finally a decision will need to be made as to what action is needed in response. This principle is important, because unless a decision is made as to how much effort to expend in responding to competitive patents, the result may be a tremendous effort, and with this effort, tremendous expense.

If a method is established by which new patent art is reviewed as it is published, patent publications will surely appear which will be of concern. Further, many of these publications will not yet be patents, so the allowed claims may very well be different from those published in the application. In any case, since there are so many patents filed every year, the number of patents which might be of concern could be substantial.

At a minimum, a decision must be made as to which areas of technology should be watched for competitive patents. One may decide to analyze any patents that might restrict future manufacturing or one may decide to review any patents which might impact a future market area, but this broadens the amount of technology that might have to be reviewed. Therefore, it is best to identify the key technical areas where new developments would have significant impact, and consider any patents or applications that occur in these areas. Other areas of lesser value can also be reviewed, but only after the major areas have been considered.

Patents to be analyzed should be reviewed by personnel with both patent training and technical training, because it is necessary to develop both a technical analysis and a patent analysis of the publication. The technical analysis will tell whether the technology is valuable, whether it has flaws or unreasonable assumptions, and should summarize the technical information obtained from the patent. The patent analysis should tell whether or not the claims are broad, and suggest where the patent is limited in coverage, or where the patent has weaknesses. The two analyses should then be brought together and a single combined analysis prepared which summarizes the impact of the patent on the business.

After a clear statement has been made on the impact of a particular patent application, a number of responses is available. For those countries that have opposition procedures, the key issue for the development of a strategy is when to attempt to oppose competitive patent applications. One can, for example, decide only to oppose patents which may impact or restrict the manufacturing processes. One can decide to oppose any patent in a technology area where prior art can be found on which to base a solid opposition. Still, one may decide to oppose any patent in a technology area even if limited prior art can be found, in an effort at least to restrict the opposed patent into a narrower set of allowed claims.

7. Maintaining up-to-date (maneuver)

Whether or not they do it, most researchers recognize the need to remain up to date in their area of technology. A principle to consider in the development of a strategy is how new information in important areas of technology will be obtained and how it will be reviewed in the organization. If patents are to be reviewed in an efficient manner, it is imperative that researchers have an access or means for obtaining recent patent art. By reviewing prior art in an area of technology, the researcher can save time by not duplicating others' work; reviewing the art will also provide the researcher with ideas, test methods, and knowledge which he may not be able to get anywhere else.

To achieve this, there are a number of printed publications which supply summaries of patent and literature activity. Also, there are on-line electronic services which will conduct a search of the published art in an area of technology on a regular basis, and the search can either be mailed to the researcher or made available electronically. In both of these cases, the search is performed using certain keywords or codes which give the researcher a broad search of all of the publications in a particular field. The researcher must then review all of the information and separate out the important references. A third way of obtaining information, which many large corporations use, is to have their own in-house literature specialists generate a particular search on a regular basis, and edit the search prior to giving it to the researcher. Using this method, the researcher doesn't have to spend as much time reviewing the search results. Even if in-house specialists are not available, the independent inventor can obtain contract searches from independent firms and achieve the same type of service. Obtaining information on a regular basis is usually superior to the researcher performing a casual search from time to time in an effort to remain up to date.

On the other hand, a particular business may not need a large effort to keep up with the prior art. The business may have simply developed a single invention and does not need to review the invention art on a regular basis, or simply does not have the funds to spend to keep up to date. In most cases, however, it is very important to keep up to date on at least that technology which is critical to the business. Keeping up with new developments as they are made means knowing when someone else either improves on an invention, or develops alternative technology. Knowing such information may allow a business a chance to license these inventions, or may help detect companies that are infringing the patents of a business. If the patent art is followed, one will be more able to take advantage of these opportunities. Therefore, in most cases, if cost is a major issue, it is better to scale back the amount of technology that is reviewed rather than eliminate the task entirely.

8. Coordination of filings (surprise)

Since patents are generally granted by countries, at some point in the patenting process one will need to make a decision both on where to file a patent application, and how to file it. Of these two questions, the 'Where to file?' question is the most difficult, because it requires a consideration of the global needs of the business; that is, where in the world will having a patent help marketing efforts or hinder a competitor? One must consider where growth is anticipated over the next 10 to 20 years, and where the business wants to grow during this same period. Coming up with the answers for these types of questions can be very difficult unless a clear business strategy has been developed. However, while having a clear business strategy can help, many times the patent application must be filed before either a business using the invention has been established, or before the current business strategy is modified to account for the invention. When this happens, it is difficult to know whether or not the right decisions are being made about the global filing of a patent application.

In this and other situations, it is useful to establish a procedure for deciding where to file patent applications globally. In general, one should know how global the business efforts will be, that is, whether or not the business will concentrate on supplying the local area, or whether it will branch out into other continents and countries. A global company should know where in the world an effort to grow the business will be concentrated. Also, since patents will hinder competitors, one will want to consider where competitors have manufacturing facilities, where they might build plants, and where they might want to grow also. Given these considerations, it should be possible to develop a list of countries that should be considered when globally filing patents. Since this list will be shorter than all the countries in the world, the decision-making process is reduced considerably.

The second major decision to consider is how and when to file patent applications. Not too many years ago filing a patent application globally required the help of an agent in almost every country in which the application was to be filed. Now, there are global treaties that make the process easier in many countries, while other countries still require, from a practical standpoint, an agent's help if a strong patent is desired. So, from the standpoint of a single patent application, a patent agent should be able to provide advice on the best route for protecting an invention, and what timing must be adhered to.

On a higher level of abstraction, if one has several inventions, one should develop a plan to coordinate the filings of the patent applications. Since most countries of the world are first-to-file countries, it is important that the filing of a prior patent application not affect the novelty of the rest of the patent applications. Therefore, the strategy that is developed may mean all of the patent applications are filed the same day, or will make sure that a previous patent application does not contain information that would affect the patentability of the subsequent patent applications.

9. Protection of unprotected property (security)

This principle concerns how to organize, or what systems to put in place, to ensure that proprietary information and rights to intellectual property protection are not compromised. This requires maintaining an appropriate level of secrecy around developments so as to maintain patent rights, making decisions on the appropriateness of the filing and content of patent applications, and establishing the method by which these applications will be filed.

Since secrecy is a vital component for gaining worldwide patent rights, one should consider how to avoid unwanted disclosure of technology. In particular, one will need to consider when during the development it will be necessary to show an invention to outsiders and how this will be done without forfeiting patent rights. The best approach, which guarantees no forfeiture of patent rights, is to establish strict guidelines to file all related patent applications before any disclosure. In many cases there are good reasons for someone outside a company to see the invention, and in these cases a confidentiality agreement may help to avoid forfeiting patent rights; however, if the outsider consciously or inadvertently discloses the invention publicly, some patent rights will be forfeited.

A system should be established to decide whether or not to disclose an invention in a patent application. If work is considered in a technology area that is new to the researcher, he should establish an initial snapshot of the intellectual property landscape through a literature search. This will give the researcher an idea early in the development as to the chances of being able to patent, publish, or retain secret the technology that is developed. The decision as to whether or not to file a patent application can be made by balancing the value of the disclosure made in the patent application (not just the invention) versus the ability of the patent to prevent others from practicing the proposed claims.

If in-house legal staff are available, or a relationship has been developed with an outside patent attorney or agent, then the mechanism of preparing and filing patent applications will be fairly well established. If such a relationship is not established, one will need to locate this assistance early in the development. It is important to have legal advice available during the development of technology to help prepare written agreements. It is also very helpful to have patent application meetings with the patent agent during the development. Reviewing results with the agent early in the development can usually be helpful; many times the agent can offer advice as to what type of research or experimental information would be useful in the patent application, and in so doing shorten the time required to develop the technical information to be used in the patent application.

10. Changing the strategy

The development of a strategy is an important process, and the strategy should not be changed unless adequate time has been allocated to the change process. The conceptual level of the strategy will dictate how often the strategy should be changed. This is not unlike the strategy for winning a war versus the strategy for winning a battle. The war strategy should not change that often, and should change only after a high-level analysis of a change in the development of the war. Battle strategy will often need to be changed often and quickly, and the responsibility for making the change should be in the hands of a few individuals.

For example, a patent strategy for a business should not change very often. The strategy should be reviewed at least once, preferably twice, a year, but the bulk of the strategy should be evergreen and remain unchanged for a considerable period, at least until the business picture changes dramatically. This strategy should not be changed unless there is general agreement among the management that the change should take place.

A strategy for a patent application, however, can change dramatically from the time the invention is first considered to the issuance of the patent. Prior art unknown to the researcher and the agent can be found by the patent examiner, new experimentation can change the invention results, and any number of other things can happen to change the strategy for the patent application during both the preparation and the prosecution of the application.

After the development of a strategy, it is good practice to consider how the strategy will be documented, communicated, and reviewed. Documentation is necessary so that the strategy can be referred to, and so that the thinking that was used to develop the strategy is not lost. Communication of the strategy will be necessary because not all of the people interested in the strategy will participate in its development. Finally, regular periodic reviews of the strategy will help it to remain useful as elements of the business picture or the technical development change with time.

The Patent Strategy Model

1. Extent of patent coverage desired

2. Method of acquiring intellectual property

3. Identifying competitive advantage

4. How will decisions be made?

5. The focus of efforts

6. Response to competitive patents

7. Maintaining up-to-date

8. Coordination of filings

9. Protection of unprotected property

10. Changing the strategy

Figure 3.1 The patent strategy model

QUESTIONS FOR SPECIFIC TYPES OF STRATEGIES

DEVELOPING A PATENT STRATEGY FOR AN INVENTION

The patent strategy for an invention concerns the issues involved in getting the best possible patent application written, filed, and issued for the invention. This is the simplest and most straightforward type of strategy to develop. To develop the strategy, the principles above are combined into a series of questions, which are designed to help identify the critical issues involved in obtaining strong and useful patents.

What?

What is the invention?

This question is so obvious, one might think it is not needed. The reason this is a good starting point is because researchers typically want to claim an invention that is broader than the invention that was actually made. In many cases, it is desirable for the patent application also to cover alternate embodiments of the invention. By considering this question with the patent agent, one will have an idea of whether or not additional experimentation will be needed. However, what will be claimed as the invention will be determined by not only the amount of work completed, but also by whatever has been disclosed previously. The prior art may require the invention description to be more narrow than expected; this narrowing may mean that the protection that will be obtained will be very limited and one may decide not to file any patent application at all. Therefore, it is best to consider what the invention is both before and after a search of the prior art has been completed.

What is to be achieved by filing this patent application?

There are many reasons for filing a patent application. In developing a strategy, it is important to identify what is to be achieved early on so that the efforts expended match the goal which is desired. If one wishes to obtain a patent so that the closest competitor cannot practice the invention, the patent application should include the competitors' manufacturing processes and products in the examples. If a patent is desired so that the novelty of the invention can be marketed and sold to the highest bidder, it will be desirable to have a patent that claims the lowest cost process. One may wish to use the patent application as a vehicle to disclose parts of a current process or possible uses for the invention to guarantee that someone else cannot obtain a patent on these same process steps or possible uses. One may wish to file an application, but delay the final decision as to whether or not to actually ask for examination (in those countries that allow delay) until it is clear that the invention will be commercially useful and successful. A motive for filing a patent application may also be just to obtain a patent for professional recognition, and in this case one might proceed with a narrowly-drafted application when others might not.

There may be several things to achieve by filing a patent application. The secret is that it is possible to achieve them all if they are identified early in the patenting process. Understanding the motive(s) for initiating an effort to patent an invention is important to the ultimate success of any patent, but many do not even consider this point when starting the effort. They get caught up in the exercise of drafting a patent application or preparing examples without any clue as to what the final patent application will look like. They are not unlike a baker who decides to bake a cake, and has all the equipment for baking the cake available, and although he has an idea what kind of cake he wants to make, has not checked to make sure he has all of the ingredients. He might begin the making of the cake, only to find out an important ingredient is not available; he must then decide to wait to get the ingredient or to continue but to make a different type of cake. In either case, the resulting cake is different, and probably less satisfying than the baker originally thought it would be. Obviously, it is common sense for the baker to make sure he has all of the ingredients before starting a cake, so that he can be sure he will be able to make the cake. However, many start the patent process thinking 'I want to stop my competitor from practicing my invention' but without any thought as to what type of development is required to actually achieve this state. In many cases, the result is like the cake which runs out of ingredients; the final patent is much less satisfying than one might initially think it would be.

What additional information is needed for the patent application?

Once a definition of the invention is completed, and what is to be achieved with the patent filing has been considered, the next step to take is to consider what additional information is needed for the patent application. A patent agent is normally an excellent guide in this process, because he deals with these types of questions with every patent application he prepares. In the preparation of a patent application, one of two situations normally arise. The first is that there is a wish for broad patent claims, but there is close art that restricts the patent to only narrow claims. One must then decide whether or not to settle for the narrow claims or to perform additional experimentation to distinguish the narrowly claimed invention over the prior art and attempt to broaden the claims. The answer to this question can only be found by considering whether or not the claims that will be received will still achieve the stated goals even though the claims have been narrowed.

The second common situation is when there is only limited prior art and one wishes to obtain broad claims, but the inventor has only done a limited amount of work in the area. To obtain a truly broad patent, additional experimentation should be done. In this case, the decision comes down to how valuable the invention is and whether or not the resources and time to fully develop the area are available. One can attempt to obtain broad claims on a limited amount of work, but in many countries the patent claims that issue will be restricted to those elements that are clearly shown in the examples in the patent application. Therefore, it is not unusual to have to conduct additional experimentation to obtain a strong global patent.

When?

When must this patent application be filed?

In general, patent applications should be filed as soon as possible after the invention has been made. However, the timing is often impacted by other technical and business issues.

The filing of an application which will result in a strong, enforceable patent is dependent on having the right type of information available for the application. In many cases an inventor makes a new invention and brings it to the patent agent so that a patent application can be made, only to find out that if he wants to file a patent application, more work should be done. Normally this extra work is either additional experimentation to broaden the claims of the patent application, or to distinguish the invention over prior inventions. After the needed experiments have been identified, one must weigh the advantages gained by the new data versus the delay in the filing of the patent application. If the experimentation is very time consuming, one may want to add resources to the invention to get this patent data completed. On the other hand, the structure of the competitive arena may be such that a narrower patent would meet both the short and the long term needs of the business. In this case, additional experimentation may not need to be performed.

Also, when a new invention is made, there is a push to get the new invention into the hands of potential customers. After all, the quicker customers see new products, the quicker the products will sell; or if the products don't sell, the quicker one learns where the new products are lacking. This business need typically over-rides the need for more experimentation for the patent application, meaning the broadness or the strength of many patent applications is compromised. While this is unavoidable in some cases, it tends to occur in more cases than is necessary. If given the proper attention in the planning stages, both the data for the patent application and the business needs for early disclosure can be met.

While it may seem foolish at the start of a technical program to set a goal to file a patent application by a certain date, it is not foolish to set a goal for filing a patent application once a truly patentable invention has been developed. By setting a goal date, efforts can be focused on identifying and completing the required experimentation, and it may be possible to complete the experimentation while the patent agent is drafting the patent application. The overall effect is that the patent application is prepared in a more efficient manner, and the goal filing date is more likely to be met.

Who?

Who is going to develop the information for the patent application?

Once the experimentation that needs to be done is identified, it is important that the responsibility for developing the required information is clearly communicated to research personnel. This is particularly important when a team of researchers is to attempt to develop an invention. Someone in the team should be assigned the responsibility for obtaining each piece of needed data so that there is no confusion about who is to do what.

In some cases, a researcher may be asked to perform new experiments or run new tests, but he may not have the expertise or the equipment to complete the experimentation successfully. In this case, the research manager may have to hire someone to help develop the needed information. Again, if responsibility is clearly assigned, the chances of obtaining the required information are greatly increased.

Who is going to prepare the application?

If in-house patent agents are available, one may want to consider which attorney or agent should prepare the application. Patent agents have different types of technical backgrounds, and while it is not strictly required that the agent be knowledgeable in the particular technical field, having an agent with such experience can help speed the drafting of the patent application.

If an in-house patent agent is not available, a relationship should be established with an agent or a law firm. Since most businesses already have an attorney for general legal or corporate matters, the most practical method of obtaining help is to ask this attorney to suggest a patent attorney or agent who will meet the needs of the business.

One may be tempted to prepare and file the patent application without the aid of an experienced agent. Inventors are traditionally very independent minded, and are inclined to think that they can write a patent application as well as a patent agent; plus, if the inventor prepares the application, he does not have to deal with lawyers. However, researchers should not succumb to these temptations. The reason inventors should not do their own patent work is that if there was ever a need to enforce the patent against an infringer (assuming a patent would issue, which is by no means guaranteed), they would have to hire a lawyer; if the patent was not prepared by a competent patent attorney or agent, the chances that the patent will be enforceable are considerably decreased. In general, inventors without patent training simply do not have the skills to draft a good patent. The time spent trying to prepare and file a patent would be much better spent doing additional technical work in the laboratory either to support the patent application or to generate new inventions.

How?

How much information should be disclosed in the application?

Almost any patent application that is filed will disclose to others exactly how to make or use an invention. In doing so, it is important to not disclose any more of the technology developed for the invention than is absolutely necessary for the patent to be valid. If one is not careful, things may be disclosed that are not particularly necessary for obtaining a patent on an invention, and in so doing, simply give away key pieces of proprietary information. Getting the right amount of disclosure in a patent application requires the expertise of an experienced patent agent. Many inventors want to obtain a patent on their invention, but at the same time, not totally to disclose the secrets of their invention. In most countries, the patent application must be an enabling disclosure, that is, the application must provide enough information for another to duplicate the invention. If an enabling disclosure is not provided, the patent can be found invalid, so the patent agent must make sure the disclosure is adequate. The United States has a further stipulation that the best mode must be disclosed. The best mode is the preferred method of operation or the preferred embodiment of the invention at the time of filing. Again, in the United States, if the best mode of the invention known to the inventor is not included in the patent application at the time of the filing of the application, any patent that might issue could be found to be invalid. In most cases, it is best to be very open with the patent agent and give him all of the information available about the invention, and allow the patent agent to select the information to include in the patent application. However, the inventor should review the application and question the amount and type of disclosure the agent makes, and make sure that all that the agent thinks is required is in fact required. If, in the opinion of the inventor, too much proprietary information is disclosed, then perhaps the filing of a patent application is not a smart business decision.

On the other hand, one may want to include additional information in the patent application, information that is not specifically required for the patent to issue. Certain attributes of the invention which are not apparent from examining the invention, or other technology that has been developed, can be disclosed in the patent application. This disclosure will help prevent others from obtaining patents on variations of the invention. Many countries interpret the disclosure in a patent application very narrowly. This means that if all possible embodiments of a particular invention are not specifically disclosed in the patent application, others may be able to obtain a patent on an undisclosed variation of the invention, assuming they can generate a convincing argument for patentability. By making extra disclosures in the patent application, information about a technology area can be put in the public domain, which can be useful in preventing others from obtaining nuisance patents on small obvious improvements on the features of an invention. Manufacturers of generic items, such as chemicals and fibers, have long disclosed in patent applications various types of end uses for their materials. These disclosures have been an attempt to prevent their customers from patenting the use of their material in a particular end use, and thereby help to assure that more than one customer will use their product in the end use. This disclosure, however, can also prevent the discloser from patenting the same; therefore, the reasons for disclosing the information should be carefully thought out before the disclosure is made.

How broadly can/should the invention be claimed?

It is only natural to want to obtain broad claims on an invention. By doing so, one can both protect ones preferred invention, but also alternate versions or functionally similar inventions. Two things will impact the patent agent's ability to write broad claims for the patent application. These are the amount of research that has been completed and the disclosures in the prior art. If an invention is taken to a patent agent so that he can prepare a patent application, the agent can probably construct claims that will get the inventor some type of patent on the invention; that is, unless someone has made the exact same invention. The agent attempts to determine how broadly the invention can be claimed and still be allowable in the face of the prior art. Even if no troublesome prior art is found and broad claims are filed on an invention, the inventor should still consider how narrow a claim he is willing to accept. It is also good practice to make sure enough information is included in the application to allow the agent the opportunity to narrow the claims in the future, if unknown prior art is found by the examiner and a narrowing of the claims is needed to obtain an allowance.

The amount of research that the inventor is willing to complete defines the opportunity. Having completed a lot of research, the inventor is provided with several advantages. The first advantage is that the inventor has a better chance of knowing in which situations the invention does not work and what are the limits of the invention. This allows the patent agent to identify these limits clearly, and when the inventor is willing to apply limits to the invention, the patentability of the invention can be improved in many cases. The second is that, by completing a lot of research, the inventor will have developed a keen understanding of the technology. In so doing, he will have a better idea as to how the invention can be applied to various situations and what elements of the invention are critical for success. All of this information is very useful to the patent agent when he is developing a draft of the patent application. The third advantage is that the inventor will be more likely to have multiple examples of when the invention works and does not work. Patent applications normally contain examples of the invention, and most countries of the world will allow patent coverage only on the technology that is specifically exemplified. If one wishes to claim a new paper that has 10–85 percent of an ingredient, but only gives an example of the paper containing 50 percent, many countries will only allow a claim to a paper with 50 percent of the ingredient. Therefore, it is important to include in the patent application, multiple examples of the technology, preferably at the desired operating point(s), and the practical upper and lower bounds. If extensive research has been conducted, the inventor should have a good idea of what are the upper and lower bounds of the technology. If the inventor hasn't any idea of the bounds, a guess will have to be made, and the inventor can only hope the patent agent can convince patent examiners that the wide range claimed is deserved, even though the entire range is not exemplified. Alternatively, instead of making a guess, the inventor can conduct specific experiments to get information on the bounds, but this takes additional time to accomplish.

Let's take an invention and see how the amount of research can affect the patent which is ultimately issued. Let's say a chemist is working in the lab developing new polymers, and one day he mixes several ingredients together and gets a polymer that has properties that have never been seen before. Based on the chemist's knowledge of what is needed in the marketplace, he realizes this polymer is exactly what is needed by several customers. The chemist adds the ingredients together again, and he gets the same result. He really doesn't know what has happened to get the new polymer, but at this point he is just happy to have developed this new material. If the chemist decides to file a patent immediately and take the new polymer to customers, he may be able to obtain a patent on that one polymer composition, but since he has no understanding of what actually happened, it will be exceedingly difficult to translate this experience to other polymer combinations and other patents. The result will be a patent with claims which are probably very narrow in scope. A competitor will be able to read the patent, and if he is so inclined, conduct in-depth research to figure out how the invention works. The competitor can then improve on the patent, or develop alternate technology that lessens the value of the patent.

If, on the other hand, the chemist chooses to research why the two chemicals reacted the way they did, and researches other polymer combinations, he will be in a better position to expand the breadth of coverage of the patent, and the chemist will be the one who will be developing improvements on his own technology. However, the development of this new information takes time, and there is always a trade-off between the amount of research which can be performed and the need to get the product to the marketplace.

Extensive disclosures in the prior art can drastically reduce the breadth of a patent application, regardless of the amount of research that has been completed. This is one good reason to have a literature and patent search conducted during the planning of a research program. Also, in most cases, if the researcher makes any inventions, another patent or literature search will be made by the patent agent to identify the prior art for the invention. This is referred to as an anticipation search. Its purpose is to determine whether or not the invention has been anticipated by previous disclosures. Before this anticipation search is performed, one can speculate how broad he wishes the claims in the patent application to be, but in most cases, some prior art will be found which will restrict the claims.

For example, let's say a duck hunter invents a wooden duck decoy with eyes which attract other ducks. The hunter immediately begins thinking about having a monopoly on duck decoys, that is, replacing all of the wooden duck decoys in the world with the new improved decoy. The hunter then quickly realizes that he shouldn't settle for just duck decoys; there could be any number of animal decoys that would benefit from his technology for making decoy eyes. He takes his new improved decoy to a patent agent for help in getting a patent. The agent suggests the hunter has invented both an eye for a decoy, and a decoy containing eyes that attract other animals. The agent performs a prior art search, and finds a magazine article on ostrich decoys that have special eyes for attracting other ostriches.

This reference could impact the hunter's application in any number of ways. First of all, the agent will probably not be able to draft a claim to a generic decoy containing eyes that attract other animals, because such a decoy has been shown to exist. However, if the technology used to make the ostrich eyes is different from the hunter's technology, the agent might be able to construct language that allows the hunter to claim a decoy with a special type of eye. 'Special' in this case means an eye incorporating the hunter's new eye technology. The effect of the ostrich reference is to narrow the claims in the hunter's patent application from very broad to more specific.

On the other hand, the article could disclose the exact same technology for making the eyes, but only discloses the technology as it was applied to ostrich decoys. In this case, even though duck decoys are not mentioned, it might be difficult for the hunter to obtain any patent. First of all, since the technology for making an eye is the same, the hunter would not be able to patent an eye for a decoy. One might think that the hunter should be able to get a patent on a duck decoy, because a duck decoy is different from an ostrich decoy. It is possible, but not probable, that in some countries the hunter's patent agent might be able to convince an examiner that the application to duck decoys is inventive and different from the application to ostrich decoys. In many countries, however, the application of the technology is so similar, no patent would issue. To obtain a patent, the hunter would probably have to add another feature distinctive to duck decoys, such as waterproofing the eye, or find some distinction between his eye technology and the eye technology disclosed in the reference. Again, the effect of the reference is to narrow the claims the hunter's patent agent should include in the application. In the case where the hunter develops a waterproofing feature for the eye, the hunter's patent might be directed to a waterproofed eye, which is much different than what the hunter initially thought the patent would cover.

Broad claims are not without risk, and the business need is sometimes best served by obtaining narrow claims. A patent agent will prepare the patent application with the broadest claims possible based on the information given to him and the content of the prior art search. Unfortunately, searches are never 100 percent complete. If a reference not found in the search is found by the examiner, the best one can hope for is to be able to amend the claims to a narrower invention. A potentially worse case is when a pertinent reference is not found in either the patent agent's search or the examiner's search. The patent may issue, but when the patent owner tries to enforce the patent against another, the pertinent reference is found and used to invalidate the patent.

In Japan, many patent applications have traditionally been very specific with narrow claims. However, the effect of obtaining a patent on narrow claims is that the patent can be very strong, and many Japanese companies have chosen to file several patent applications of limited breadth rather than file one or two broad patents. In this way, if an invalidating reference is found, the entire patent position is not compromised.

However, patents normally contain independent and dependent claims. The dependent claims are included to help maintain the validity of the patent. If the main claim is found to be invalid, the dependent claim, which narrows the main claim, may still be valid. For example, let's assume the patent search mentioned previously did not find the magazine article on ostrich decoys even though it was in the prior art, and the magazine article disclosed an eye made using a different technology from that of the hunter's. If the examiner misses the same magazine article, the hunter will probably obtain a patent having (1) a main claim to a decoy having eyes that attract animals, and (2) a claim depending from the main claim that claims a decoy having eyes where the eyes have the specific technology the hunter has invented. If at some point the hunter attempts to enforce his patent, and in the process the magazine article is found, the main claim of the hunter's patent will probably be invalid because the type of decoy described in the first claim was disclosed in the magazine article. However, the dependent claim would probably be ruled to be valid, because that particular decoy, the one with the hunter's technology, was not described in the magazine article.

Now consider two additional possibilities about this example. First, let's make the same assumptions as before, but in addition suppose that the person whom the hunter wishes to stop by enforcing his patent, makes decoy eyes using a process different from that claimed by the hunter. Since the first claim is invalid, and the second claim is not infringed, the hunter has no way to enforce the patent. Second, let's suppose that the technology disclosed in the magazine article and the hunter's technology were the same, and as before, the article was not found in the prior art search. Then, both of the claims in the hunter's patent would eventually be shown to be invalid because the content of both claims would have both been disclosed in the magazine article.

Where?

Where is patent protection wanted?

The selection of countries in which to file a patent application is dependent on the perceived value of a country to a business, the perceived effect the patent application has on the business, the enforcement climate in the country, and the willingness of the business to spend money on patents.

The perceived value of a country is determined by the business strategy and the perceived strategies of competitors. A business strategy should either identify the countries where products will be sold, or at least identify where the growing and lucrative markets for products are located. Normally, patents will be wanted in these countries to restrict competition. Even if products are to be sold globally, the patent filing should be selective; rarely should it be necessary to file a patent application in every country of the world. Filings should only be needed in those countries that make up most of the market for a product, or that have markets that are growing at a rapid pace. There may also be value in filing some patents in the countries where competitive products are manufactured, regardless of the market size of the country, in an effort to hinder the efforts of competitors to produce these competitive products.

Each patent application filed has a different effect on a business. Intuitively, important applications should be filed more broadly, that is, in more countries than less important applications. Unfortunately, many times an application must be filed long before a commercial readout of the success of the invention has been obtained. So, in many cases, an application must be filed based only on the perceived effect the patent will have on competitors. The principles developed around the value of an invention can be used to help better pinpoint this perceived effect and lessen the amount of uncertainty.

The ability to enforce a patent in a country should be considered when selecting countries in which to file patent applications, but this by itself should not outweigh all other issues. The enforceability issue has traditionally been used to justify the filing of patent applications in only a few countries that have very stable legal systems. In so doing, the patent agent was dealing with a known situation and could predict the response that the court system of a country would make to a legal challenge of the patent. However, by filing a patent, one is starting a process that could last for 20 years or more. Legal systems can change in countries, and most countries have realized that improvement in intellectual property protection is critical for foreign investment. In response, countries that had gained a reputation as having bad intellectual property climates have implemented new laws to give patents more teeth in their judicial systems. Communist countries like China, and the former communist countries of the Soviet Union, which have discouraged the concept of personal property rights, now seem to want to embrace these concepts on at least a limited scale to attract foreign investors and increase the standard of living in their countries. If there is a business reason for filing in a country it is best to go ahead and file in that country, regardless of the enforcement climate. On the other hand, if one must choose between a country which has a good enforcement climate, and one which doesn't, it is clear that the country with the good enforcement climate is the better choice.

Global filing of patent applications is expensive, and companies do not always need to broadly file all applications. In particular, a small business may not be financially able to file in as many countries as it would like. On the other hand, if the business situation is such that the invention can generate a lot of money, one might be advised to spend money to get some global insurance through patents. The key issue to realize, however, is that different countries charge different fees to file patent applications and to obtain and maintain patents. Cost, like enforcement climate, should not be

---

Developing a Patent Strategy for an Invention

What is the invention?

What is to be achieved by filing this patent application?

What additional information is needed for the patent application?

When must this patent application be filed?

Who is going to develop the information for the patent application?

Who is going to prepare the application?

How much information should be disclosed in the application?

How broadly can/should the invention be claimed?

Where is patent protection wanted?

Figure 3.2 Developing a patent strategy for an invention

ignored, but also should not be the only consideration in filing patents globally. Scandinavian countries have gained a reputation as being expensive countries in which to file, although most countries of the world in recent years have increased their fees, so that filing in almost any country is now expensive. In any case, if there is a business need to file a patent in a Scandinavian country, this should outweigh any consideration of the cost of fees. Cost becomes a major issue to consider when the value of a patent application is uncertain, but the business believes some global coverage for the invention is appropriate. In this case, it may be appropriate to be very frugal with both money and effort, and file only in those countries where a major opportunity for the product line in general is perceived.

Constructing the strategy

The patent agent, along with a patent liaison or intellectual property professional, if one is available, play a major part in the construction of a strategy for a patent application. If the patenting team consists of the inventor and an agent, the agent should recommend how broadly the application can be written, what additional experiments are needed, and how much disclosure will be needed in the specification. A good patent agent will also suggest ways the inventor might improve the scope of the claims, if the inventor is willing and able to do the additional work. The researcher/inventor can play a major role in performing these additional experiments, informing the agent as to the business need for the patent filing, and reviewing the application with an eye toward the amount of disclosure in the application. All have an important role in deciding whether the amount of disclosure is worth the opportunity for obtaining a patent.

DEVELOPING A PATENT STRATEGY FOR A SERIES OF INVENTIONS

In-depth research normally does not result in only one invention, but a series of inventions. The result is the need not only to prepare strategies for all of the individual inventions, but also an overall strategy that will act to coordinate the individual filings and filing strategies. Unless an overall strategy is developed, the chances increase that a disclosure in an earlier patent application could needlessly compromise the patentability of a subsequent filing.

Key players in developing this patent strategy are the current business, marketing, and technical leaders for the product line, assisted by either a patent liaison and/or a patent agent. It is the business and marketing leaders' responsibility to provide market trend information, while the technical leader should provide technical trends that could be to the advantage of the business. The patent liaison provides input on the extent to which patent coverage has been provided for in the area, and what possibilities exist for strong patent protection on the areas of interest. His job is to help decide whether a strong patent position can be achieved. The patent attorney can provide valuable guidance for resolving adverse patents that are found and providing all types of advice about patent matters, in addition to the tasks associated with preparing, filing, and prosecuting patent applications.

The simplest situation, where an overall strategy of this type is appropriate, is when one is developing several different but related inventions within a short time span, and all of the inventions are believed to be patentable. The most complicated type of strategy is needed when one is considering a patent strategy for a particular product line or market area. We will again use the questions What?, When?, Who?, How?, and Where? in developing the strategy. In this situation, the patent strategy becomes tied closer to the technology strategy; in fact, the best way to develop a patent strategy for a series of inventions is to develop this strategy as one is developing the technical and business strategies.

What?

What is the vision for the product line or the series of inventions?

It is important to have some idea where a business is going with a product line. If efforts are directed at improving a product line or developing a series of inventions, it is important to understand how the individual developments fit together to enhance the entire business. As one goes about planning a strategy, the key will be to use the individual patents that are filed as a series of legal barriers to the competition. Therefore, the vision for the product line will need to be clearly established and the resources available to make the vision a reality.

If the product line is viewed as a series of mature products, then the strategy may either by to reduce the cost of the products, or to develop new products to replace the mature ones, or some combination of both strategies. If a new technology or a series of new products are being developed, then one may have a strategy to obtain as much protection as possible for the technology. The strategy might also be to totally ignore patent protection. Process technology can be licensed from others or new products can be disclosed as they are developed; the business can rely on an ability to respond quickly to the marketplace and continuously develop products as they are needed. In each case, however, having a vision of the future helps the business establish how it will approach the establishment of a strategy to handle invention. If there is no specific idea as to what the business ultimately wants to achieve with a product line, the business may end up with patents that do not cover useful inventions, or more importantly, the patents may disclose information that will be very helpful to competitors.

What technologies will provide the product line with a proprietary position?

In almost any technology area, there are always new developments that could radically improve or change the state of the business. While patents on minor improvements in products and processes can be helpful, a true proprietary position, which can provide a business with a competitive advantage, is obtained by developing step-change improvements in technology. One should consider what these step-change improvements might be, and what the impact might be if competitors were to develop them first. The goal is to develop a clear understanding of the new technologies that can provide the business with a competitive advantage.

If that competitive advantage is in the form of a cheaper product, then one may be able to develop a proprietary position on the lowest cost process. If a new product functionality will be an advantage, then one can consider whether or not the functionality can be provided. If competitive advantage can be had by developing a totally new and different product, but a business cannot or chooses not to make this product, it is possible to build a successful block of the new technology through patents; or, these patents may be licensed to others for fees and royalty payments. Remember, patents enable the patent owner to exclude others from practicing. If a business can patent potentially competitive processes and products, then that business will be in a position to exert patents against any competitors that try to practice these same inventions.

When a researcher is working in an area where he has previously obtained patents, he may not be able to obtain a strong proprietary position with a single new patent. That is, it may not be possible to construct with one patent a direct barrier that will prevent competitors from the technology area. However, the researcher may be able to construct an indirect barrier by obtaining a number of patents, which may effectively work together to provide the barrier.

For example, let's say a company makes and sells plastic trash cans, and the company also makes the plastic that forms the trash cans. The company patented the plastic long ago, and the patent has expired, and now anyone can make this plastic or a plastic trash can from the plastic. A researcher at the company believes a particular chemical additive to the plastic will make the trash cans tougher, and the researcher is able to demonstrate in the lab that the additive does in fact make tougher trash cans. However, the company is unable to file a patent on the additive in the plastic, because it is known to use the additive for plastics – that is the application for which the manufacturer sells the additive. When commercial use of the additive begins in the manufacturing plant, the process engineers have many difficult problems in making the additive work in the process, and in response, the engineers develop a series of new processing equipment which allows the use of the additive and the efficient manufacture of the new improved trash cans. The engineers are convinced that the only way to use the additive in trash cans is to use this newly developed equipment and the processes developed for preparing and adding the additive to the plastic. The company files a series of apparatus and process patent applications, which taken individually do not seem very important. However, when these patent applications issue as patents and are combined together, they effectively prevent competitors from using the additive in the production of trash cans. Now competitors may be able to develop alternative equipment and processes, but in the meantime, the company is able to use the legal monopoly to increase their market share of the sales of trash cans.

What technologies will match the vision of the future but will not be proprietary?

A technical development that will have the potential to provide a proprietary position through patents may not agree with the vision for the product line, or there may be multiple opportunities using known technology to improve the product line, which all fit well with the vision, but that are not patentable. Since no one has unlimited resources to spend on new developments, the technical resources that are available shouldn't necessarily be focused only on developments that will provide a proprietary position.

Obtaining a better proprietary position may not be the best option for a particular business. If a person owned a business manufacturing horse-drawn wagons at the beginning of the twentieth century, what was needed was a vision to phase in the manufacture of automobiles, which were to become more and more popular, while maintaining or slowly phasing out the manufacture of wagons. Additional patents on new types of horse-drawn wagons and new processes for producing wagons would have been of limited use at that time, because one could have improved their proprietary position and still see their business falter. However, if a business developed a version of the automobile, their business might thrive even though they might not have anything potentially patentable.

Obviously, the vision and the business strategy should be consistent. If possible, it is always great to develop technology that can be patented; however, the desire for patents or a proprietary position must be consistent with the business strategy and must support the vision of the future. The development of an improved but worthless proprietary position signals the technical strategy for a business is out of alignment. The technical strategy must be in agreement with the long range vision for the business.

What claims are wanted for each case?

Given a long-range vision, and a technology area, one should be in a position to describe what they would want to claim in any patent applications that might be filed. Now, it may seem silly to do this in the early stages, but a researcher should be able to formulate what inventions should result from the research, assuming the research is successful. These mental inventions, if combined with knowledge of the prior art in the technology area, should enable the researcher to formulate not only the invention, but the desired claims which would be included in patent applications.

This is an interesting and useful exercise for the researcher to undertake, because it can help him consider what types of experimentation and testing are needed to generate data to support not only the desired invention, but also a patent application. It can also serve as a check of the potential proprietary position one can expect as a result of the research.

Where?

Where in the world are the stoppers?

It is important to know if there are patents that can cause a business trouble, and where these patents have issued. Stoppers can be either patents that have strongly supported claims, which prevent one from practicing an invention; or even could be detailed disclosures of a technology area, which prevent one from obtaining strong patent protection. If another has a strong patent position, one might decide to try another technology area or try to license the technology. One may find that certain countries of the world are covered by patents in a technology area, while other countries are not, so an estimate of the negative effect of the stopper can be generated. On the other hand, if one finds that there are other patents that disclose a lot about the technology and they have expired, one may come to the conclusion it is no longer possible to create a proprietary position in this technology area. The issue then becomes one of whether or not a business is in a position to compete with many different competitors on a cost basis.

Where in the world should a patent estate be developed?

Part of a business strategy and vision is an expectation for the sales growth of the products in the various countries around the world. Since patents are valuable for about 20 years, a fairly long period of time should be considered in the business strategy. While a set of countries may be targeted for a particular invention, a consideration should be made as to where comprehensive patent estates will be developed for the series of inventions. If a country is vital to the business, one will want to develop a patent estate in that country, because in so doing, the patents in the patent estate help to protect an area of intellectual property greater than the individual patents. By developing a patent estate, instead of just one wall being erected to hinder competition, several different walls are erected that work together to form a more impenetrable defense of the technology area. A competitor may be able to engineer around a single patent, but is less likely to be able to engineer around several patents. The sheer number of patents may be enough to stop even a determined competitor.

When?

When will the development of a technology area end?

It is useful to consider how success will be measured in the development of a series of inventions. In particular, what has to happen or at what point the organization will stop research or development work in an area of technology. As patents are obtained and more and more information is disclosed in a particular area of technology, the potential scope of any patent claim necessarily becomes more and more limited. Good patents may still be obtained in a heavily patented area, but the likelihood that several marketplace-affecting patents can be obtained in a heavily patented area is normally very low. Therefore, one needs to consider when the development might reach the point of diminishing returns.

One may decide to try to 'reserve' a certain section of a technology area through research and aggressive patenting, so that this program will be successful once a specific list of research work is complete and the patent applications have been filed. On the other hand, one may decide to concentrate efforts in one area of technology for a specific period of time and then re-evaluate the potential for a major positive business impact, and if this potential is low, consider developing another area of technology. When developing a series of inventions, the researcher typically has in mind two or more inventions on which to file patent applications. One may decide that after the two patent applications are filed, it is in the best interest of the business to do research on other things. However, a whole portfolio of patents may be needed for a true competitive advantage; if this is the case, additional work must be completed and additional patent applications must be filed before the program is stopped and work in another technology area is begun.

Who?

Who needs to work on these inventions?

In the development of a strategy for a single case, one of the questions was 'Who would generate the information for the patent application?' The question needs to be asked in a similar manner for a series of inventions, especially since each individual case will require its own effort. If one intends to file a number of patent applications at the same time, so as to avoid having one application contaminate another, a single inventor, or even a research team of a couple of people may not be able to develop the needed information at the pace required for the filing. Likewise, more than one agent may be required to draft all the applications at one time. All of these efforts must be thought out and coordinated.

The development of a series of inventions will also require more input from persons other than the inventors. Technical personnel who have expertise in specialized areas may be able to add useful insight in the development of one or more of the inventions. Also, people in the marketing or sales force can provide a customer's perspective of the developed inventions. While all of this input is helpful, all of the people involved with the development need to understand the need for security around the invention. They must understand that an inadvertent or premature disclosure of the technology could forfeit patent rights in many countries.

How?

How much money is the business willing to spend?

In a very basic sense, the speed and breadth of development, and therefore the ability to develop a patent estate, is dependent on how much money a business is willing to spend. By assigning more scientists to the task of developing a series of inventions, and providing them with the resources needed, a business increases its chances of first developing in-depth knowledge about a technology area, and then second, the ability to deliver the resulting technology sooner. The result of this fully supported effort is more information that can be used to develop well supported, strong, patent applications. All this comes at a cost, however, so the expected benefit must be great enough to justify the allocation of resources and effort.

In developing a series of inventions, sometimes money can be saved by obtaining just those patents that provide basic coverage of the intended technology area. For example, if one develops a new chemical composition, he might be tempted to file separate patent applications on the composition, a process for making the composition, the equipment used to make the composition, and something made from the composition. However, one should consider whether, if a patent on the composition is obtained, a patent on the process for making the composition is really necessary. Clearly, the process patent is not nearly as important as the product patent, and may involve more disclosure of the manufacturing process. Likewise for the equipment used to make the composition and something made from the composition. The money spent on these patent applications might be better spent on researching other inventions, since these additional applications only tend to augment the overall coverage of the invention to a very minor extent.

How will consistency be maintained from case to case?

As applications are prepared and filed, it is important that they are consistent on the basics of the technology and the definitions used for the technical terms. If at all possible, names for common items should not be changed, or different versions of the same tests should not be used, from application to application. By being consistent, the overall patent estate is strengthened; should there ever be a need to enforce a patent, the technical terms in the patent will have clear and consistent definitions in the patent estate.

More importantly, the content of the initial applications should be carefully monitored to make sure that information that will be useful in subsequent applications is not inadvertently disclosed. Also, the information in later applications should be checked for disclosures that might weaken or

Developing a Patent Strategy for a Series of Inventions

What is the vision for the product line or series of inventions?

What technologies will provide the product line with a proprietary position?

What technologies will match the vision of the future but will not be proprietary?

What claims are wanted for each case?

Where in the world are the stoppers?

Where in the world should a patent estate be developed?

When will the development of a technology area end?

Who needs to work on these inventions?

How much money is the business willing to spend?

How will consistency be maintained from case to case?

Figure 3.3 A patent strategy for a series of inventions

cast doubt on the validity of prior patents. The easiest way to develop consistency is for someone to assume the role of making sure that the applications are consistent, and this can be a researcher in charge of the program, an intellectual property professional, or an agent. Where possible, the best way to maintain consistency is to have the same agent write and prosecute all the cases. That way, the agent is aware of the history of the product line, and can help maintain consistency.

DEVELOPING A STRATEGY FOR AN EXISTING PRODUCT

When a company has a valuable existing product the need for an intellectual property strategy becomes an important part of the long term health of the business. Such a strategy provides a useful balance to a tendency to focus on the short term. Normally, an existing product will already have a business strategy. What is needed is a specific intellectual property strategy that will work within the business strategy. People working with an existing product will have some knowledge of competing products, marketplace trends, and unfulfilled customer needs. Many of the researchers and managers will have their own opinions on where research should be conducted and what inventions are needed. Generating an intellectual property strategy will help focus the overall efforts of a research team and will help the organization reach an agreement on how to proceed.

What follows is an outline of a method which seeks to generate a strategy for an existing product by focusing on a few simple but powerful questions.

This particular strategy development uses both internal and external views of the product to add additional perspective. These questions are good starting points for subsequent discussions, however, these can be changed or augmented should a business have different needs. Ideally, a multi-functional group of experienced personnel would generate this strategy. The only practical requirement is that at least some of the members of the group have specific knowledge about the product, the competitors, and the marketplace. Development of the strategy proceeds as follows.

What is the current situation?

It is helpful to start with a realistic assessment of the current business. This assessment can include many different types of facts, concerns, and opportunities.

It may involve a statement about the intellectual property climate for the product, and summarize patents that are in force. It may discuss patent applications that have recently been filed and how they will affect the marketplace. It can outline the perceived needs of major customers or segments of the market. Finally, the various opportunities and concerns already recognized by the people in the business can be voiced. Generation of this summary of the current situation allows a common understanding of current pressures on the business, the important recent technical developments, and the opinions of the organization's members.

What is the vision?

The strategy should also include a statement of the overall vision for the business. Most businesses already have a vision of where the business is going. Therefore, normally a vision statement is not something that must be developed in an intellectual property strategy. However, if one is not available, such a vision statement should be generated. The vision statement acts as a reminder to those who are generating the strategy; it helps as a checkpoint in understanding whether or not the proposed strategic actions are in agreement with where the business is going.

The next steps in this process generate those proposed strategic actions. It is a two-step process. In each case, certain advantages, needs, or trends are identified, and then a series of focused actions that have the most impact are specified; these become the working strategy. The overall idea is to generate an ongoing process which helps the business focus on what new developments will really be important to the bottom line.

What are the existing competitive advantages?

The strategy development starts by identifying the competitive advantages of the business or its products. What does the business or product do better than competitors? Why do customers prefer the products of the business over competitive products? Competitive advantages can come in many forms, from product performance to service to pricing. The first step is to identify what are the primary competitive advantages that truly separate the business from competitors.

Once identified, these product strengths become the starting points on discussions of how these strengths can be improved, or how one improves on something already done well. The idea is not to over-engineer, but to understand the competitive advantages and then seek to improve those advantages. If inventions are made in the process of improving those competitive advantages then patents on those inventions can provide increased protection of the business. It is important, however, that the business concentrates only on the strategic actions that will have major impact. The idea is to focus the efforts, not create a laundry list of possible action items.

For example, one might decide that product color is an important competitive advantage. Therefore, the business might decide to implement process improvements to make color more uniform or more vibrant or more longer lasting, any of which would improve the competitive advantage.

What are the existing market needs that could be met by a determined competitor?

Next one identifies the key needs that are not being met in the marketplace. There are always things that customers wish could be changed, or product performance or attributes which they wish were different. The existing needs in the marketplace that must be identified are those needs, which if met by a determined competitor, could dramatically change the business climate or market share. Competitors hear the same desires from customers, so a determined competitor might be able to make headway on some product flaw and gain market share.

Once these substantial market needs are identified, then the question becomes what strategic actions should be taken to develop the technologies or systems to meet those needs. Again, the effort should be focused on substantial needs that could have major impact, and if inventions that are made to meet those needs, they can be patented to protect those inventions and the subsequent market share they bring.

What are the major enduse trends and thrusts?

The third item in the strategy concerns the technologies competitors are developing and the trends in the marketplace. It involves understanding how the marketplace is evolving and how the drivers in the marketplace are changing. This understanding should reveal whether or not the current business focus drives toward the future marketplace or if some new actions need to be taken. It may reveal that the organization should take actions to avoid being blocked from some key future technology area.

Once this has been understood, the next step is to identify the strategic actions to take advantage of the perceived trends. Also, strategic actions should be developed to lessen the impact of the developments of competitors. For example, suppose a market need is being met by two types of product supplied by two different companies. Further assume the marketplace trend is to products which have several new features. A strategic action for one company would be to not only invent and patent, if possible, their new product with the new features; but also seek to invent and patent the version of the product with new features that their competitor would probably develop. In this way, the company can either reserve the technology or license it to the other company to obtain additional revenue. As with the other parts of the strategy, the key here is to focus on those strategic actions that are felt to have the most impact.

The statements on the current situation and vision are combined with the strategic actions to form a three-part strategy for an existing business. The first part lists the major competitive advantages and what strategic actions will be taken to improve those advantages. The second part lists significant major market needs, and what specific actions will be taken to meet those needs. Finally, marketplace trends and competitive thrusts are identified along with what actions will be taken to impact those with a positive result for the business. The result is a strategy document which has a simple message of focus and intent so that it can easily be communicated and understood by the organization.

Developing a Strategy for An Existing Product

What is the current situation?

What is the vision?

What are the existing competitive advantages?

What are the existing market needs that could be met by a determined competitor?

What are the major enduse trends and thrusts?

Figure 3.4 Developing a patent strategy for an existing product

DEVELOPING A STRATEGY FOR LICENSING PATENTS

The licensing of patents is a complex topic and big business. If one has a patent, one may use it to prevent others from practicing, or may be able to license the patent to another for a fee. Likewise, one may want to use an invention patented by another, and want to license that patent. In both cases, it is important to establish clear bounds on what is to be licensed, and how much the technology is worth or how much someone is willing to pay for it. The ins and outs of licensing would fill up an entire book; for our purposes, we will make the following points:

Licensing patents to other companies

If a business has patents on inventions which have a substantial non-competing use, the licensing of these patents is superior to either just retaining the patents and continuing to pay maintenance fees, or abandoning the patents to save payment of the maintenance fees. Once the patents for licensing have been selected, there are any number of ways in which to attempt to license them. If another company is known to work in the area, and perhaps has expressed an interest in the patent, then they can be contacted directly to see if they are interested in pursuing a license.

On the other hand, on-line databases can be used to see if any patents owned by a business are cited in the prosecution of an issued patent owned by another company. The claims of this subsequent patent can be reviewed to see if this is an improvement patent and is dominated by one or more of the patents owned by the business. If the patent is dominated, then the business has a strong position from which to negotiate with the other company, if the other company wants to practice the invention in their patent. If after reviewing the patent claims there is no domination, if the patents relate to the same technology areas, it may still be worth approaching the company because they could have an interest in pursuing a license.

Another method of licensing patents is to let someone else do it. There are firms that will 'shop' patents in the technology markets for a percentage of the licensing fees. The advantage of these firms is that very little effort must be expended by the patent owner to get the word out that a patent is available for licensing.

Licensing patents from other companies

If a company holds a patent on an invention that is of use to a business, the business may wish to approach this company concerning the possibility of licensing the patent so the invention can be used without infringement. Each licensing case is different, so a patent attorney will play a major part in helping to negotiate a license with the other company. An analysis of the patent will need to be done to confirm the patent is valid, and that the invention to be used is really claimed in the patent. Negotiations of the license should also include some consideration as to whether or not the license agreement will include some type of provision for the other company to supply technical know-how or equipment in addition to the use of the patent.

DEVELOPING A STRATEGY FOR HANDLING A POTENTIALLY ADVERSE PATENT

If the products of a business are successful, there will be competitors, and therefore a business will have to deal with competitors' patents. At some point, if a business is reviewing the published patent art, researchers will come across patents which will be of concern because they may appear to restrict the freedom of the business to operate. To handle these potentially adverse patents, an overall approach for evaluating these patents should be developed. After it has been determined whether or not the patent is a threat, a strategy for handling the patent can be developed.

The overall strategy when faced with an adverse patent is to:

1. Determine the status of the patent publication.
2. Determine what is claimed.
3. Determine whether it is a shield or a sword, or neither.
4. Develop a strategy for taking action.

1. Determining the status of the publication

In Chapter 1, we discussed that in most countries in the world patent applications are published 18 months after their original filing or priority date. Therefore, there are at least three types of patent publications. These are:

- patents;
- examined patent applications which have been published, just after issuance, for the purpose of public review (and the initiation of opposition or revocation actions by others that believe the patent to be invalid); and
- published patent applications.

The strategy that is initiated will depend on the status of the patent publication.

All patent publications have a number for identification. A patent agent or patent liaison can determine what type of patent publication the researcher has found, based on the publication number. It may very well be a published patent application and not an issued patent. However, since most companies are globally oriented, the global status of the application should be considered. It is possible that the patent application has actually issued as a patent in another country, or the publication the researcher has found is not the most recent publication of the patent application from that country. For example, the researcher may have a copy of the published patent application, while in fact the application has already been granted. By accessing on-line electronic databases, one can determine the breadth of filing and status of the application, with two provisos; first, one needs to realize that if the application was filed within the last two years, getting an accurate and full readout of where the application has been filed will be difficult. Applications are generally published 18 months after filing, and time must be added to allow for the abstracting services to enter the application into their database, which can take a few months. The second proviso is that some databases do not enter in the number for the patent grant, just the first publication. A patent agent or liaison can find out the actual status of the application in various countries, which in some cases will require contacting agents providing this service in the actual countries. If the publication is a patent, a patent agent can also determine whether or not the patent is still in force.

Therefore, the first task is to identify what type of publication has been found. Next, a complete analysis of the publication should be performed.

2. Determine what is claimed

Most patent publications have claims. The title of the application should be reviewed and then the claims found, which will either be the first section in the patent application or the last, and they will be numbered. The claims should be carefully read in order to get an understanding of what the applicant is trying to claim, but it may be difficult to understand completely what the invention is. As we described in Chapter 1, the claims are the legal description of the invention. The rest of the application serves to describe and explain the invention. After the claims have been read, one should return to the beginning of the application. Typically, the first part of the application describes the problems in the prior art, next comes a short summary of what is to be claimed, and then come the details, including drawings and examples about the invention. By carefully studying the application, the researcher should be able to determine exactly what the invention is and what has actually been claimed.

3. Determine whether it is a shield or a sword, or neither

The owner of the adverse patent has filed the patent to be either a sword or a shield, that is, he either wishes to disclose his particular invention and nothing more, thereby creating a shield which protects his particular process; or he wishes to disclose and claim more than his original invention, and thereby use the patent as a sword to prevent others from practicing related inventions. Now that the claims are understood, one can go about the task of evaluating whether they are of a concern. If the patent discloses a fairly specific invention, the owner probably wants to use the patent as a shield. In most cases, if the business is practicing a different invention, then the patent is not of concern. However, there are issues about equivalence, particularly in the United States, where it might be prudent for an attorney to give an opinion of whether or not the business practice will infringe the other company's patent. If what the business wishes to do is claimed in the patent, then the business must decide whether or not (1) to ignore the patent and risk legal action by the patent owner, (2) to attempt to obtain a license for the use of the patent, or (3) to change plans and not practice this invention.

4. Develop a strategy for taking action

If the patent is of concern after the previous analyses, then a business is in the position where it may infringe another's patent. In this case, it is best to confirm these fears with an attorney, who can interpret the claims and tell exactly whether or not the patent is infringed. If the attorney believes there is an infringement problem, then two final tasks should be undertaken before making the final strategic decision. The first step to take is to have a comprehensive prior art search performed for the attorney to review. It may be possible that published references can be found which will make the patent invalid. The second step is to obtain a copy of the file history or the prosecution of the application from patent offices from around the world for the attorney to review. It may be possible that these files contain information the attorney can use to reach an opinion of invalidity. It is important to work closely with the attorney during this phase, particularly because the issues involved are primarily legal issues, not technical ones, and most researchers or research managers are not trained in this area. If the attorney believes the patent is invalid, then the business may decide to ignore the patent and risk legal action from the patent owner. Again, the attorney is the best person to guide the business as to all the possible ramifications of ignoring a patent. The patent owner may initiate litigation, so a business needs to be aware there are legal risks even though internal studies have revealed the patent to be invalid. It is possible, even though a business believes a patent is invalid, that in a judicial setting the patent will be judged to be valid and infringed. Therefore, ignoring the patent is not a simple decision.

If the adverse patent has no apparent flaws, a business must then decide whether or not (1) it is willing to risk litigation by the owner of the patent, (2) it will try to license the patent, or (3) it will change its plans and not practice the invention. Since competitors are least likely to license their patents, the most common method chosen by ventures when the patent is owned by a competitor is to change plans. Instead of doing nothing, however, the business will normally develop alternate technology that will perform the same function.

Now, whether or not a business will be able to develop alternate technology which is not covered by the adverse claims, depends entirely on the exact invention description and the prior art. If successful in developing alternate technology, that is, technology that is not covered by the adverse patent, the business might actually be able to file its own patent.

In determining whether or not the alternate technology is covered by the adverse patent, the business needs once again to solicit advice from a patent attorney. While many countries have literal interpretations of claims, the United States has the long-standing concept of the 'doctrine of equivalence'. That is, if the alternate technology performs the same act in the same way with essentially the same result as the invention in the adverse patent, but this alternate technology is not specifically claimed in the patent, the alternate technology may be found to be 'equivalent' to the invention claimed in the patent and the patent to be infringed. Therefore, either before alternate technology is developed, or shortly after it is developed, a patent attorney should be consulted as to whether this new technology is clearly outside the grasp of the adverse patent, and it can be used without liability. The patent owner of the adverse patent might still initiate legal action; however, if the attorney has given good advice, then the owner of the alternate invention should prevail.

DEVELOPING A STRATEGY FOR ODDBALL INVENTIONS

Suppose a business make widgets, and has a research organization and research programs to develop new types of widgets and new processes to make widgets, and one day a machine operator invents a new tool which helps him do his job, but has nothing to do with the venture's competitive position concerning widgets. Perhaps the operator invents a new basket for moving widgets, but the basket is useful for groceries, or almost any occasion where one would use a basket. The point is, here the business now has an invention which may be truly valuable, but it is difficult to see how this invention will provide any improved competitive position in view of widgets. This invention is an oddball, but it may have true value. What should the business do with it?

The most important thing to do when there is an oddball invention is to give it proper attention and make a conscious decision whether or not the business will 'do' anything with it. Typically, the invention initially gets some attention when it solves a problem and perhaps the person who developed the invention gets some award; however, this attention soon dies down and later people will say, 'You know, we should have patented the such-in-such, I wonder why we didn't'. The reason it was not patented, nine times out of ten, is because since it was either not a research program or it did not fit an established research area, patenting was not even considered.

The next thing the business should do is decide whether a patent on the invention would be worth anything to the business. Here the particular situation of the business must be considered; specifically, the practical matter as to whether or not the legal resources are such that working on this invention is feasible. The business will have other, more important patent cases that are critical to the business, and a decision may be made early on that the legal resources will be devoted entirely to these inventions, and time will be spent on the oddball invention only after all of the other work is complete. However, if the business has more than a passing interest in the oddball invention, the most important thing that can be done to help decide whether or not to patent the invention is a prior art search.

A prior art searcher, given the topic of the invention, can identify what has been previously published that is close to the oddball invention. Typically, this search does not have to take a lot of time, and for a few hundred dollars or less a compilation of abstracts and patents can be provided for review. A patent agent or liaison can then determine how surprising the oddball invention is, and perhaps see how others have tackled this same problem. The inventor of the oddball invention might even get hints as to how he might improve his invention! In any case, with a search the research manager should be able to answer two basic questions, which will lead to an answer as to whether or not a patent should be filed.

The search should show whether or not what has been invented has already been disclosed or patented in a previous patent application. If it has been, then the analysis and decision process for filing can abruptly end. Even if someone else did not specifically claim the invention in their patent, if the invention is disclosed it will not be possible to obtain strong patent protection. If there is any confusion as to whether or not the invention is already claimed in another patent, a patent attorney should be contacted. He should consider whether or not there is any liability in using the oddball invention. If, on the other hand, the search does not turn up anything reasonably similar to the invention, the first test for patentability has been passed, the item is 'new'.

The second thing the search should reveal – and this requires some very open-minded analysis – is whether the invention is worth anything. For example, if a different invention is found in the search, which solves the same problem, and this invention makes more sense or is more practical than the oddball invention, then it probably does not make sense to patent the oddball invention. So one should look in the search for inventions that perform the same function in a better manner. This can be difficult, because the inventor will, no doubt, fall in love with his invention, as all inventors do, and may not see the superior logic of other inventions. If no better ideas are found in the search, then at least two tests have been passed; the invention is 'new' and the invention is 'useful' – in a practical sense.

The last piece of data needed to make a decision is the history of the use and disclosure of the invention. We went into the requirements for secrecy in Chapter 1; if patent rights have not been forfeited by inadvertent disclosure or use, then a valid patent may be obtained. If, on the other hand, patent rights have been forfeited, or the business is barred from obtaining a patent, the decision process can abruptly end. If security has been maintained, or some patent rights remain, then the business can still obtain a valid patent and the decision process continues.

Armed with these four items – some idea of availability of personnel and monetary resources, some idea of the 'newness' of the invention, some idea of the practicality of the invention, and a determination of the status of patent rights, a business should be able to discuss intelligently whether or not to file a patent application. If the process has reached this stage without identifying any reason not to file the application, reasons to have a patent should now be considered.

There are only two reasons to need a patent on an invention that is not critical to the business. The first is to provide a sense of achievement for employees. By filing and obtaining a patent, the business encourages employees to develop other inventions, and one of these other inventions may be critical to the operation and make a hefty return to the business.

The second reason to file a patent application is possibly to license the invention to another company and make money off the invention. The chances of licensing the invention are directly proportional to the assessment of the practical value based on the prior art search. However, since this invention is not critical to the process, the business should consider actively trying to license the invention to others to recoup the investment in the preparation and prosecution of the patent application. One should beware that the business does not get caught up in its own paradigms, however. The oddball invention may be the start of a new product line for the business if there is a willingness to manufacture and market the invention.

After considering all of these angles, the business may decide that patenting the oddball invention is not worth the trouble. However, if there are no stoppers to patentability, and there is the belief that the patent can be licensed, the possibility exists that extra revenue and even substantial sums can be obtained if the business is willing to devote the resources.

DEALING WITH INVENTORS WHEN PATENT APPLICATIONS ARE NOT FILED

Unfortunately, a business cannot file patent applications on every invention made by its inventors. Sometimes the invention simply is in a technology area not important to the business. Sometimes because of limited funds a business must choose to file only those patent applications that are expected to have the greatest impact, leaving unpatented some good inventions. These good inventions might be profitable in the long run, but may require more development than the business is willing to commit to.

Sometimes there are problems with the patent application itself. Many times there is a concern that the proposed claims for an invention are too narrow, that they will do little to stop a competitor from duplicating the invention in some way. Other times there are previous inventions very close to the new invention, and there is a concern that the new invention may be thought to be obvious in view of these inventions by the patent office examiner. In either case, the perception is that obtaining a useful patent is something of a long shot.

So, what is a business to do for the inventor of these unwanted inventions? One option is to grant a release to the inventor. Many corporations require employees to agree to assign inventions made by them to the corporation. If that is the case, the inventor can be granted a release from the corporation, allowing the inventor to personally pursue the filing of the application. In many cases, the corporation will want to retain the right to a royalty-free license of the invention just in case the invention turns out to be of major importance. Therefore a release is an excellent option when the new invention is clearly outside the realm of the company's core businesses.

When an inventor has done good work that is important to the business but no patent application is likely to be filed on the inventions that came from that work, the situation becomes much more delicate. A manager must understand that many inventors see their inventions as an extension of themselves. If possible, the inventor should be a part of the decision process. The worse thing possible is for an invention to be rejected and the inventor to have no idea of the real reason it was rejected, because the inventor will be sure to make up a reason if one is not given.

Also, if the inventor is a part of the process, a couple of good things might happen. First, the inventor might make a good case to the managing structure for proceeding with a patent application. Many times an inventor understands the technology landscape better and has more knowledge than say, a patent committee. Given a chance to show why the invention is important, the managing structure might decide to proceed with an application after all.

Another possible good result of incorporating the inventor into the decision process is that the inventor will see why it makes sense not to file a patent application. Most inventors are pragmatic and can see that certain patent applications will have little effect on competitors, or that other inventions have more potential. The inventor may still feel bad that no patent application will be filed, but will be much less likely to make up some absurd reason why this happened, and may actually be energized to go and invent something that will have more impact.

Finally, one last thing that managers can do when no patent application will be filed on a invention is to award the inventor the same as if a patent application had been filed. If good work has been done, recognize the good work. Concentrate on acknowledging the effort made by the inventor. If it makes sense to explain to the organization why no patent application will be filed, do this. If this is done in a open and genuine way, chances are the inventor will harbor fewer negative thoughts about the process and will be able to start to invent again sooner.

COORDINATION OF OTHER STRATEGIES AND PATENT STRATEGY

A patent strategy needs to be consistent with the business and research strategies of the organization. Although typically the business strategy and research strategies are first developed, if they are not clear in their focus they need to be clarified either before (preferably) or during the development of a patent strategy. A business strategy typically outlines the desired financial performance and the market focus, while the research strategy typically outlines the development of the technology required to meet the business objectives and support future growth of the business.

If the business is entering a new market or wants to develop a new product, it is best to develop the patent strategy in conjunction with the business and research strategy. Since this is a new market, one may not be familiar with the intellectual property landscape. Others may have patents that dominate the technology or market area and legally prevent or restrict the market presence of a business, that is, it might not be possible to sell into the market area without infringing the patents of others. Without knowing such obstacles up front, a business could expend a fair amount of effort and money in developing a product which it cannot legally sell. On the other hand, knowledge of the intellectual property landscape can give researchers insight on what parts of the technology or market area have not yet been exploited. By developing a patent strategy, a research manager may be able to steer research efforts toward a proprietary position where patents can legally exclude others from practicing.

If a business is developing a new product in an existing or familiar market and technology area, the business managers can make an initial business and research strategy and then later construct a patent strategy. This assumes there is a prior knowledge of at least some of the intellectual property landscape and there has been a fairly stable research strategy for a number of years. Even if the likelihood if a new product development effort is less, one still runs the risk that a patent exists that could impact entry into the market. In well-worn technology areas where much of the technology is in the public domain, a patent strategy may be of little use. The business will need to compete on speed, or quality, or some aspect other than patent protection. However, this may never be known unless the business goes through the exercise to develop a patent strategy.

4 Researching with Intellectual Property in Mind

INTRODUCTION

Ask an average person to name an important inventor and there's a good chance they will mention the name of Thomas Edison, who made important life-changing inventions. Ask the same person to name a researcher, and they might not have an answer, even though Edison surely conducted research to make his inventions. The popular image of a researcher is of a highly educated person in a lab coat working in a modern laboratory making discoveries that are hard to understand and explain. The image that has been fostered for inventors, however, is that of an average person who is stubborn but creative and willing to work all hours of the day and night in his garage to perfect his invention. During their lifetime, both inventors and researchers have the potential to obtain many patents for their inventions.

If one is a member of a research organization, there are probably a few individuals in that organization that have patents; some may even have a significant number of patents, and some of these patents may have been crucial to the success of the business. However, the average researcher may never be named as an inventor on a patent, much less on a significant number of patents.

Likewise the independent inventor may have many ideas which might be turned into inventions, but many of the projects or inventions an independent inventor might devote considerable time to may never be patented for one reason or the other. Regardless of whether the research is done by a research organization or an independent inventor, the stark reality is that those inventors that do have patents typically have very few that are important to any business. However, when a patent is valuable, its importance can outweigh the effort and expense of all of the inventor's other inventions. The exercise of creativity along with the lure of the profitable patent continue to inspire both researchers and inventors and they continue to invent and patent their inventions.

In this chapter we will attempt to identify some characteristics of researchers who have become prolific inventors. We will review the components of the inventive processes used by these inventors, and suggest ways to foster inventiveness in a research organization. Finally, whether one is an independent inventor or a member of a research organization, we will consider how to conduct research so as to develop the right information with which to construct a strong patent application. In so doing, we hope to give researchers and research managers insight as to how to research to obtain stronger patents and more of them.

CHARACTERISTICS OF PROLIFIC INVENTORS

Anyone can invent, but some people are able to generate many inventions over their lifetime. Prolific inventors can fit the classic image of the independent tinkerer, or they can be a member of a prolific research team, or fit anywhere in between. Therefore, it is risky to have any hard and fast requirements for being a prolific inventor. However, there appears to be some traits that many prolific inventors seem to share.

Synthesizing Concepts

We know the traits of many successful inventors because there are numerous books on successful inventions that describe or interview the inventors. The picture one develops is that these inventors usually have the capacity of combining two or more different technologies or ideas in a way that the combination is greater than the individual parts. They are said to think 'laterally', that is, to think across a number of different technology areas, and then make the mental associations that result in an invention. In so doing prolific inventors are able to see what others overlook. Many times the combination of technologies is not logical at first glance but then the resulting invention from this combination seems obvious in hindsight.

Many inventors seem more willing to embrace the unconventional. Their thinking and research utilizes but is not restricted by accepted thought. In so doing, they are able to prepare their minds to be more receptive to embracing astonishing new insights – the insights that are key to a new invention. Perhaps because they do not ignore the unconventional, they are more likely to work with seemingly mad ideas for a while longer than the typical researcher, who might automatically discount those same ideas.

Many prolific inventors point to their ability to combine information from multiple sources to solve whatever problem on which they are working as a distinct characteristic that allows them to invent. Since many inventions fall between two technology areas or disciplines, it is helpful if inventors acquire skill in several technology areas. Even though many prolific inventors are experts in more than one technology area, actually being the expert in many different areas is not a necessary requirement if the needed expertise and advice can be obtained from others.

Many prolific inventors cite better preparation as a secret to inventing. They claim formal education is not the key, but knowledge of the technical subject they are working on. A part of this preparation is to be very proficient with the information that is developed. Many inventors must deal with critics and naysayers, and many times these naysayers are very smart and well trained. An inventor must be able to back up the important points of his invention to these critics with real facts or the inventor's credibility will be in question.

Clearly there are complex inventions that require advanced education and a highly technical background, but there are many other inventions that only require a creative mind. Still, an inventor must be well trained in the area he is working in. One cannot combine concepts from multiple disciplines if one doesn't have any good ideas to begin with. An invention can result once an inventor knows how a thing works, and then learns something new about it. Inventors can obtain this needed background by learning at least some information about the previous inventions in the technology area in which they are working. Otherwise, they may make some invention only to find out it was made many years before.

In some respects, combining different technologies to make inventions is like an art form. Many prolific inventors are visualizers. They can imagine and visualize the details of the proposed invention in their heads. Both the inventor and the artist combine new concepts and work with them and develop them until they work. Sometimes this takes considerable time and it is at this point that having patience and the ability to keep an open mind become valuable traits for the inventor. Rarely do ideas come to prolific inventors from nowhere. Invention is usually the culmination of many different thoughts that provide a better understanding of the problem and ultimately a solution.

Getting Ideas

So where do prolific inventors get ideas? First of all, inventors need ideas for things that the world needs; they also need to identify inefficiencies in what has previously been invented. Second, once target inventions are identified, or a problem is identified, inventors need ideas on how to actually make the inventions and solve the problems.

If prolific inventors have more ideas than other researchers this may be due to the degree of curiousness the inventors have, and the type of ideas that pop into their minds. For example, prolific inventors are typically not only curious to see how or why a machine works the way it does, but they are also eager to develop ideas on how to make the machine work better. Perhaps the object of their curiosity is to improve the world, not just to learn about the world.

In any case, ideas for invention are everywhere. Prospective inventors can get ideas for inventions by constantly looking for problems that could be solved. These are problems they might run across in their daily routine or problems presented by someone else, or something one comes across by listening to television or reading a newspaper. Some inventors claim one should not try to predict the future, but rather look to the present and think about how current inventions perform their functions, whether they are efficient, and if not, how one might improve those inventions.

However, inventing is more than simply thinking up something to invent, despite the fact that many potential inventors believe they have invented something when they have just come up with a concept for an invention. Prolific inventors carry the process further. Many will read up on the problem to learn as much as they can before they do any additional work. Some prolific inventors spend a lot of time working out problems on paper. Others will jump right into the problem, attempting a solution without much thought. Many inventors make the mental exercise of thinking through possible concrete solutions to the problem, concrete solutions which may be the actual invention. Finally, prolific inventors actually try out the solutions that up to that point have only been mental constructions. Later they will see if their invention has been done before.

Other inventors that work primarily as part of a research team say they like collaboration to generate ideas. This group can have more value for brainstorming for ideas. Just as an independent inventor can believe the kernel of an invention comes from within, another inventor may believe the kernel can be arrived at by meshing the collective consciousness of several individuals.

Some prolific inventors say that having a deadline helps in the generation of ideas. They believe that having a deadline forces the mind to concentrate and arrive at a solution in a shorter amount of time. Many inventors, particularly independent inventors, may find it useful to set up an internal personal deadline for themselves, while other inventors might have a deadline imposed on them by some external situation or person. In any case, if one works best with a little pressure, apply that pressure to upgrade the seriousness of what is being attempted.

As always, a key to this process of idea generation is the critical self-examination of the ideas conceived. Prolific inventors seem to have the right balance of self-criticism, creativity, and confidence. Creativity to come up with ideas, self-criticism to objectively evaluate those ideas, and the confidence to continue even though good ideas are difficult in coming or others may not believe the ideas are good. A prolific inventor realizes good ideas are never exhausted, and with patience and perseverance anyone can have an endless stream of them.

Most prolific inventors agree that to invent one must have an idea of what problem is being solved or what is being created. While exactly how the invention will look is not entirely clear, one should have a goal for what is being attempted. While chasing that goal, another invention might be found which was not expected, and the original goal might be abandoned to pursue this new line of inquiry. However, many prolific inventors say that even though it is not uncommon for the solution to a problem to come from an unlikely source, the majority of their inventions have come by proceeding long past the time others would have given up with an idea.

How Prolific Inventors Invent

One of the most important ingredients for prolific inventors is their attitude. Prolific inventors have a can-do attitude about invention. Their attitude is that there are no barriers, just challenges. Cautious optimism helps them overcome the negativism of critics and colleagues. They charge ahead with energy and the confidence that they have invented in the past and will be able to again. One characteristic seen in many prolific inventors is a high energy level and a willingness to work. Inventing is asserting oneself on the world. It takes energy and determination, and perseverance to see the invention through to a successful product or innovation. Most inventors talk about the need to stick with a problem, continuing to work on a problem even though they have not had much success. They cite the need for confidence to continue despite having so little success on the problem. Perseverance and persistence may be the most important parts of inventing.

Researchers who receive a large number of patents seem to place a high value on obtaining patents in the first place. They seem to enjoy either the personal satisfaction or the fame associated with obtaining a patent and having their name permanently associated with an invention. While these inventors, if asked, might publicly downplay this aspect of their personality, if one is observant one will notice that prolific inventors will either have their patents prominently displayed on the wall or collected in some form. To them, patents represent accomplishment and may even represent a validation of themselves as scientists or their scientific work. Consequently, they think about obtaining patents on their work and are willing to do extra work to generate the information necessary for the preparation of a patent draft.

Since prolific inventors value the attainment of patents, as they succeed in obtaining patents, they get better at the exercise. As time goes on, they tend to understand what is needed for a patent application and conduct those experiments naturally. They become knowledgeable about the legal lingo that patent attorneys use. They become more efficient and comfortable dealing with attorneys. Finally, they are able to tell the patent attorney exactly what they think they have done that is different and patentable, which is more difficult than one might expect. Their experience makes the entire process of obtaining a patent more efficient.

When it comes to patent applications, most prolific inventors will tell you they understand the fundamentals behind their invention. They know not only the scientific fundamentals, but they know the prior art and how their invention is fundamentally different from those that came before. Before the creative juices can work, an inventor must know enough about the area in question. Prolific inventors may not be able to sketch out the fundamental mathematical equations behind the invention, but they have a fundamental knowledge of how the invention works and where it will work and where it will fail. So, prolific inventors take the time to learn the background necessary for inventing.

Some inventors are hands-on inventors. They would never think to have their work done by assistants. Others see assistants as necessary resources in the development of an invention. Still others see a research team as necessary for invention. Many of the complex inventions of today have to have input from various special disciplines so that collaboration is an absolute necessity. Whether an inventor goes it alone or forms a team of some type totally depends on both the inventor's personality and the type of invention. One would not expect, for example, for a new space vehicle to be made by a sole inventor in a garage. This type of invention would require a research team.

Prolific inventors try to consider practicality with their inventions. This can be in two different forms. If the invention is not practical, then very few will want the invention, and the inventor will get very little support from others for the invention. The other aspect of practicality is in the work done to arrive at the invention in the first place. Some prolific inventors try to identify the defining experiment or test that will show if the invention will work. That is, they will skip some minor steps, looking for the key experiment or showing which would indicate whether or not the invention is possible. They see that if they can just make a key part of the invention work, the entire invention will work. If the key step can be found, one can decide very quickly whether or not a solution has been found, and can move on to other routes if the result is negative.

Prolific inventors tend to know what is potentially patentable in the technology area in which they are working. They have this information because they have typically studied what others have patented and reported in technical papers. Some inventors want to approach problems without being influenced by those that have tried to tackle the problem before, and therefore downplay the benefit of learning from previously published sources. While some important inventions may have been made in this manner, for prolific inventors this is the exception instead of the rule. Perhaps prolific inventors are able to digest the published information without it unduly leading them in the wrong direction. In any case, they certainly use published information to avoid duplicating work that has already been done, and perhaps it is this saved time which allows these inventors to become prolific!

Prolific inventors are not always highly respected by their peers. Perhaps their success in obtaining patents makes other researchers jealous, but the more likely reason is that prolific inventors can be highly individualistic and sometimes idiosyncratic. Inventors that have numerous inventions are driven by a desire to improve the world, and therefore their first responsibility is to busily work on whatever task they have before them. They are so single minded that they like to work by themselves or with an assistant, but in any case, be in charge of the development, rather than part of a committee or team. They do not seek to advise others, although they normally can provide excellent advice if asked to do so.

Inventing in a team situation can have its challenges also. Different members of the team may contribute differently to the total effort, and a small contribution by one may be the key to the entire invention. Therefore, all members of the team need to keep in front of them the goal for the team so that a balanced perspective is maintained.

Some prolific inventors like to work alone to obtain the ideas for solutions to problems and think that inventing is a lonely art form. They look to others to help them understand specific aspects of the problem, but they feel they need the solitude of their own thoughts to come up with the ideas for solutions. They have little value for brainstorming ideas. These solitary inventors say ideas for solutions just come to them from their subconscious. They come from daydreams or from constant study about the problem. Sometimes technology learned long before surfaces in their minds when it is needed.

In my experience, many prolific inventors are organized in appearance and in their thinking. They have a sense of urgency about what they are doing. Many great inventions come as the result of the unshakable convictions of a single champion, and these inventors are fully willing to be that champion. They are dissatisfied with the *status quo*, and can see the inadequacy of previous technology. Organized thinking, combined with a since of urgency, and the ability to see the problems in the prior technology are the qualities that make up an individual who can succeed as a prolific inventor.

CHARACTERISTICS OF CASUAL INVENTORS

Just as there are prolific inventors who have numerous patents on inventions they have developed, there is another type of innovative researcher. These researchers could be called casual inventors. These are researchers who have been named as an inventor on only one or two patent applications. Researchers who have many years of excellent research and a wealth of contributions to a research organization, but have never been named as an inventor also fall into this category of a casual inventor. Independent inventors who never file patent applications on their inventions would also fall into this category. So, what is the distinction between those prolific inventors who actively go after patents on their inventions and those casual inventors who do not?

In my experience, the most striking difference between researchers that do not have many patents and those that do is the personal value the researcher assigns to the patent. Casual inventors don't particularly get turned on by the idea of obtaining a patent, they don't particularly want or need the type of validating 'fame' that a patent hung on the wall provides. Casual inventors realize the competitive advantage a patent can bring, and will work to provide the data when it is clear that a competitive advantage will result. However, they are less likely to continue to work to develop the data for a patent when the effect of obtaining a patent is unclear. Since patents are normally filed long before a commercial or competitive response can be obtained, in many cases the situation is unclear. A prolific inventor is probably more willing to continue working on an invention when the ultimate situation is unclear, and therefore obtains more patents, regardless of their value.

Other differences between casual and prolific inventors are less universal. It is dangerous to try to claim all casual inventors have the same traits. However, every organization has some casual inventors who are the major contributors of technology to the organization. By all standards, these major contributors could be prolific inventors, but typically they are not. The reason these major contributors do not have many patents may lie in how these major contributors view their position within the organization and how the organization in turn reacts to the major contributor.

Perhaps casual inventors tend to be more at ease in their professional life, more confident in their position or their ability to obtain or maintain their position. Prolific inventors tend to worry about completing their invention, even though they are also important contributors, and are driven by some inner force to 'hurry' which is evident to those around them. This does not mean they are in a haphazard hurry. They just seem to be driven, and this shows.

Another common trait of many casual inventors who are major contributors to a business is that they can come across to the organization as much more intellectual than the prolific inventors of that business. It may be unfair to characterize them in this way, but many major contributors assume the role or are treated as 'thinkers', and are valued for their judgment in the organization. Many of these major contributors interact well with people and want to be part of a team effort. They see their role as not only developing technology, but also providing advice. Prolific inventors, on the other hand, can assume the role or be treated as primarily 'doers', and are perhaps less valued for their judgment. This does not mean that the thinkers are not doers, or vice versa; however, these casual inventors tend to be more well respected by the organization than many of the prolific inventors.

Casual inventors can obtain more patents. In a research organization, the most effective way is to simply give major contributors more time to invent. They certainly have the skills to invent even though they may not have obtained the patents over the years to show the result. If the personalities are compatible, casual inventors can be paired with more prolific inventors so they can learn how prolific inventors invent. Finally, casual inventors of all types should be encouraged to complete their inventions. Emphasize the need for protecting the technology developed by the researcher and that the inventor should not be too quick to abandon an invention without a full analysis of the potential value of both that invention and a patent on that invention.

THE INVENTIVE PROCESS

Defining Invention and Discovery

When thinking about inventing it is useful to understand the distinctions between invention and discovery. It has been said that to discover is to recognize that which has always been but went unnoticed. Invention, on the other hand, is at least a mental construction of something new. From a practical standpoint, one might think of discoveries as universal truths that are detected, while inventions are tangible constructions or combinations which have not been known to exist previously.

Invention and discovery have much in common. Both involve acquiring knowledge, solving problems, and conducting experiments. However, invention requires the conversion of this experience into a tangible object or process, while discovery may be the gathering together or the organizing of that which was already available. They both can arise when a problem that should be solved by using known collective experience or intelligence resists being solved, or some machine fails to perform in an anticipated manner. When this happens, and the problem is solved or the machine is made to work, a new set of experiences is added to the technological experience library. Discovery and invention work side by side, and there are any number of researchers that have made a discovery and in turn created an invention that utilized that discovery. There are even more researchers who

made a discovery and continued to make discoveries without ever constructing an invention. For one to make an invention, one has to exert purposeful
effort to make a usable and successful product or process. Normally the
reason for this effort is for economic gain.

Two Types of Invention Processes

Conceptually, inventions normally result from one of two invention processes. The first invention process is initiated when a researcher attempts to
force nature or a discovery into one of the established conceptual boxes and
finds it does not fit. This, in turn, forces the researcher to establish a new
conceptual box. If the researcher translates this new conceptual box into a
tangible form, he may have a patentable invention. The researcher doesn't
even have to be entirely correct about the conceptual box; as long as the
translation of the discovery to an invention is successful, the exact nature of
the conceptual box is not required. Clearly, however, the more in-depth the
understanding, the more likely the invention will be on a firm technical
footing, and the patents which result are more likely to be valid.

The reason new conceptual boxes must be formed is because the advancement of technology itself creates new demands and expectations in the
marketplace and in the technical community. Before a new invention is
made, there is a certain set of experiences in the collective technical community – that which was done before. However, there is no real guide or
recipe to tell how to specifically improve on these past experiences. There is
no easy way to evaluate the method one might take to make an improvement. However, once the invention has been made, the method that was
used in making the invention becomes part of the collective experience. The
invention, and the method for arriving at the invention, become the new
standards by which future inventions are judged. This is the reason reviewing the patent art, particularly patent claims, is so crucial to the prolific
inventor. It is not just to determine what has been done before, it is to
determine by what standard subsequent inventions will be judged. When the
researcher knows the prior art, and comes across an experience that doesn't
fit, the researcher then knows he has a possible invention.

The second invention process is when the researcher takes pieces from the
ever-growing technology stockpile and combines them in a new way to add
something new to the stockpile. Since the scientific method helped create the
stockpile, a modified version of this method is helpful for making inventions. The scientific method can be described as being composed of the following steps:

1. stating the problem to be solved;
2. hypothesizing a cause of the problem;

3. designing an experiment or experiments to test each hypothesis;
4. predicting the results of the experiments;
5. conducting the experiments and observing the results;
6. making conclusions as to the suitability of the hypotheses based on the experiments.

The purpose of the scientific method is to guide the researcher's thoughts and actions; that is, to provide a structure so that the researcher will be less prone to errors. The real power of the method is in that if it is followed and the hypothesis fails, it will provide new information which will improve the chances of succeeding in subsequent attempts. In fact, if one uses the scientific method, one should expect and welcome initial failure, because failure means things are not working as might be expected. One is therefore increasing the amount of information available about the technology.

The scientific reasoning required by the scientific method is useful in the invention process because it requires a mental dialogue between what is possible and what may be attained. Therefore, many inventors follow, whether consciously or subconsciously, a modified scientific method in making inventions:

1. stating what is to be achieved or improved;
2. hypothesizing a means for making the achievement or improvement;
3. designing an experiment or building a prototype to test the proposed means;
4. predicting the results of the experiments or the operation of the prototype;
5. conducting experiments or operating the prototype and observing the result;
6. making conclusions as to the suitability of the means.

The most difficult steps in this modified scientific method are the first two. Recognizing that the established invention has a shortcoming is the first major hurdle to conceiving a solution for that shortcoming. Almost anything can be improved. While the previous invention might perform its primary function, it will have some sort of limitation – all inventions do. It is impossible that the previous inventor anticipated and accounted for all the limitations of the invention; inventions are used in many situations which were never considered by the original inventor. Engineering is most like inventing in this respect. Engineers are constantly looking for ways to take an existing design and make it better, make it overcome the limitations of previous designs, while retaining all of the good design features which have already been incorporated.

When attempting to improve on an invention, another issue to consider is that although a previous invention might perform several functions, it had some primary function that was critical to its usefulness or success. Unless one builds a new conceptual box, that is, unless the invention is totally replaced with a radically new invention that in some manner obviates the need for the primary function, the improved invention must perform the primary function of the previous invention at least as well.

Assuming a researcher can identify something 'to achieve or improve', and can competently conduct experiments and draw conclusions, the other key to obtaining inventions using this modified scientific method is in the researcher's ability to generate a possible solution to the problem. Some inventors generate a series of solutions in their minds and then mentally find fault with each one until they generate one which appears to be the correct solution. Others are able to design 'quick-and-dirty' experiments that immediately show whether or not they have a viable means for achieving their goal. In fact, some inventors claim that they don't have a successful invention unless it is clearly obvious from these 'quick-and-dirty' tests.

The Role of Serendipity

Read about the great inventions of the world, and more likely than not serendipity will be given the credit for many inventions. The idea that the key to an invention is the unexpected result that was not sought makes for a very satisfying story. However, it is important to understand how serendipity normally occurs in the invention process or one is likely to give it too much credit. While the idea that a researcher gets to make an amazing invention by accident or chance is very entertaining, most inventions are the result of conscious work toward the achievement of some end.

Even when serendipity plays a part in the invention process, in most cases the researcher, by his previous effort, has prepared his mind to understand and accept the unexpected. Look at almost any invention that has made a difference and one will see the researcher had initially made a hypothesis on how something works, and subsequently conducted experiments to confirm or disprove the hypothesis. The process of inventing requires the interweaving of knowledge and theory and experimental result. Many times when serendipity does step in, it is the result of the researcher attempting to interweave that which has never been done before; but in almost all cases the researcher was making the attempt to develop either a new invention or a new understanding. Seldom does invention come up and tap one on the back.

FOSTERING INVENTIVE ACTIVITY

In a research organization, to encourage successful invention and subsequent solid patents, managers should attempt to understand the creative needs of their inventors and foster an inventive environment in the workplace. Also, if possible, they need to delicately balance the personality of the individual researcher with the task to be accomplished. In addition, even the most independent of inventors will need help to ultimately succeed. Even the most brilliant inventor cannot succeed commercially on just a vision and an invention; the inventor needs others to help complete the effort and make a commercial offering. So, to encourage innovation, managers should consider the following issues in their organizations.

The Creative Needs of Inventors

One of the most important traits for prolific inventors is curiosity, the act of looking at something and wondering 'What makes it work?' or 'Could this work better?' Many prolific inventors can see that the *status quo* is inelegant, and that they can find an elegant solution if they put their minds to it. Many inventors don't get interested in a problem unless others have failed or there is general agreement there is no solution to the problem. They like the challenge. Therefore, to stimulate an inventor, challenge him to invent a way around the problem. Expect him to succeed. Once that solution is found and the invention is made, find some way to utilize it. Instead of putting a good invention or a patent on the shelf, license that patent to another that will do something with it. In so doing a manager helps to confirm the efforts of the inventor, and that inventor will invent again.

Organization and Freedom

Researchers need some freedom to research on what they feel is most important, and freedom to research using the methods that make them most effective. Many inventors are able to invent because they are able to try out ideas without having to gain an inordinate amount of approval by management or committees. This can be difficult in some large organizations. At the same time, however, there must some understanding as to what are the goals of the business or the research. A research manager cannot plan inventions, but he can increase the probability that researchers will develop new inventions if they have a research organization founded on the concept of personal freedom and flexibility.

Clear objectives are critical to inventive success. While freedom is important, the idea that someone can invent without a lot of effort, or that an invention will just come to them, does not work for most prolific inventors. It may seem that there is no rhyme or reason to their work, because inventing can sometimes require an empirical approach where multiple things are tried. However, just because many things the inventor has tried have failed, does not mean he is not expending the effort required or that the inventing is haphazard.

A clear deadline can also be useful. Deadlines, whether imposed externally on an inventor, or imposed by the inventor himself, help to focus the mind. They motivate the inventor to find a solution to whatever problem he is working on. It's not surprising that for some people a deadline can stimulate if it is imposed in the correct manner. Inventing can be like solving a puzzle, and some inventors work well with some time pressure. The key here is that expectations are communicated and the personality of the inventor is taken into account. Some people work better when they are calm and comfortable; many work better when they have a deadline or an expectation of a delivery date.

Having said objectives and deadlines are important, an organizational approach should not be so rigid so as to eliminate the opportunity to pursue unplanned discovery that occurs during the invention process. Accidents or unexpected new information might actually result in even more promising inventions. An inventor needs to have the support and understanding from his management that promising new leads can be followed until they are understood.

Systems Development

Edison was successful with the light bulb where others failed because he thought in terms of systems to deliver light, which required not only new technology and inventions but also the marketing and promotion of the technology and inventions. If a researcher concentrates on developing a single invention without considering how this invention will be used, the invention may not be a success. If one creates a successful invention, but cannot translate the invention into truly usable results, no one will ever want the invention.

A commercial success requires more than a great invention. It requires that all the pieces needed to bring that invention to the marketplace are in place. So, a company that can be flexible and can act like an entrepreneurial firm from the inventor perspective will encourage more inventions from their research personnel.

Larger companies are good at developing systems and normally have the experts required to make a complex operation work, even if this process is slow at times. Sometimes this slow pace cannot be avoided because of the complexity of the project itself. Additional time may be needed to bring a large team up to speed on the various aspects of the project. However, once a working level of knowledge is obtained, the collective experts can stimulate new inventions and the systems needed for that invention. In a small company, there is normally less red tape, and an inventor can be more entrepreneurial with more responsibility for the systems.

In most large corporations one normally has larger financial and intellectual resources on which to rely. Most inventors would like the resources of a larger company while retaining the flexibility of a smaller company. Many inventors say that a good laboratory in a small company is the best place to work. Perhaps that is why many small startup companies can have very important and ground-breaking patents that establish their business.

Encouragement and Acceptance of Failure

For inventors to develop the all important trait of self-criticism without detracting from their creative natures, someone they respect has to encourage them and compliment them when they do something right. They may need even more encouragement when things don't go right. It is surprising how far a little praise can go in encouraging inventors. Many prolific inventors remember many years later how their manager or a senior colleague complimented them on their work. This is because most prolific inventors have a strong commitment to their work and inventing is a very personal experience for them. Therefore, this kind of encouragement is vital to the inventive process.

If the emotional climate can be established with the right balance of creativity and criticism, increased inventiveness will result. Negative feedback can be a demotivating experience. However, we have all had times when we were given truly constructive criticism, and it contributed to our work instead of detracting from it. Inventors especially want to know if they have overlooked some component or key point. By pointing out that oversight, you are doing the inventor a favor that will not go unnoticed as the inventor continues to work to make his invention a reality.

Accept failure for what it is – new learnings about technology. Research work in scientific fields and technology is based on possibilities, not certainties. No one ever accomplished anything without taking some risk, and in taking risk some detours are bound to occur. Use setbacks to learn more about the potential for invention.

Acceptance of Personality and Skills

For research to be successful, each phase of research may require different skills and one researcher may not have either the disposition or the skill to do all phases. Even the most independent-minded inventor in a research organization may need some help with an invention. Inventing to them may be a somewhat selfish act, but they may still find it useful to talk or even to work with others because sometimes they need someone with them if for no other reason than to help absorb and spread some of the frustration every inventor experiences while inventing.

Also, the person that can simultaneously manipulate the information from several different technologies and ultimately combine them into an invention may not be able to catalog and analyze hundreds of data points to develop a statistically sound sample. Many of the most inventive people lose interest very quickly after successfully inventing a solution to a problem. Managers need to recognize that at the appropriate time these people need to be combined with others who can do the work required to achieve a robust process or generate patent examples. Sir Alexander Fleming discovered penicillin would kill bacteria, but the task of making the discovery useful, that is, the use of penicillin as a therapeutic agent, was not completed until long after the initial discovery was made, and it wasn't done by Fleming. If, after the discovery was made, a team had been formed with people having the expertise in developing lab processes into commercial processes, penicillin might have been made available long before it was.

Expecting Inventions

Researchers need to feel that patents are important to their management. They need to know that their inventive efforts are supported by their management. One key part of fostering inventiveness is simply for research managers to have the expectation that their researchers will make inventions and will do the work required to obtain strong patents on those inventions. If possible, this should be communicated from the highest possible managerial level. If the organization values inventions and patents, and when inventions and patents result these positive results are recognized, the creative members of the organization will invent even more.

The simple act of a research manager asking whether or not a new development is patentable can result in a patent analysis if one has not already occurred; if the manager makes a practice of asking such questions, the researchers will automatically learn to question whether or not the new development will likely generate proprietary information that could be the subject of a patent.

SUGGESTIONS ON HOW TO CONDUCT RESEARCH FOR STRONGER PATENTS

A researcher's actions in the laboratory or workshop during the development of an invention impact the breadth and strength of any patent applications the researcher may file on his invention. Unfortunately, the information needed for broad and strong patent coverage isn't always apparent to a researcher until after the researcher has essentially completed work on the invention and begun work with a patent agent to file a patent application. In some cases, it is not convenient for the researcher to return to the laboratory to conduct some missing experiment(s) that the agent believes is needed for the patent application. So, an outline of the things a researcher should consider and practice during the research process for the preparation of a patent application should make the application process smoother and place any patentable inventions on a firmer foundation.

There are three major things a researcher can do to make the subsequent preparation of a patent application more efficient and the resulting patents strong. First, the researcher should become aware of the general state of the art in the technology area in question. Second, the researcher should seek to define the ranges in which critical elements operate and the best operating point, and any additional alternative inventions; and third, the researcher should carefully document his results.

Know the Technology Area

During the preparation of a patent application, the researcher will be responsible for explaining his invention to the patent agent and answering any questions the agent may have. Although the agent will have some type of technical credentials, the attorney may not know the basics, much less the state of the art in the researcher's technology area. The researcher will be relied upon to provide the technical information that the agent needs in order to prepare a complete and accurate patent application.

The most efficient method for the researcher to obtain an understanding of the state-of-the-art in the field he is researching is by conducting a literature search before he starts his research. Although this might seem an obvious step in the research process, many researchers do not bother to take this step. Therefore, when the researcher creates what he thinks is a patentable invention, he has, in fact, no basis on which to decide whether his invention is new, since he has no idea what prior references have disclosed in this technology area. The result in the best case is the researcher must go back to the laboratory and conduct more experiments; in the worst case the researcher must start over because his invention was already done by someone else.

Some researchers deliberately choose to tackle a problem without reviewing how others have sought to solve the problem. They may not want the prior publications influencing their work or may want to look at a problem from a fresh approach, and therefore make a conscious decision not to investigate what work has been accomplished in their field of inquiry. This is an entirely appropriate approach to research as long as the researcher realizes he risks duplicating someone else's work, and is willing to take that risk. However, after the invention has been made, the researcher should arrange to have a literature search performed so that he can confirm to himself he has in fact made a new invention. Armed with this search, he can confidently discuss the case with the attorney, or go back to the bench to improve on what others have done.

By reviewing the literature in the technology field one is researching, one does more than just learn the technology. Reviewing the literature will also give one ideas for features which may be included in the invention. Sometimes these features can be the critical difference which allows a patent to be obtained on an invention.

Even when a search of the prior art is made before the research is begun, that search may be too narrow or flawed in some manner. Therefore, after the invention has been made, the researcher should consider whether the search that was made reflects what is truly inventive about his work, that is, he should question whether or not the search is still applicable. If it is not, then another search should be made.

Best Mode and Operating Ranges

After a researcher succeeds in developing a new product or making a new process work, the next task is usually to try to find the optimum combination of properties for the product or the optimum operating point for the process. Therefore, the ultimate invention that the researcher believes he has invented is the commercial offering. However, the commercial offering is just an optimized version of the invention, and patent claims to that optimized version may be so narrow as not to stop any competitor from duplicating the invention with a slight modification to avoid the patent claims.

To obtain broad patent claims, a researcher should attempt more than just to optimize his invention. He should also determine the range of parameters under which an invention performs. Now, the issue of where the invention performs can be somewhat subjective, because one must make a judgment as to when 'something less than optimum' performance actually becomes unacceptable. However, the ability to clearly identify the ranges of operation of an invention is critical to the patent agent and the construction of claims. If the invention has only been optimized, and little has been done to push the operating envelope to determine where the critical elements of the invention fail to perform, the best the agent can do is select what the inventor feels to be appropriate bounds for the invention. This has two problems, the first of which is the inventor might be incorrect and leave out a substantial area of coverage which a competitor would find and exploit. The second problem is that unless the research has been done, it will be very difficult to generate examples of the limits of the invention. Many countries will only allow claims to areas of operation that are clearly exemplified in the patent application. Therefore, if the only example in the patent application is the optimum set of conditions, in many countries the claims will be restricted to that particular set of conditions. Again, a determined competitor will most likely develop a product that will be acceptable, all because no experimentation was done on the ranges of the invention. Therefore, the researcher must first seek the solution of a practical problem, but at the same time, perform those experiments which will illustrate how broad the solution truly is.

This is not to say the optimum point is not useful. As stated before, it is useful as the commercial offering, and at the time of this writing, some countries, the United States in particular, require the patent applicant to disclose the best mode, that is, the best version of the invention, which is known to the applicant at the time of filing.

Finally, as the researcher is attempting to define the limits of the invention, he should consider alternate forms of the invention and how a competitor might bypass any patents he might obtain. For example, if the researcher generated an invention which uses a particular plastic, the researcher should examine whether or not the type of plastic is critical to the invention or whether or not there are other plastics which will also perform in the invention. In so doing, the researcher should look at both in-kind or similar materials, but also materials which compete in a functional nature. For example, if an invention requires a metal part, the researcher should also consider whether or not a composite part might also be applicable. If it is, the patent agent should be told that the description of the part can be very broad and not restricted to just metals.

All of this research requires a lot of effort. However, if the research is approached in this manner, not only will the patent application that is eventually prepared be stronger, it will pave the way for even more patents and the establishment of a patent estate in the technology area. Therefore, the effort which is expended to generate one patent application is normally useful in the preparation of other applications, so it is not as though an extraordinary amount of effort is being expended for one patent application.

Documentation

There are several reasons every researcher should document his work. From a patent law standpoint, at the time of this writing, the United States is a first to invent country, versus a first to file country, which means that the documentation of inventive work could be useful in proving one researcher made an invention before another. This documentation needs to be witnessed and credible, and many companies have special notebooks for researchers for this purpose. There have been predictions that this first to invent system will change to the first to file system already in place in most of the rest of the world. If the law is changed, researchers will still need to document their work to have some proof that they are the true inventors that should be listed on the patent application. Again, at the time of this writing, some countries like the United States require the correct inventors of the invention be listed in the patent application. If the correct inventors are not listed, the patent could be found invalid. Therefore, documentation is important to correct identification of inventors.

Documentation is just good research practice. Research can take years to complete, and no one can remember all of the work which is conducted over the year. The documentation of both successful and unsuccessful results may be useful in a patent application, and unexpected or unexplained results, if documented, may one day be explained by further experimentation. Further, researchers that follow the research of others can avoid duplicating experiments if the previous researcher kept a good research notebook. However, if there is no documentation of research, none of this is possible.

5 Infringement and Freedom to Operate

A patent gives one the right to exclude others from an invention for a period of time, however it does not give the patent owner the right to practice the invention. Even if a patent is granted for an invention, practice of the invention may require the use of someone else's patent. If that is the case, the other patent is said to 'dominate' the new patent.

It is no wonder that the word 'infringe' is used to describe the use of another's patented claims, infringe meaning 'to transgress' or 'to encroach.' If one must use another's patented claims in the practicing of an invention, the patent owner can legally stop the infringing activity and demand the infringer pay damages.

Therefore, in addition to obtaining patents for inventions, an inventor must decide whether or not the invention can be practiced freely. In fact, freedom to operate issues can be the most challenging patent issues one can face, because many times a decision must be made without having complete information on what types of claims will issue in pending patent applications.

TYPES OF INFRINGEMENT

What constitutes actual infringement of a patent is dictated by the laws of the country in which the patent is granted. However, there are some common ways patents can be infringed. The most obvious type of infringement is called direct infringement. This is when someone actually practices the claims of that patent without the patent owner's permission. One might be making, using, or selling an exact copy of the claimed invention. One might be making, using, or selling a product that has never been made before, however, might still be directly infringing another's patent because the patent claims were very broadly worded. In any case, in direct infringement, the infringing activity occurs by the person actually making, using, or selling the claimed invention.

Contributory infringement can occur when someone manufactures a product that is specially designed to be used by others in an infringing manner. For example, let's assume a person gets a patent on the use of a new ingredient X in food. Note the patent does not claim the ingredient X, or the manufacture of X, but the use of X in food. Another person would directly infringe that patent by making a food having ingredient X. However, a person that manufactures X might be guilty of contributory infringement. Contributory infringement occurs when the product has no substantial non-infringing use; that is, the product is essentially only used in the enduse claimed by another's patent. In this example, the manufacturer of X could be a contributory infringer if the only substantial use for ingredient X is in food! If there is substantial non-infringing use, the manufacturer normally has a good argument that the manufacture of the product is not contributory infringement, but this is no guarantee the owner of the patent will not sue for infringement. While one can never be fully protected from possible lawsuits from contributory infringement, one can help one's position by making sure one's products have substantial non-infringing uses.

Another type of infringement is induced infringement. This can occur when one knowingly or unknowingly encourages another to do something which infringes someone else's patent. For example, a salesman, in helping a customer use his product, may tell the customer how to modify his equipment so that the product processes better in his plant. The salesman could be guilty of inducing infringement if the changes he suggests have previously been patented by another and the customer implements the changes and begins using the patent invention. Therefore, one must be careful as to what actions are recommended to others.

Another type of infringement deals with imported products made by the patented process of another. Note that one is a direct infringer if one imports a product into a country and someone else already has a patent on that product in that country. However, infringement can also occur when a patented process is involved. If one has a patent in a country on a process for manufacturing a product, and another makes a product using that process in another country, importation of that product into the patented country constitutes infringement of the process patent. The owner of the process patent can prevent the products made by that unauthorized duplicate process from being imported into the patented country.

The penalty for infringing a patent can vary from country to country. If found guilty of infringement, one normally must pay damages to the owner of the infringed patent. What these damages are and how they are figured varies from country to country and case to case. However, the damages can be quite severe. For example, if a person is found guilty of willful infringement in the United States, this person may have to pay treble damages, that is, three times the determined amount of damage caused by the infringement. The damages could be in addition to the total cessation of the infringing activity. In fact, the ability of a patentee to work through the courts to totally stop the manufacture of a product by an infringer is an important deterrent for potential infringers.

AVOIDING PATENT INFRINGEMENT

Freedom to Operate Searches

So, there are good reasons to be concerned with whether or not another's patent will impact one's operations. By checking to see whether or not there is an adverse patent when introducing a new product or changing a process, potentially devastating expenses may be avoided. One of the expenses to avoid, or to be in a better position to avoid, is the cost of patent litigation. This can be a potentially high drain on the financial and human resources of a business.

In addition, much of the money and time invested in a project can be lost if some part of the project or the product being made infringes a patent and the project must be stopped. By identifying patent problems early in the project cycle, time is then available to determine whether or not the potentially adverse patent is a major concern, and if it is, whether or not the patent owner would be willing to grant a license. Then the potential cost of handling an adverse patent can be dialed into the project's financial calculations.

Sometimes an invention is patented in only a few countries. This means one can practice the invention in other countries where a patent was not obtained. A freedom-to-operate search can reveal where those troublesome patents have issued, which can help with decisions on where to manufacture or market a product. Knowing the extent of worldwide coverage also helps in determining whether or not there are enough available markets to achieve adequate business results.

A freedom-to-operate search is normally conducted by a competent professional searcher. The searcher may use any number of methods to search the patent art. The searcher will normally search the patent classification codes and also search keywords to find whether or not there are patents that involve the same materials, concepts, or arrangements as the invention being searched. Once these potentially close references are identified, these patents, particularly the claims of these patents, will be reviewed.

This type of search is not a patentability search. Here the searcher is looking for patents that might impact the legal practice of the invention. In one sense, the searcher is looking for the same invention in the patent art, however, the searcher must also look for patents that have broader claims that might cover the new invention even though the invention is not specifically mentioned.

If the search does not turn up any references the patent owner can feel some satisfaction proceeding with a clear conscience. However, no search can be 100 percent correct. It is always possible that patents may have been missed by the search strategy or were misinterpreted when reviewed. One option is to have more than one search conducted, but this is not normally practical except for exceedingly high value inventions or when the original search is thought to be incomplete. For example, if the original search returns essentially no close references, but the inventor is familiar with the technology area and feels that some references should have been found, one would almost certainly want to have the search redone. Any time no close references are found in a search a warning light should go on. It may be the searcher did not fully understand the invention being searched or that the search methodology was inadequate.

Even if multiple searches are completed, they can never guarantee the practice of a new invention will be free from problems. The owner of the new invention will pay experts to review the patent art to determine whether or not the invention in question infringes any patents. Then, assuming no infringement is recognized, the invention will be commercialized. Once the invention appears in public, other patent owners may have their experts give opinions on whether or not the new invention infringes any of their patents. Unfortunately, experts can differ in their interpretation, and the possibility exists that patent infringement problems may emerge. However, a freedom-to-operate search helps immensely in avoiding infringement problems. At a minimum, the fact a search was made can help to show that responsible steps were taken not to infringe the patents of others.

Interpreting Potentially Adverse Patents

When the search turns up patents which might appear to be infringed, an analysis of those patents should occur. It is a mistake to take lightly the exercise of reviewing the patent art found during the search. This analysis should be conducted by or with the help of an intellectual property professional.

The analysis is done by carefully and objectively reviewing each of the claims of each patent to determine whether or not the invention to be made, used, or sold is included in the patented claim. Many times the claims will have terms which are ambiguous. A trained professional will need to consider the information provided in the patent application itself and may have to refer to the record of communication between the patent offices and the inventor.

This record is sometimes called the 'file history' and is available from the patent offices in the various countries where the patent was granted. In these documents one can see how the application was amended during prosecution and one may find statements from the applicant further explaining the invention. The inventor, in an effort to obtain the patent, may have made admissions to the patent office that the invention only applies to certain operating areas or may consist of only certain things. These admissions can be very useful in sorting out shades of meaning when resolving infringement questions.

If lucky, these statements can reveal that the patent is actually not a concern, that the claims do not extend to the invention one wants to sell. So, interpreting patents is not just reading the claims of the patent; it is important to understand the complete prosecution of the application. A patent professional like a patent attorney should be able to interpret the shades of meaning in a patent and help determine whether or not a patent is a major concern to the business.

Early in this analysis a patent professional should check to see if the potentially adverse patents found by the search are still in force. As covered previously, most patent offices require that fees be paid to maintain a patent in force throughout the granted term. If the owner of a potentially adverse patent previously decided to save money and allow the patent to lapse through the lack of payment of maintenance fees, the patent claims are deemed to be in the public domain in that country and can be used by anyone in that country. Therefore, a patent professional can first check where in the world the patent has issued and where it is still pending, and can also determine whether or not the patent's maintenance fees have been paid. It is a great feeling when one finds out a potentially adverse patent is no longer in force and will not affect one's freedom to operate.

Dealing with Adverse Patents

If, after a full review of a potentially adverse patent, a patent attorney believes the patent would be infringed if one were to proceed with making, using, or selling an invention, several options can be considered. One may try to obtain a license from the patent owner; that is, buy permission to use the patent owner's invention. Of course, after spending many days, months, or even years developing an invention, it is difficult to have to pay another to make, use, or sell the hard-earned invention. Also, the patent owner has no obligation to give a license, and the terms under which a license could be obtained may involve a very large sum of money. If a license is not obtained there are still options.

One can, after all, ignore the patent. In doing so, one risks the legal costs of litigation which can be very costly, along with the damages which would be paid to the patent holder if a court determines the patent has been infringed. Rarely does one ignore the patent without some legal opinion that the patent, in itself, is defective in some manner and is therefore invalid. By going through the effort to get an opinion of invalidity, one avoids the assertion that the patent is being ignored without any regard for the patent laws and that one is willfully infringing the patent. This can impact the amount of damages awarded in some countries should there be litigation and the patent is found to be valid and infringed.

Now, one might think that to obtain an opinion of invalidity is a simple procedure. However, since the patent office has granted this patent it has already survived an examination by a presumed capable patent examiner and so there is a legal presumption of validity. Proving all the claims of a patent are invalid can be very difficult because patents are normally written with claims of different scope. One may be able to find invalidating art for the broadest claims, but may have trouble locating invalidating art for more narrow or specific claims. So, obtaining substantial evidence of invalidity of all the pertinent claims in the potentially infringed patent can be very difficult. One must also remember that even though an attorney has given an opinion of invalidity, which remains confidential between the attorney and the person requesting the opinion, the patent owner may still decide that the patent is valid and being infringed. Therefore, one can still be sued for patent infringement even though one has an invalidity opinion in hand.

DEALING WITH INFRINGERS

If another is thought to be infringing a patent, one will need the help of a patent attorney if there is a desire to enforce the patent and to stop the infringement. The attorney will want to know what type of information or evidence is available showing that infringing activity has taken place. The attorney will review the patent and the evidence and take one of four positions.

1. Infringement is not conclusive and more evidence of infringement is needed.
2. The patent is infringed.
3. The competitor is not infringing the patent.
4. The patent is infringed, but the enforceability of the patent is questionable.

Depending on the attorney's position, one may have to do more analysis to generate evidence that clearly shows infringement, or the management of the business may have to decide whether or not to initiate action against the infringer. If, after initial contacts, the infringer continues to infringe and a decision is made to take legal action, the business must be ready to allocate some technical resources to work with the attorneys in addition to the obvious hefty legal fees.

Infringement actions take a lot of attorney time and many times the attorney needs to hire additional counsel in various countries around the world if the patent action is brought globally. Litigation of a patent dispute is similar to the filing of a patent application in that legal action will be conducted on a country by country basis. Evidence of infringement will need to be established in every country, and actions in each country must be conducted in accordance with the patent laws of that country. Clearly, enforcing a patent can be an expensive exercise. Still, it makes no sense to obtain global patents and then not to enforce them when one's rights are at stake.

RESEARCH DISCLOSURES AND JOURNAL ARTICLES

Putting technology in the public domain is one inexpensive method to help obtain a degree of freedom to operate. Publications describing inventions should normally prevent the issuance of patents claiming that specific invention. This is dependent, of course, on the examiner locating the disclosing reference during the prosecution of the patent application. Therefore, published patents and applications are the easiest for the examiner to find. Major technical journals are also convenient routes for publishing information. Abstracting databases are sure to abstract papers from these major journals, making the disclosed information broadly searchable. There are also speciality journals whose purpose is to publish compilations of invention disclosures and then mail copies of these compilations to patent offices around the world. In these specialty journals the invention descriptions can even be published anonymously.

So when should one publish an invention rather than, or in addition to, patenting the invention?

These invention disclosures can be very effective in preventing another from patenting the exact invention described. They can also be somewhat useful in preventing others from patenting a use or application of a product. For example, suppose one invents a fiber F that has potential use in many different applications, but someone else obtains some of F and uses it for the first time in furniture, with surprisingly good results. This person could then obtain a patent claim to furniture made with F, therefore preventing anyone else from making furniture with the fiber. Therefore, the use of F in furniture is not controlled by the manufacturer of F, but the manufacturer of furniture! If the furniture maker decides that some other fiber is better in furniture, or simply does not want F to be used in furniture, in many countries the patent-holding furniture maker can effectively prevent the use of F in furniture. A potentially major market for the manufacturer of F could be effectively eliminated by another's patent. By disclosing that fiber F is useful in furniture in a published disclosure prior to the other person making the invention, the breadth of the possible patent claims that another might obtain is potentially reduced.

However there are some criticisms to making research disclosures. One criticism is a disclosure can suggest to others where they might work to obtain patents. A second criticism is the difficulty in making the disclosure truly effective in meeting the needs of a business.

Let's look at the first criticism, pointing others to where they might obtain patents. For example, to continue the furniture analogy, if the disclosure states the invention can be used in furniture, but does not indicate what type of furniture, this leaves the opportunity for an enterprising inventor to show that certain types of furniture using the invention are special and obtaining a patent on that specific selection of furniture. As we discussed in Chapter 3, one could then develop a number of specific patents having broad reach collectively, while the invention disclosure still exists. The other possibility is that one would optimize the invention for the application. For example, if different types of fiber F were available, say having different widths, and the maker of F had already published that fiber F is useful generically in furniture, an inventor might be able to obtain a patent on new types of furniture that had a critical need for fiber F of a certain width. Therefore, broad generic disclosures can leave open the door for patents on special subsets of the invention or optimized inventions.

The other difficulty with a disclosure is the inherent concern with its effectiveness. One has to be very careful not to have unrealistic expectations about the freedom to operate granted by the disclosure. One may be able to disclose one or several possible inventions in a publication but will be unable to identify all possible related inventions. The door is left open for others to file patent applications on technology not disclosed or anticipated by the disclosure, however, one can be reasonably confident about freedom to operate the specific inventions disclosed in the publication.

So, the decision to publish a research disclosure should be considered carefully and the disclosure should always include enough specific information to be effective in its intended use. There are many times when a publication can achieve the intended result at a very little cost to a business. In particular, certain types of inventions lend themselves more naturally to public disclosures rather than patents. Specifically, some common instances where public disclosures may be very effective are:

1. The invention is critical to a business but is only slightly different from previous inventions and therefore may have limited patentable dignity. Publishing prevents another from patenting that invention and impacting operations in countries without prior user rights.
2. The business does not want to spend money on developing or patenting new inventions in a particular area, but wants to obtain some degree of freedom, realizing that the disclosure will not assure total freedom to operate.

3. Whenever one believes that a suitable disclosure can be drafted which will be specific enough to be effective. This requires an understanding of the expected markets, the technology, and the possible useful commercial variants in that technology.

PUBLISHED PATENT APPLICATIONS AND PROVISIONAL PATENT COVERAGE

Most countries publish the patent applications that have been filed 18 months after the priority date. This allows the public to know what inventions are pending in the patent office. However, this disclosure of the invention could give others the opportunity to practice the pending inventions without penalty unless there was a provision for protection before patents were granted. So, most countries provide what is called provisional protection for published applications. That is, anyone that uses the invention prior to the patent being granted will be liable for some damages should the patent actually be granted in the future. Now each country has different remedies for provisional coverage. Many require a reasonable fee or royalty for the period between the publication and the issuance of the patent. Also, once the patent has been granted, the patent holder has no obligation to actually grant the infringer a license to continue practicing, although this can happen.

Published patent applications can be quite a challenge when trying to determine freedom to operate. This is because it is difficult to be certain about what claims will issue. Many times the applicant will include claims which are too broadly worded and it is obvious these claims will not be granted. The same application can also include claims to a very specific invention which might be found to be patentable.

Published search reports, like those published by the PCT searching authority and attached to world patent applications, indicate the initial references that will be considered by the examiner during the examination of the claims. This PCT search report will give one a clue as to how difficult the examination will be. If the search report was favorable, that is, the PCT searcher did not find any references which were particularly relevant to the issuance of a patent on the invention, some claims will probably issue, and in fact, the claims will probably not change much. On the other hand, the search report may be very negative and reveal several references which are particularly relevant to the examination and which indicate the claimed invention is not novel. Even with this negative search report, effective claims could issue. The applicant may be able to amend the claims so that a patentable invention is described. Someone interested in this published application can only review the references and imagine how the applicant may respond to those references. If an obvious amendment will eliminate the examiner's concerns, this will probably happen and the patent will issue. Someone worried about freedom to operate should decide with the help of a patent attorney whether or not the resulting amended claim would still affect their ability to operate, and if so, proceed with a decision process as if the patent was granted.

Therefore, when trying to make a commercialization decision while being faced with a potentially adverse patent application, a patent attorney can help advise on the viability of the adverse patent application and any potential problems with any provisional protection. If it seems clear some claims will issue which will hinder the ability to operate, the decision may be made to initiate talks to license the technology prior to the patent issuing, in hopes of obtaining a lower royalty rate. Alternatively, non-infringing technology may be developed to avoid all patent complications. In any case, a patent attorney or agent will be very useful in explaining the specifics of the countries in question and outlining the possible options available and is indispensable in this process.

6 Working with Attorneys, Agents, and Patent Liaisons

INTRODUCTION

While in some countries a researcher can file a patent application on his invention, in most cases to get a patent that will be of value, one is advised to use the services of a patent attorney or patent agent. In the United States, a patent attorney is someone who has a degree in law and has passed the examination to practice before the United States Patent and Trademark Office (USPTO). A patent agent is someone who has some type of technical certification, as required by the USPTO, and has passed the examination to practice before the Patent Office. Both patent attorneys and patent agents can prepare, file, and prosecute applications in the patent office, along with appeals in the patent office. However, appeals in the legal system, and opinions of infringement and other legal issues are best addressed by a patent attorney. In what follows, we shall use 'agent' as a generic term for either an attorney or an agent, and 'attorney' only when we are referring specifically to someone with a degree in law.

Large corporations and universities typically have either in-house agents or have retained a legal firm to help file and prosecute their patent applications. Some companies, in addition, have special intellectual property managers or patent liaisons to help manage the filing of the organization's patent applications and help facilitate communications between the agents and the scientists. There are other specialists, such as literature searchers, which also work with the agents to identify prior art. While the exact job responsibilities may differ from organization to organization, in today's world a researcher must interact with at least one patent agent in order to have a patent application filed. In many cases, particularly in large companies, the researcher also interacts with an intellectual property manager and a prior art search specialist. Since the world of law is very different from the technical world, unless the researcher has some experience in filing patents, the researcher may be confused about the roles these people play in obtaining patents for the organization, and why they ask the questions they do.

Many researchers would like their world to be filled with clear distinctions – yes or no answers, but in reality very little of the world is that way. This seems particularly true in the legal world, at least when the legal world is viewed through the eyes of most researchers. In a very real sense, many patents succeed because of the presentation of the information and the arguments made in support of the information. For patentability, it is most important to have a compelling argument; good agents will work with researchers to make sure the patents they file have a compelling argument for patentability.

PREPARING FOR THE LEGAL WORLD

Many researchers find that dealing with legal issues and with patent agents and attorneys can be confusing. Patent agents and attorneys are asked by organizations to provide advice on any number of issues, and attorneys are trained to render advice based on their knowledge of law and their past experience in dealing with similar issues. In so doing, attorneys provide organizations with judgment. This combination of experience and legal understanding confuses researchers because researchers tend to feel more comfortable with absolutes. Many legal issues, however, are not so easily sorted out, and must deal with the various shades of gray between black and white.

Still, when an attorney or agent is asked to file a patent application, they will try to accomplish the following in the quickest manner with the least possible effort, and in so doing may place different emphasis on the content of the technology and the content of prior publications. They want to:

1. understand the invention,
2. understand why the invention is inventive, and
3. adequately describe the invention on paper.

Normally, the agent will first want the researcher to describe what has been done, and why the researcher thinks it is inventive. The agent wants first to understand, in a general way, the technology and the invention. Next, the agent wants to understand what is absolutely critical to the invention; that is, what parts or steps, if left out, render the invention useless or unworkable. By determining what is absolutely critical, the agent is fixing in his mind the elements of the invention which he will later put in the patent application.

The agent will next want to know what parts of the invention are known to others. He will initially use the researcher's knowledge of the technology area to give him a sense of what has been publicly disclosed and what is publicly known. Later, the agent or the patent liaison will obtain a search of prior publications to confirm there are no other references which disclose critical elements of the invention. If new references are found, the agent may have additional questions and will look to the researcher to identify what differences exist between what has been published and what was done by the researcher.

It is important to be accurate, precise, and truthful with the patent agent. Accuracy is important, because if the statements made in the patent application are not accurate, the patent may be shown to be invalid later. Adequate precision is desired in the patent examples so that the work can be reproduced. When there is a need to distinguish an invention from a close prior art reference, precision in experimentation can become a necessity. Truthfulness with the patent agent is necessary because in some countries, including the United States, the researcher will be required to make either an oath or a declaration that he is an inventor of the claimed invention and the researcher has disclosed to the patent office the most pertinent prior art.

It is also important that the researcher does not hide details of the invention from the patent agent in an attempt to maintain the secrecy of the invention. The researcher, realizing that the invention will be disclosed in the patent application, might be tempted to hide certain important details. This is a risky game, because the resultant patent might be found to be invalid due to inadequate or misleading disclosure. It is much better to provide the agent with all of the details of the invention along with those details that have been deemed trade secrets; the agent must then decide whether the trade secret is necessary for the invention. If the secret is necessary, the agent will need to disclose the secret in the patent application, if a patent application is filed. In many cases, however, the secret will not be necessary to the invention and the agent can draft the patent application without a disclosure of the secret. Remember the patent system is a 'method of promoting the useful arts', and the contract that the researchers makes with the government is that if the researcher discloses the invention, the researcher secures the right to prevent others from practicing the invention for a limited time.

ACTIONS TO TAKE BEFORE MEETING WITH THE AGENT

Once an invention has been made, but before meeting with a patent agent, the researcher should refer back to the references found in his literature search, and attempt to do two things. The first is to identify the critical elements or features of the new invention; and secondly, what is specifically disclosed about those critical elements in these prior publications. Patents in the literature search are excellent sources of information, because in patents the critical elements are clearly identified. By comparing the new invention to patents on prior inventions, the researcher can get an idea of what makes the new invention distinctive over these prior inventions. These distinctive features should be pointed out to the patent agent, because these features represent the set from which the critical elements of the invention will probably come.

Also, as the list of distinctive features is developed, the researcher should note what is stated in the prior references about these features. That is, the researcher should look for specific disclosures or teachings of the parts of the new invention in the previously published references. This information will be useful to the agent because a combination of references might disclose enough information about the new invention to make the invention unpatentable. On the other hand, it only takes one new feature to make a patentable invention, so one of these distinctive features may be the patentable kernel of the invention. In either case, the patent agent needs to be aware of all of this information early in the discussion of patentability.

Typically, a researcher at this point in the patenting process will be reviewing a patent and wondering how a patent issued on an invention that the researcher believes to be well within the skill of an ordinary researcher. While patent examiners can make mistakes, the reason for the issuance may become clearer if the researcher looks specifically at the date of the patent filing or carefully reads the claims of the patent. In most cases, the researcher will find the invention was made before the accepted skill was common in the art, or will discover some critical element or kernel on which the entire patent is based. While this kernel of patentability may be small, the patent holder evidently put forth a strong enough argument to the patent examiner for the patent to be allowed.

One of the most difficult concepts for the researcher to accept is the literal reading of the prior art references, which is what patent examiners and patent agents do. Some researchers tend to get caught up in the research or technical themes given in the patent, and fail to see what is actually disclosed. For example, a patent may issue on an invention only remotely related to the researcher's new invention, and in this patent there may be a disclosure of the researcher's new invention. So, although the prior patent did not claim the researcher's new invention, the patent application disclosed information which now makes the new invention unpatentable. Unless the researcher is careful, his initial reaction to this other patent may be to state that the previous researcher was working to solve some other problem and this patent has nothing to do with the new invention. However, frequently some feature of a new invention will be disclosed in a reference, and even though the reference might deal with some entirely different issue, the disclosure acts to prevent a valid patent from issuing. When this situation arises, it is sometimes helpful for the researcher to look at the prior art reference from a higher conceptual plane – one where the reader does not have any experience in the details of the technology – and read the patent for the particulars which are specifically disclosed.

TYPICAL WORKING ARRANGEMENTS WITH AGENTS

The actual work with the patent agent to prepare and file a patent application follows a predictable pattern for most inventions. While speed in preparing applications is always desired, few cases require the patent agent to draft the patent application for immediate filing. When this happens, the same steps take place, just at an accelerated pace.

The time required to prepare and file a patent application will depend on the complexity of the invention, the completeness of technical information and data which has been generated, and the workload of the attorney. Unless the patent application must be filed immediately, it is wise to plan on having at least three meetings with the agent and/or intellectual property professional prior to the filing of the patent application. The purpose of these meetings is to:

1. define the invention,
2. review the draft of the patent application, and
3. sign the finalized patent application for filing.

The first meeting will normally consist of the researcher describing to the patent agent what is believed to be the invention. The agent will ask questions for clarification and will ask for data which confirms the invention works as stated. This type of questioning serves two functions; one, by asking for clarification, the agent is making sure he truly understands the invention so that he can eventually draft a patent application. Second, by asking for confirmation, the agent is ascertaining how much evidence or data has already been generated which could be used as examples in support of the invention in the patent application. By asking these questions, the agent is also getting a feel for how the research was carried out, which may indicate how much additional work will be needed before a patent application can be filed.

The agent will also ask the researcher what is known about the invention in prior publications and what is the closest 'prior art'. If the researcher has made a literature search, he should give that search to the agent along with a summary of what the researcher believes to be the references which disclose inventions most like the new invention. Based on the information shared in this initial meeting, the agent and researcher should agree on a proposed invention definition. This definition may be the initial claims for the invention, or it may be a general agreement on the limits of the invention, with the agent to submit actual proposed claims at a later date.

After the meeting, the agent will normally have another prior art search commissioned that will attempt to find any references that might affect patentability and that might not have been found in the literature search performed by the researcher. If a new reference is found the attorney may ask the researcher to review the referenee and tell him how the new invention differs from the reference. Also, after the initial meeting, the researcher may be asked to submit sketches of the invention or additional data for use in the patent application. After all of the questions about the prior art have been answered and sufficient technical information has been generated, the patent agent will prepare a draft of the patent application for review by the researcher.

The second meeting will normally consist of a discussion of the draft patent application to iron out any inconsistencies or final questions in the draft application. At this point, the business implications of the patent filing and strategy issued should be addressed. In particular, a decision should be made at this time whether or not the expected claims will be worth the disclosure of the technology in the patent application, or if additional work should be conducted to generate support for broader claims in the patent application. If the decision is to continue with the filing, the agent will ask for information on who should be considered an inventor of the technology, and at this point may ask the researcher to provide information on when the invention was conceived and reduced to practice, and what other researchers were involved in the development of the invention. After the meeting the patent agent will take the comments on the draft application from the meeting and incorporate them into the final draft of the patent application for the researcher to review. If drawings are needed for the application, the agent will convert the researcher's sketches into acceptable drawings to be included in the patent application. The agent will also take the inventorship information supplied to him and identify who should be listed as an inventor on the patent.

The third meeting will normally be the final meeting before the filing of the application in the patent office. The claims are reviewed for a last time for correctness, and assuming all are happy with the application, the agent will probably need oaths or declarations to be signed by the inventors listed on the patent application, stating they are in fact the inventors. If the rights to the patent are to be assigned to another, like a corporation, the agent will probably need those papers signed at this time also. The attorney will then file the patent application with all the required documentation in the patent office.

THE RESEARCHER'S RESPONSIBILITY FOR TECHNICAL DETAILS

Some agents have more technical experience than others. In any case, the researcher should assume the patent agent is not terribly knowledgeable about the technology area in which the invention was made. The researcher should make sure adequate time is spent providing background for the agent and making sure the agent not only understands the invention, but also the language of the technology area.

After a draft of the patent application is written, the researcher should check over the draft for technical correctness and completeness. Correctness should be foremost in the mind, for the researcher is the person involved in the preparation of the patent application who is most knowledgeable about the technology area. If the agent makes a mistake in the technical description it is up to the researcher to detect that mistake at this point.

Also, while different countries have different requirements for the extent of disclosure required, the researcher must make sure that the patent application is operable; that is, the application could be used by another to make or reproduce the invention. Therefore, the researcher should read the draft, making sure all of the critical elements of the invention are included. Note that only the critical elements must be included – a patent application is not a technical report where all of the technology must be taught! The application should contain the critical elements and an adequate description of these elements and how these elements work together to form the invention. The researcher is disclosing in the application 'how to make' the invention work, and reasons 'why' the invention works are not always needed. Reasons 'why' are only needed if the researcher is trying to convince the examiner that the invention is different from a seemingly similar invention. However, even in these cases, some agents want to retain the 'why' arguments until the examiner has reviewed the application. The thinking is that it is possible that the examiner may not think the inventions are similar; perhaps the examiner will allow the application without any challenge of patentability. If the examiner does issue the challenge, the agent can still use the arguments in his response to the office action. Should the agent succeed in convincing the examiner, the final published copy of the patent will contain only the 'how' part of the invention, not the 'why'; however, the 'why' can be obtained by reviewing the correspondence with the patent office in the patent office file for the patent. This takes a fair amount of effort, so the casual observer of the art will not normally make this effort unless the patent is of an infringement concern. Therefore, wide distribution of the explanation of 'why' the invention works is lessened, and the researcher has done what could be done to retain the technical expertise in a less accessible form.

ALOOFNESS

Some patent agents, especially patent attorneys, seem aloof to technical professionals; that is, the agents do not seem to be particularly interested in the researcher's invention. It is important that the researcher realizes that the agent's reaction to the invention is not because the invention is not a good invention, but rather because the agent sees new inventions all the time and processes patent applications every day. Most agents care just as much as researchers do about bringing their clients value through the issuance of patents on important inventions. Unfortunately, patent agents have to deal with lots of good ideas which never pan out, and researchers who never deliver what they promise. This tends to make the attorneys a bit cautious before getting excited about a particular patent application.

Part of the perceived aloofness on the part of patent agents is that sometimes it seems as though the researcher can never satisfy them. An analogy might be helpful in understanding why this happens.

Most agents would like all researchers to conduct research the way a chef might make a good-tasting cake. To make such a cake, the chef would decide what ingredients would make a good tasting cake, assemble all of the ingredients, and then put the whole thing into an oven to bake the cake. The agent would like to be the person who writes down the recipe; he wants the researcher to supply him with all the information he needs at one time so that he can sit down and prepare the patent application and then send it away to the patent office.

The problem is that some researchers do not do research like baking a cake. A researcher may take an empirical approach, starting with a list of ingredients and adding them one after the other until the resulting cake tastes good to him. The researcher, if successful in making a tasty cake, may not know why he was successful, much less be able to identify what were the critical ingredients. Plus, even after making a cake that tastes good, the researcher may continue to add ingredients to make the cake taste even better. If the researcher sits down with an agent to record the recipe, all the researcher can say is that he added certain ingredients together and the result was a tasty cake. He may not be able to tell the agent what critical ingredients are needed and may have to do additional work to be able to identify clearly which of the ingredients make for a tasty cake. That is, the agent will want the researcher to make several more cakes, if that is what it takes, to completely settle on a recipe.

The reason for this analogy is that when starting the preparation of a patent application, many researchers do not have a clear idea as to what are the critical components of their invention, something patent agents will want for the application. Given what has been accomplished by the researcher, the agent may want some additional experiments performed to better define the critical components and improve the value of the patent application.

When the agent makes these requests, it is important that the researcher listens and understands exactly what the agent is trying to ascertain. If the researcher does not understand after first listening, he should continue to probe the agent until the researcher understands what the agent would have him do. If the researcher follows the agent's requests, the agent should help him improve the patent application which results.

On the other hand, some agents are quite willing to prepare a patent application given only the information the researcher brings to them initially. That is, if it is apparent that the researcher has a novel invention, an agent can draft claims that will be allowed by a patent office based solely on the limited information provided by the researcher. However, the real value of a patent is when the claims will not only stop someone from practicing the exact invention, but also other inventions which have a similar quality. If the agent seems perfectly satisfied with the initial information the researcher provides, the researcher should question the agent and ask where the patent is weak and how the researcher might broaden the invention. Given the answers to these questions, the researcher must then decide whether he is willing to undertake this additional work.

EXPERIMENTATION FOR THE PATENT APPLICATION

Should a patent agent need the researcher to perform additional experiments for a patent application, the researcher should understand that the agent is looking for three things in this data. These are the practice of good science, the generation of distinctions that can be justified, and true comparisons with the closest prior art.

The idea that the agent wants the researcher to practice good science should not have to be mentioned. Researchers should automatically practice good science – science is their business, after all. Good science involves conducting research in a manner which can be duplicated by another and have the same result. Good science involves the proper design of experiments to show clearly where the invention does and does not work, and the gathering of data in a manner which allows a researcher to make clear and correct conclusions about the experimentation. Good science means the researcher did not take shortcuts in the research that could affect the scientific basis for an invention or assertion, or the researcher did not make conclusions without adequate scientific basis for those conclusions.

The phase 'the agent is looking for distinctions that can be justified' means that if the researcher is to distinguish an improvement over or a difference from the prior art by conducting comparative experiments, the results of the experiments should clearly illustrate exactly why there is an improvement or distinction. The difference between the results of comparative experiments in the best case are statistically significant, that is, the differences between the results should be real, not due to procedural or testing error. If the researcher is making the case that the new invention is distinct over another invention, the test data should show that there is a clear, substantial difference between the prior invention and the new invention.

Finally, the agent expects the researcher to compare his invention, through experimentation, to the closest prior art. Note that is the closest prior art, not the closest commercially practiced art. In many cases, an invention is developed that is an improvement over what people are commercially using. However, when the prior art search is performed, there may be something disclosed in that art which is actually closer to the invention than the technology commonly practiced commercially. Comparisons with the closest commercial art are of virtually no use to the patent agent; what the agent needs is a comparison with the closest disclosed invention, regardless of whether or not it is commercial and used widely. Sometimes the closest invention will be the one used commercially, and in that case, the comparison is proper. It is not the use of the invention which is the key, it is the public disclosure of an invention close to the new invention which will be of interest to the patent examiner. The researcher must recognize this and generate the information to show clearly a distinction or improvement.

PATENT LIAISONS AND OTHER INTELLECTUAL PROPERTY PROFESSIONALS

Large corporations tend to have technically trained personnel in positions referred to as patent liaisons or intellectual property professionals. These liaisons serve several functions but their main function is to make the acquisition and maintenance of intellectual property more efficient. Liaisons, no doubt, arose from the need to make sure the needs of the business were considered and coordinated during the patenting process for all of the inventions that a business might have, and to help make both the agent and the researcher more efficient by handling some of the more routine tasks associated with preparing a patent application.

Liaisons understand what sort of information is needed for the agent to begin to prepare an application. The liaison can be a ready source of information and advice during the initial stages of the research and can help the researcher decide whether or not he has enough information to initiate a patent filing. In many cases, these patent liaisons or intellectual property professionals decide when and what cases are filed.

If an organization has patent liaisons or intellectual property managers, the working arrangements with the patent agent will be slightly different. Typically, the researcher first describes his invention to the liaison, who in turn proceeds to generate a prior art search and to locate the closest prior art. The liaison can also point out if the researcher lacks some obvious data points which will be needed by the agent, and can help the researcher to summarize the information or data which will be needed for the patent application. When the researcher, the liaison, and the agent meet to discuss the invention, the agent is more likely to have most of the needed information, and the filing of the patent application is made more efficient.

The liaison may establish the priority of the applications on which the agent works. Therefore, if the researcher wishes for his application to be worked on at a faster rate, the researcher needs to make sure the liaison understands the business needs involved. While good liaisons can make the filing process more efficient, bad liaisons can slow down the process for no apparent reason. Therefore, the researcher should monitor the progress of his patent application, and if in his opinion the needs of the business are not being met, he should work with the liaison to provide for additional resources or alternate priorities to make sure his application is filed in a timely manner.

The researcher may also interact with information specialists. These specialists, or prior art searchers, sort through the available information for prior art for inventions and useful references for oppositions of other patents and applications. These searchers will search on-line computer databases for disclosures of technology that are close to the invention and will normally provide the researcher or patent agent with a listing of abstracts and actual patents that should be considered. Occasionally, these searchers will perform hands-on searches of actual patents in patent offices. In the past, the main reason this hands-on approach was required was the lack of any alternate methods of searching the prior art. However, the total content of many countries' patent publications are now available on-line. It is now possible to obtain both the full text and the figures disclosed in those publications electronically, so hands-on searching of patent applications may become a thing of the past.

If the researcher is working with an information specialist, he should make sure that the searcher understands what types of references are needed. Often it is helpful to provide the searcher with several descriptions of the invention at different conceptual levels. For example, if one developed a water-treatment membrane to remove lead from drinking water, the researcher could ask the searcher to search on:

1. synthetic membranes that are used to remove contaminants from water
2. synthetic membranes that are used to remove contaminants from drinking water
3. synthetic membranes that are used to remove lead from drinking water
4. synthetic membranes that are used to remove 'X' amount of lead from drinking water.

Note that by providing the searcher with different conceptual levels on which to search, the searcher can start with a broad conceptual level and narrow the search as needed to get a reasonable number of abstracts to review. By starting with a broad conceptual description of the invention, chances are the resulting search will contain the closest prior art and the search will be comprehensive. The searcher will normally review the abstracts found, remove any non-related abstracts, and provide the edited search to the researcher and/or the patent agent. Occasionally, the searcher will miss the point of the invention, and the search will have no applicability to the invention; in this case, the researcher should go back to the searcher and clarify the invention and have the searcher redo the search. In particular, if the searcher does not find any related references, the researcher should proceed very cautiously and review the basis for the search. In many cases, if no close art is found, the search should be repeated, perhaps with another searching technique so that any and all possible references are identified.

7 Disclosure and Filing Decisions

INTRODUCTION

Patents are an excellent source of information on how companies make their products and run their processes. Patents can disclose why prior inventions are flawed and can indicate the preferred elements of new, improved inventions. They disclose what parameters are important to a patented process and disclose preferred operating points for processes. Competitors can learn valuable information about each other's technology and business from each other's patents. Since patents play such a major role in the development of technology, companies must monitor the patent art to make sure they are aware of current developments. Because competitors will be reading and studying patents one should try to avoid disclosing any more information in one's patents than is absolutely necessary. However, controlling the amount of disclosures is not a simple exercise.

Along with controlling disclosure, the decision whether or not to file a patent on an invention may be critical to the success of a business. This is because the invention will be disclosed regardless of the success of the patent application. If a patent on the invention is granted, the assignee will obtain a limited monopoly on the invention, but only in the countries where the application is first filed and the patent is subsequently granted. If the patent doesn't issue, the assignee has no reserved rights in the invention, and since the invention is disclosed anyone can use the invention. We will examine two issues; first, the need to control how much information is put in a patent application, and second, the decision to file the application.

CONTROLLING THE DISCLOSURE OF TECHNOLOGY

The basic rule for the amount of disclosure in a patent application is only to disclose that information which is required to obtain a valid patent. In addition, in those countries without prior user rights, the patent application should provide enough disclosure to prevent others from obtaining a patent on a somewhat similar invention should no patent issue. This means the patent application should have a minimum amount of superfluous writing.

Each detail included in the application should be used to support the critical elements of the invention.

To avoid excessive disclosure, first examine the application and identify all items in the disclosure which may not be critical to the invention. Second, to check if these non-critical items are truly not needed in the application, remove them and see if the invention is still operable. Third, if the application will be filed in a 'best mode' country like the United States, check to make sure the critical elements include the preferred elements for the invention. Fourth, consider adding information back into the application on items which are non-critical to the invention, information on how someone might operate, but refraining from disclosing non-critical details about the commercial process. This may help to cloak the true commercial process from competitors.

A word of caution is appropriate. The desire to protect information should not be so great so as to misrepresent the invention or attempt to hide or not include in the patent application the critical elements of the invention. The invention disclosed in the patent should work, or the effort to file and obtain a patent will have been wasted. If a flawed patent is granted, other competitors will quickly determine that the patent is unworkable and therefore invalid.

The researcher should disclose to the patent agent the entire invention early in the patent drafting process. Later a review of the application can be completed and certain disclosures can be challenged. By giving the agent drafting the application the entire story, the final patent received will be stronger.

Finally, before the completed application is filed, assume competitors will read this application. Assume the role of a competitor and read the application and identify the new information which will now be available to the competitor when the application is published; new information which is not now available in previous patents and publications. Reconsider whether disclosure of this new information is necessary to obtain the patent; if it is, it must be included in the application. If it is not necessary, take it out.

THE FILING DECISION

The decision of whether or not to file a patent application requires a consideration of the business need and the impact a patent will provide. Also, there is a need to determine whether the protection obtained from having a patent is worth the disclosure of the technology. To some extent, the value of the patent will depend on the type of invention and the effort required to detect infringement to eventually enforce the patent claims.

Most product patents are very useful as offensive tools to enforce the patent rights of the owner. Product patents are patents which claim the exact item which is sold, whether it be a bulk chemical or a machine. If the patent contains product claims, infringement should be easily detected. The infringing product will, no doubt, be on sale, and can be purchased and analyzed in secret to determine whether the product, in fact, does infringe the patent in question. If the product is found to infringe the patent, legal maneuverings or actual legal action to stop the competitor from infringing can then be initiated.

In contrast, process patents tend to provide the patent owner with defensive capability unless the process can be identified directly from the product. In general, patents on processes that leave the equivalent of a fingerprint on the product are more useful as offensive tools than those process patents that do not. The fingerprint allows the detection of infringement of the process by analysis of the product, thereby allowing one to develop a firm case for legal maneuverings or action.

Some patent professionals question whether or not process patents which do not leave fingerprints in the products are of any value at all. The thinking is that the patents probably disclose more technology than the amount of protection that is obtained, and competitors who do not respect patents may practice the invention in secret and will never be caught. However, it is not wise for companies to ignore and willfully infringe any patent. Most companies will attempt to develop a legally supportable position which will allow them to practice. However, the development of this position over a solid, seemingly valid patent takes time and resources to complete. Therefore, at a minimum, process patents can have definite nuisance value. Also, process patents can and have been enforced. The effort required to detect infringement and develop a legal case against an infringer, however, is much more involved than with a product patent.

There are some generally accepted thoughts about the value of certain process patents. Broad patents on processes are more valuable than narrow patents. Patents on the cheapest method of making a product are valuable. Process patents that can be monitored by industrial discharge or waste reporting are very useful. Process patents in English law countries are useful; should a legal action on a product patent be initiated, the discovery phase can provide a method of collecting evidence of infringement of process patents. On the other hand, process patents which are very narrowly claimed or can be easily bypassed are not as useful to the patent owner.

One concept which is heard when discussing the value of patent applications is that of 'engineering around' a patent. The phase is used in conjunction with the practice of developing a process or apparatus which is not covered by the claims of a known process or apparatus patent, but can achieve a similar end. Many will base the value of a patent application on the perceived susceptibility of someone being able to engineer around the patent. However, almost any apparatus or process patent can be engineered around, and the single fact that a process might be engineered around should not be the only reason for not filing a patent application. Most companies will honor patents if they feel they are valid. The fact that a patent has issued on a process will at least preoccupy some of the competitor's resources to identify ways of engineering around the process.

Patents on machines that are developed by a company to be used in their proprietary processes but are not to be sold, have the least value. Do not confuse this maker of machines with a manufacturer and marketer of equipment or machines. For the company that makes and sells machines, the patents on their machines are product patents, and the information on product patents applies. However, if a company develops new equipment in-house and does not intend to sell it as part of the business offering, then a patent on this equipment has the least practical use. The reason one might want a patent on such a machine would be to prevent competitors from making and using the same machine in their process. However, these types of apparatus patents are the least easy to detect – most companies will not show their proprietary equipment – and are the easiest to engineer around. A team consisting of a patent attorney to interpret claims and an engineer to design and build the new machine, can normally develop an acceptable alternative machine which can be used quietly in a competing process. Therefore, in many cases it is best to keep these types of apparatus inventions secret unless they are so special that it is doubtful one could engineer around them.

FILING GLOBALLY

One of the more difficult tasks involved in filing a patent application is the selection of countries in which to file the application. Theoretically, a company can obtain patents in all of the countries of the world so as to prevent others from making or using that company's inventions anywhere without a license. In most cases a company will want to file its most important inventions worldwide, so that the inventions provide the company with a global competitive advantage. This decision – the actual selection of countries in which to file the application – can be difficult because in filing an application globally, the cost of the patent application escalates many times over the initial cost of filing in the home country.

Let's walk through the process. A researcher makes an invention that he thinks is valuable, plus he believes broad patent claims can be obtained on the invention. Therefore, the researcher has a patent application prepared and filed in his home country, starting the effort to obtain strong claims in that country from the patent office. However, before the examination of the application is complete in the home country, that is, before the researcher knows whether or not the patent will be granted, decisions on whether or not to file the application in other countries must be made. The decision as to whether or not to file, the decision on where to file, and the actual filing of the application is normally made within one year of the first filing to take advantage of the Paris Convention. Therefore, within a short period of time the countries in which protection may be obtained are set, long before a reading of either patentability or commercial success can be obtained.

In deciding whether or not to file globally, it should be obvious that the business need should be the first consideration, and there are three concepts to consider. They are the competitive value of the patent, the competitive value of the country, and the marketing value of the invention.

The competitive value of the patent is the most obvious and easiest to determine; patents prevent competitors from practicing, using, or selling the same invention. If restricting a competitor from the invention will provide a significant competitive advantage, then global filing of the patent application is warranted. For example, if the patent is on an improvement to a manufacturing process, but competitors use another process to make the same product and cannot use the improvement, the patent will have little value to competitors. Global filing of this patent may not be wise, unless competitors are expected to switch processes in the future.

The competitive value of the country involves a consideration of the type of patent application which is to be filed, the location of competitors, the location of the desired markets, and the enforcement climate of the country. The pinpointing of countries of value has become more important because the cost of obtaining and maintaining patents seems to rise each year. For equipment and process inventions, patents will be most useful in countries where competitors manufacture products using similar processes and equipment. For product inventions, patents will be most useful in those countries where the product or competitive products will be marketed. For a widely sold product, this might mean filing applications in most of the largest and most populous countries. For a specialty product, this might mean filing applications in a few select countries where the majority of downstream processors are located. In either case, most countries have importation laws which prevent importation of products which either infringe existing product patents or which are made by processes which infringe existing process patents. Therefore, it is necessary to file patent applications in only those countries which provide the most lucrative situations.

Considering the marketing value of the invention means considering the intangible values that obtaining a patent in a country gives to the marketing representative in that country. Some countries have a bad enforcement climate, and there may not be any real legal reason to obtain a patent in that country. However, filing a patent in that country may also help marketing efforts. Depending on how the patent filing is used, it can show customers that the company has an advantage over competitors, which in turn translates into the customers having an advantage over their competition. The patent filing can be used to show customers that the company is serious about building relationships in that country. It can be used to show that the company has a technical staff which is ready to make more inventions and support the current line of products. The filing can be used to show the company has 'special' or cutting-edge technology which competitors do not have, which in turn will help make the customers more special in the marketplace. Finally, some customers derive a sense of security from patents; some assume their suppliers' patents protect both the supplier and themselves. However, this is a false sense of security; if the customer is not able to generate adequate business, the supplier may easily find other customers in the same country who will.

THE COST OF BROADLY FILED PATENT APPLICATIONS

It might be surprising that monetary cost is a major concern in the filing of patent applications globally. If an inventor has enough money, he can obtain patents in all the countries of the world that issue patents. As businesses have become increasingly more globally focused, the desire to have worldwide protection has also increased. However, countries have consistently raised the cost of obtaining patents to generate more revenue for their treasuries. Therefore, the total cost of filing a patent application in many different countries has increased to the point where a decision to file in a handful of countries can easily cost more than a hundred thousand dollars over the life of the patent.

While the fees are different from country to country, there are almost always fees for both obtaining and maintaining patents. It will seem to the new inventor that at every turn there is a fee. There is normally a fee for filing the application, and if the patent is allowed, a fee for issuance of the patent. In many cases, a patent agent may need to use the services of a patent agent in a foreign country, so these additional costs must be anticipated. Additional costs include translating the patent application into the language required by the country in which it is filed, translations of the examiner's office actions from the country's patent office, and translations of the applicant's written responses to these office actions. Just communicating with the patent office of one country can generate a sizable bill.

After the patent has issued, many countries require the payment of maintenance fees on a periodic basis to keep the patent in force. If these maintenance fees are not paid, the patent lapses and the technology is in the public domain in that country. Some countries require the patent owner to 'work' the invention in these countries, or require compulsory licensing of the technology. This 'working' can take the form of additional, albeit small, fees to the country.

Finally, the intent in filing an application in a country is to obtain a patent in the country to prevent others from practicing. If someone in that country does decide to practice even if faced with the patent, the patent owner needs to be willing to expend the effort to challenge the infringer in court. If the patent owner is not willing to enforce his patent should the need arise, or there is some reason to be concerned about the enforceability of the patent, the patent owner may be better off not wasting the money for the filing and issuance fees.

The types of fees mentioned above are the normal fees one encounters. The patent offices of the world like the usual and dislike the unusual, so whenever an applicant needs to do something slightly out of the ordinary he should expect to pay additional and higher fees.

Now, while one might think that these individual payments are not prohibitively expensive, if the application has been filed in many different countries the cost can add up to a considerable amount. These costs may be justified for a very valuable invention, however, from a practical standpoint, the inventor will need to be on guard or he will tend to file applications in too many countries. The reason is that inventors tend to become enamored with their invention and believe it is more valuable than perhaps it is. Unless inventors are careful, they will equate their inflated value of the invention with an equally inflated number of countries in which to file the application. Many companies take on this extra cost, thinking that the cost, spread over about 20 years (the life of the patent, in most cases) is cheap insurance. It has been said that about one out of 10 patents is commercially significant. When one of these 10 patents pay off, however, they can really pay off, returning to the company more than just the cost of the other nine patents. The key is to try to examine critically each patent application and determine objectively whether or not it will be a true source of competitive advantage. This is especially true if there is an expectation that the company will continue to invent and have many different patents, because the accumulated cost of all of the applications and patents can place a tremendous burden on the cost of doing business.

THE LEGAL SYSTEMS OF INDIVIDUAL COUNTRIES

The reason there may be a need to use an agent in another country is that each country has its own laws concerning intellectual property. Although progress has been made to harmonize or make more uniform certain aspects of the global filing of patents, the patent laws and the enforcement climate in various countries seem to be in a constant state of flux. Since this is not a legal book, we will only touch the surface of this issue.

Since patent attorneys live in the legal world, they approach patents from a legalistic viewpoint, with the prevalent issue being how enforceable a patent will be in a country should someone infringe the patent and an attempt be made to legally stop them. That is, how receptive will the country's legal system be to the contention that the patent holder has been wronged? The legal world is based not only on the law, but also precedent and judgment. In the best case, to arrive at a decision as to whether or not a patent holder will be treated fairly in a country, an attorney will consult specialists, review the law, and study the legal precedents on how others have been treated when they have tried to enforce their patents. This seems a very satisfying method of predicting how one will be treated in a country, however, the past is not always an accurate forecaster of the future. Many countries that formerly had very bad reputations from an intellectual property standpoint have implemented changes because they realize the benefits of having a well-functioning patent and legal system. The past history may indicate the climate is not conducive to patents, when in fact the climate has changed substantially. Therefore, the filing decision may conclude that the gamble for protection is worth the money spent, even though there is no precedent and no guarantee the patent will be treated fairly.

In the worst case, an attorney may assess the enforcement climate of a country, and therefore its value, based only on preconceived notions or very subjective issues which may have no basis in fact. It is important to determine the reason the attorney does not recommend a country, and make sure the attorney has researched and understands the current trends in the country, and what legal developments are anticipated.

There is one school of thought prevalent in the legal profession, especially those of English-speaking countries, which places a lot of value on patents in countries whose legal systems are based on English law. There are two important issues which may be helpful in understanding some of the positions an attorney may take. The first issue is the right of an individual to private property. The concept is that countries which do not appreciate the individual right to private property will not have a strong legal enforcement climate. In other words, since a patent is a form of private property, countries which do not respect private property will not respect the rights of individuals to enforce their patents. The second issue is the process of discovery in a legal action. This concept allows for examination of certain private records of the other litigant. These records may contain information useful to legal experts in preparation for trial, and on a rare occasion there may be previously unknown information on other patents the other litigant is infringing. Therefore, a lot of emphasis is placed on English-based legal systems by some attorneys. Now this thinking is not necessarily wrong, but global business needs may dictate filing in countries other than those which are derived from English law.

One method of approaching the problem of deciding where to file patent applications is to generate a list of countries to consider, and then weigh the current legal climate in each country versus the amount of money the inventor or business is willing to spend on the patents for the invention. This decision will be made knowing full well the legal or the enforceability climate may change before the patent expires. However, at least an analysis of the information available will have been performed and the risks involved would have been considered.

TECHNIQUES FOR DETERMINING WHICH COUNTRIES WILL BE OF VALUE

Where in the world should an application be filed? Here are some techniques which can be used, based on the competitive situation and the type of patent which is being filed.

If the invention is a new product and any infringement of the invention could be seen in the marketplace, one will want to file for patent protection in those countries where a market presence is desired, especially those countries which will have the largest market for the product. If a patent is obtained in those countries, competitors will not be able to legally sell or make the product in those countries. Since the invention is a product, one will be able to clearly detect if another company starts to infringe the patent, because the product can be bought in the open market and then examined to determine if the competitor is in fact infringing the patent. In general, product patents are normally filed very broadly to reserve the larger markets for the patent holder.

If the invention is a new process or a new machine which is used to make a product, and the use of the process or the machine can be detected in the product, then patent protection will be wanted in the same countries that would be filed for product protection. The key here is that because infringement can be detected, albeit indirectly, the value of the patent increases, because it is now similar to a product patent.

If the invention is a new process or a new machine which is used to make a product, and the use of the process or the machine cannot be detected in the product, and a decision is made to file a patent application in the inventor's home country, there may be a desire in turn to file the application globally to attempt to restrict competitors' ability to use the new invention as much as possible. If a competitor uses the same general manufacturing process as the patent holder, then process patents may be of value in the countries where the competitor has production facilities, or where there is a reasonable expectation he will install production facilities. However, if different processes are used, filing an application in the countries where a competitor manufactures will not be as useful. It will only be useful if there is some thought that the competitor may want to use the technology in some manner.

Enforceability of a patent is a common topic when considering the filing of process or apparatus inventions. In many cases, a competitor can use these types of inventions behind locked gates, and unless the particular attributes of the manufacturing process can be tied to the product, infringement may never be detected. This has led some to avoid filing applications for process and apparatus patents. In actuality, if a decision has been made to file the patent application in the home country of manufacture, the application might as well be filed in the countries where competitors manufacture. If the patent issues in the main country of manufacture, then competitors will learn the technology anyway; if one is able to obtain a patent in countries important to competitors this will, in most cases, cause competitors to carefully consider the patent before infringing. Most companies, from a practical standpoint, cannot haphazardly ignore their competitors' patents because of the potential liability involved with being found guilty of patent infringement. Most companies have policies to avoid infringing valid patents, and, if a patent is obtained in a competitor's country the competitor will normally initiate a study to develop an argument for the invalidity of the patent. If no good argument is found, then the competitor will have to decide what course of action to take; whether or not to ignore the patent and practice, to license the patent, or to find an alternate process which does not infringe. In any case, the effort expended by competitors in this analysis, by itself, may be worth the money spent in obtaining the patent.

If an invention has been made and the potential competitors are unknown, or it is not clear where to file the patent application, there are techniques for obtaining information from electronic on-line patent databases which will help in the making of filing decisions. By searching for information on patents in the technology area, one can obtain the names of other companies which might be competitors for the invention, in addition to obtaining information about their inventions. After developing a list of potential competitors, one can then proceed to examine in which countries they file patent applications that are involved in the technology area. If it is assumed competitors make logical, well-informed decisions, which is probably a reasonable assumption, then one can usually pick out the inventions a competitor thinks highly of – these are the ones that are filed in many countries. Now one must consider that the PCT procedure allows one to file in many countries in a very simple manner, and one may want to take a closer look to determine which of the originally selected countries are finally designated by the patent applicants. However, this list of countries can be used as a starting point for developing one's own filing strategy. This list will also indicate where in the world a competitor thinks the markets are and perhaps where competitors intend to target their efforts.

WORLD GROWTH AND ECONOMIC POWER

Earlier we stated that one will want to file patent applications for new products in those countries where the largest markets are believed to be. Also, when filing an application globally, one is trying to forecast where the markets will be in the next 20 years. To attempt to make an adequate decision, it is useful to consider both where current markets are and how the world is expected to change in the future. Forecasting the future is very risky and fraught with errors. Still, it is useful to consider what has been forecasted so that potential opportunities can be considered.

The World Bank has forecast how populations will change between 1995 and 2030. They forecast the majority (60 percent) of the world's population will continue to be in Asia, and Africa will be the continent that will experience the greatest percentage growth in population. Europe is forecast to have a fairly substantial percentage decrease in population, while the Americas will experience a slight decrease.

Today, the majority of patents are filed in three major patent offices – the United States, Europe, and Japan. Clearly, the United States and Japan will continue to be popular filing countries for many types of technologies. However, if one considers only population growth, the forecast for Europe might indicate the need for reduced patent filings, while increased acquisition of intellectual property in the African continent would be called for. However, population growth does not mean that economic power or the ability to buy newly patented products will also increase; with increased population the standard of living might decrease instead of increase. The countries also need the ability to develop and sustain markets.

So, one would also want to consider which countries are favorable for trade and business. For example, *World Trade Magazine* annually ranks the top 30 countries for trade and expansion, considering several different criteria. In the lists for 1999 and 2000, half of the countries listed were European and a third of the countries came from the Pacific Rim. Most of the larger countries in the Americas were listed as well as well-known Asian exporting countries like China, Taiwan, Japan, Singapore, and South Korea. Other Pacific Rim countries like Australia and New Zealand were also listed. No African countries made the list and the only Middle Eastern country listed was Israel.

Near term, as many of these Asian countries continue a path toward freer markets, increased acquisition of intellectual property in Asian countries should be considered. The combination of growing trade power and growing population cannot be ignored. At the same time, one cannot ignore either the larger countries in the Americas or the countries of Europe because they will continue to have economic power for many years to come. Likewise, even though the African continent should experience a large increase in population, the current economic situation means one has to be exceedingly selective as to what countries are needed there for their business.

Therefore, in the future having a global presence will mean more than just having patents in the United States, a few countries in Europe, and Japan. To be truly global, one will have to have patents near term in a number of countries throughout Asia, the Americas, and in the longer term, Africa. In addition, one will have to consider whether or not a global presence makes sense for their business, because there will be increased cost for the increased number of patents.

TEMPLATES

If the patent strategies and business strategies of a product line are well developed, the country selection process can be simplified somewhat by the use of 'filing templates'. Templates, or lists of countries which are most important to the business, can be generated for generic apparatus, process, and product applications to reflect the differences in the type of coverage obtained by each type of patent. Once these templates are developed, they can be used in a straightforward manner to select countries without too much debate. Using templates can help control the cost of global filings because the template is a preselected subset of the world. One can first consider which of the template countries are not needed, and then consider whether or not any additions should be made. Starting the process with a subset of countries makes the selection process easier because one does not have to start with all the countries of the world, and the most important countries to the business are considered first. All in all, fewer countries are considered, and the chances are good that the global patent estate will be uniformly built in the countries that are most important to the business.

TIMING OF APPLICATION FILINGS

Once it has been decided that a patent application will be filed globally and the countries have been identified, the next decision is how to time the actual filing of the application. In doing so, the following should be considered:

- whether or not to take advantage of the Paris Convention and file within a year
- when to file in non-Paris Convention countries
- whether or not to file the applications via the PCT or nationally

In most cases, the original patent application will be filed in the home country of the inventor (or of the business), with the remaining global filings occurring within one year under the provisions of the Paris Convention. Remember, the chances are that the applicant will not know whether or not a patent will issue until after the Paris Convention one-year time period has passed. However, the applicant should also have some idea as to whether or not to expect an issuance based on the prior art found in the patentability search. In most cases, the applicant believes the invention to be patentable (or he would not file the application) and that the patent that issues will be strong; the major consideration then becomes the maintenance of absolute novelty of the invention and the priority date. For these reasons most cases are filed taking advantage of the Paris Convention.

Some countries are not signatories of the Paris Convention. Most of these countries are also absolute novelty countries. Therefore, in a very strict sense, if one wishes to obtain valid patents in these countries, one must file in the countries as soon as possible after the initial filing in the home country, while avoiding disclosure of the invention between the time of the original filing and the filing in the non-Convention country. Some countries, like the United States, require foreign filing licenses for technology developed in the country before filing applications globally. Obtaining these licenses must be dialed into the timing, because sometimes they are not granted as quickly as would be desired.

Finally, one should consider whether or not to file the patent applications nationally; that is, in the national patent offices, or via the PCT. The PCT system was discussed in Chapter 1; the key issue to consider is that the PCT has built-in periods of delay before the patent application examination process actually begins. This delays the issuance of a patent, and also delays aggressive legal action in the courts to stop an infringer. Even though the PCT provides some provisional protection during this delay, if one wishes to initiate serious action against an infringer, direct filing of the application in the national patent offices will be the quickest method of obtaining a patent.

Another issue to consider is cost. The PCT system, while convenient, can be more expensive. The system is attractive in that the costs of filing nationally are delayed, and time is available to decide whether or not an invention is a success and a patent is needed. However, filing via the PCT requires additional fees because of the additional steps involved. If coverage in only a few countries is needed, filing the application directly in those countries may be cheaper.

GLOBAL EXPERTS

The best initial source of information about the practices and intellectual property climates of countries will be an experienced patent agent or attorney. He or his firm probably has experience in prosecuting cases in a number of countries worldwide. He may rely on the services of an agent in a foreign country to help prosecute the application if he does not have experience in that particular country, or if he believes it is in the best interest of the client to do so. A qualified agent in the country in which the application is filed is by far the best resource of specific information about the practices and enforcement of patents in that country.

Recently, a number of magazine articles have appeared which criticize the patent systems of the world, and extol the virtues of the system in the United States. Many of these articles seek to convince the reader that patents or the patent systems in various parts of the world, particularly Asia, have limited value. In particular, many of the articles seem to have a hidden agenda to blatantly attack the Japanese patenting system. While the articles may have some valid points, in general, it is not only unfair to bash other systems, it is misleading. All patent systems have flaws, and complaining about these flaws will not help develop a proprietary position in these countries. It is much better to develop a business plan, ask advice of a patent agent, and seek professional intellectual property help in the countries in question to make the vision of a business a reality.

AGREEMENT WITH STRATEGY

The ultimate decision for the filing of an application should be that the filing agrees with the patent strategy, and should be consistent with business strategy. Anything other could waste money and the valuable time of patent agents. However, researchers do not always make inventions which fit exactly into either strategy. When this happens, the technical and business leaders should consider whether or not this technology or invention is a major breakthrough and the patent strategy should be revised, or the patent strategy is still adequate and a patent application on this new invention is not needed.

If the invention does agree with the patent strategy, one must consider whether or not a competitor would pay to license a patent on the invention.

If there is better, more attractive technology, a patent application is probably a waste of money. However, if a competitor would be likely to pay to use the invention, an attempt to obtain patent coverage and license the patent should be strongly considered.

The researcher may be the only person to detect that the new invention is a major and lucrative development. Therefore, the researcher has an obligation to question the strategy when a major new opportunity comes along which is not recognized by the management.

8 After the Filing

INTRODUCTION

After making the invention, and then working with a patent agent to review prior publications, generate additional data for the patent application, and review drafts of the patent application, it is not unreasonable that most researchers feel they have finished when the patent application is finally filed. However, after the filing the researcher still has a role to play in obtaining a patent. Any number of issues can arise after the filing, in what is called the prosecution of the application. Even after the patent has issued, the researcher may still be called upon to help determine whether or not the patent should be maintained; that is, should the assignee continue to pay fees to governments worldwide to keep the patent in force. While the researcher may have spent a year or more inventing and filing a patent application, several more years may pass before the application issues, and 20 years from the filing date may pass before the patent expires. Clearly, filing a patent application is a long term commitment. Let's start after the filing and trace what can typically happen with a patent application.

ANTICIPATING THE FIRST RESPONSE FROM A PATENT OFFICE

It is surprising how long it takes to get a patent, and depending on the country, the wait for the first substantial response from a patent examiner can take from several months to several years. A 'substantial response' means either a rejection of the patent claims or an allowance. The applicant has some control over this timing, because some countries require the applicant to request examination. The United States automatically begins examination, and the result is that the first response from the patent office is usually made within a year of filing. In Europe, receipt of the search report takes about the same amount of time as receipt of the first office action in the United States. After seeing the search report, if the applicant still wants the patent application examined, he must ask for examination within six months of receiving the search report. Obtaining the first office action from a European patent examiner will normally take more than a year, and in some cases the time is substantially longer. At the time of this writing, the Japanese patent system gives the applicant seven years from the priority date to request examination, however, in October 2001 this time period is scheduled to be reduced to three years. Applications pending at the time of the change will continue to have seven years to request examination. At one time, after requesting examination in Japan, the applicant typically waited two to three years to obtain an office action from the examiner. However, this time has been significantly reduced and now one can expect to have an office action in about half that time. In almost all patent offices some of the applicant's possible patent term is spent waiting for a response from the patent office; that is, waiting for the examiner to actually examine the application and issue an office action. The major patent offices worldwide realize part of the patent term is sacrificed and are working to be more responsive and to shorten their response time despite increasing numbers of applications filed every year. Therefore, there is good reason to expect that these response times will be reduced in the future.

The timing seems to work out that, if the application is filed in the United States or Europe, the applicant will receive the first reply from a patent office about the time the researcher starts forgetting the application was filed in the first place. The exceptions to this are those applications filed using the Patent Cooperation Treaty (PCT), in which case the timing is longer. As discussed elsewhere in the book, the PCT is a global procedure which allows convenient patent filing in many countries simultaneously. PCT applications will take at least 20 months before an examiner sends either an allowance or a rejection.

MODIFICATION OF CLAIMS

In the office action, the examiner will either allow the claims in the application, reject the claims, or object to something in, or missing from, the application. If allowed, a decision must be made by the applicant as to whether or not to pay the issuance fee and have the patent issue. This may sound like a silly decision, because of the extent of the effort expended up to this point; however, the invention may no longer be as exciting as it once was or the need for a patent may be gone. The invention may have been found to be defective in some respect, a serious downturn in business may require the funds which would have paid the issuance fee, or the business may have had a change in strategy. Conversely, there may be a strategic reason not to pay the fee. In some countries, and particularly in the United States, if additional work has been completed since the filing of the application which expands the original invention, the applicant may be able to file a continuation-in-part application so that the claims in the original application are broadened. A continuation-in-part application allows the applicant to add new disclosure to the patent application and expand the claims or add new ones. In essence, this means that the applicant files a new application, and the allowance is forgotten and the examination of the application starts over. The application then has multiple priority dates; the original date for the original information, and the new filing date for the new information. The additional information must be of high importance to a business because in filing a continuation-in-part, the applicant forfeits the original allowance and there is no guarantee that the original claims will be allowed in the second application.

Normally, however, the fee is paid. The application is then either granted or provisionally granted, depending on the country. In provisionally-granted patents, the implication is that this application has been examined and a patent will exist unless a reason can be shown that the invention described is not patentable. The provisionally-granted patent is said to be 'published for opposition' and there is a short period of time where the public can raise patentability issues and oppose the grant. If no issues are raised the patent then exists as published.

On the other hand, if the examiner does not allow the application in the office action, the application will typically have either a formality problem or patentability problem. A formality problem normally means something is missing or is not in the form required by the patent office. Many times this means the agent was not specific enough in the application about a key component in a claim. These types of formality problems are normally taken care of by the agent without the need for technical help from the inventor.

However, if there is a patentability problem, the agent may need the researcher's help in answering the examiner's rejection. The researcher's help may be in several different forms. The examiner may have found a prior art reference that was not found by the applicant's prior art search, and consequently, the agent may need the researcher to read the reference to help distinguish his invention over the disclosure in that reference. The agent may need the researcher to perform an additional experiment to clearly show the examiner that the new invention is different from the disclosures in the prior art. The agent may not feel comfortable with the technology and may want the researcher to review the arguments in the proposed response to the patent office and confirm that the technical points used in the arguments are valid, and perhaps contribute other points which could be made.

Based on the content of the examiner's office action and the effect of any newly cited prior art, the agent may need to amend the claims in the patent application. In many cases, this will mean narrowing claims to avoid the newly cited art or modifying the claims to reflect the real invention. This is another instance where the researcher's expertise can be very helpful to the patent agent. The researcher needs to fully understand why the change is needed, and what is the practical effect of the claim change. The agent will normally suggest possible changes to the claim which would make the claim acceptable to the examiner. The expertise of the researcher puts him in a good position to understand the practical impact of the claim change, and he may be able to suggest from a technical point of view which of the proposed claim changes has the least negative effect on the patent coverage. Occasionally, a claims restriction 'reads' more restrictive than it is from a practical standpoint. For example, if a patent claim is initially drafted broadly enough so that it covers a large operating area for an invention, but the examiner will not allow the claim to such a broad operating area, the claim must be narrowed. However, if from a practical standpoint no one would ever want to operate in certain parts of the originally-claimed operating area, and if the narrowing of the patent claim consists of changes to remove these impractical areas from the claims, then the practical coverage of the invention does not change. When these situations arise, the modified claim seems on paper to be a major concession by the applicant when in fact a very small concession was actually made. Even if the narrowing does restrict the invention, if the practical effect of the remaining modified claim still meets the overall strategic vision of the business, then the practical effect of the change is small.

However, sometimes the required narrowing will reduce the coverage of the patent to make the patent practically worthless; that is, the resulting patent will do little to stop a competitor from operating in a competitive manner because the competitor has many options for technology that will provide for a similar result as the invention, but will be outside the allowed claims. If this is the case, a decision should be made as to whether or not the restricted claims will have any value to the business. If the modified version still has adequate value then proceeding is appropriate; however, if no value or limited value is found, abandonment of the case to save money may be the most prudent course of action.

The analysis that was made prior to the filing and the strategy for the case may have to be rethought if new prior art is found during prosecution, or the examiner finds some fault with the application. This is the reason it is important to have a thorough search performed before the patent application is drafted and have the inventor involved throughout the patenting process.

RESEARCH AFTER THE FILING

Use the time after the filing of a patent application to improve the primary invention and develop improvement inventions while the primary invention is secret to the world. After filing a patent application, if the invention is not purposely disclosed by the inventor, there is a period of time during which the technology of the invention will remain secret. This period of time will normally either be the automatic publication of the application 18 months after the initial filing date, early publication in the United States, or the publication of the issued patent in a country. While it is not unheard of to have a patent issue before 18 months, in many cases the automatic publication is the first disclosure of the invention technology. The publication of the application is noted by on-line computer services which supply information to patent professionals, so soon after publication of the application, anyone in the world can obtain and read exactly what is disclosed in the patent application.

The 18 month period can be used by the researcher to develop additional inventions which can extend the patent monopoly on the technology. These additional inventions can be improvements over the primary invention, or other inventions in the same technology area. The inventions can also be in the same field, but in different technologies. For example, suppose a new polymer is invented, and a patent application is filed on the polymer. The inventor can work on improvements of the polymer, that is, he can develop variations of the polymer and patent those if they are novel over the primary or first invention. The inventor can also work on new forms of the polymer, say the use of the polymer in injection molding or fiber-making processes. Either route could provide the inventor with a strong competitive advantage; however, if the inventor waits to start developing these new inventions until after the technology of the original invention is already disclosed, he will lose the 'competitive pace' which was his by having developed the polymer first.

In developing new inventions, the patent laws around the world need to be remembered. In most countries where the initial application is filed, the invention claimed in the unpublished application will be prior art against any subsequent patent applications that are extensions of the primary patent. After the application is published, it is then prior art against any subsequent applications in almost all countries. However, the researcher has the advantage of knowing what is in each application, and as new improvements on the invention are developed, the researcher can meet with the patent agent and develop new patent applications that are patentable over the original application.

The competitive pace is the least utilized form of patent strategy. In chess, one dynamic element which impacts the strategy of the game is the development of a player's pieces. In chess, both players start out with the same number of pieces, but one player can obtain an advantage if his pieces can be deployed to a strong position on the board without any loss in time. Also, once a piece is in a strong position, it should not be moved to another position unless there is a good reason to do so. When a chess player has a dynamic advantage in the development of his pieces, he can take this transitory situation and change it into a permanent material advantage by capturing the other player's pieces, or convert the superiority into a massive winning attack on his opponent's king. However, any superfluous move prior to the material conversion can result in a loss in this superiority, because it is a dynamic advantage and can be lost as quickly as it is obtained.

The concept of competitive pace is similar; as long as an invention's technology is not widely known, the inventor has a lead in development, a strong dynamic advantage, to build on the technology through related inventions and patents. After filing a patent, the inventor, or the team of researchers which worked on the initial invention, will normally be in a great position to build on the initial dynamic advantage. However, like chess, the dynamic advantage can be quickly lost if the nature of the advantage is not recognized and not used to develop a sustained advantage. The publication of patent applications and the eventual disclosure of technology is beyond the researcher's control if patents are desired. The competitive pace, however, can be controlled by identifying on which technologies a strong patent estate is desired, and establishing the organization and the expectation to create such a patent estate.

A necessary concern with developing and filing improvement patents is that these subsequent patents will have narrower coverage than the initial patents. The amount of disclosure builds with each successive application until predominantly narrow patents are obtained in the technology area. Narrow coverage can be beneficial if the invention is critical to the business situation. However, narrow patents also indicate competitors may have more room to operate in the technology area. In order to assess whether or not the research program, from a patent point of view, has reached the point of diminishing returns, one must look at the invention in the way a competitor would. Ask whether or not a competitor would be interested in buying this technology. If the answer is no, a patent is of little use, and the research efforts might be better placed in a new technology area.

MAINTAINING COHESION

An important function that a patent liaison, an intellectual property manager, or a patent agent attempts to perform is to maintain cohesion between the patent applications that are filed. Cohesion in a patent estate is developed by avoiding contradictions between newer and older applications. Contradictions occur when a principle or a fact in a subsequent application is different from principles or facts stated in prior patent applications. Test methods and definitions should be consistent from application to application. By maintaining cohesion, difficult questions during examination and enforcement are avoided, questions which might weaken prior patents. If a test must be introduced which has been invented by the inventor for a particular patent application, make sure this test does not make prior patents weaker.

Another concept encompassed by cohesion is the idea of maintaining trade secrets. Typically, an organization will identify what items they want to maintain secret. It is important that these trade secrets are not accidentally disclosed in patent applications. As stated before, a patent liaison is normally extremely helpful in pointing out what aspects of the technology have traditionally been kept secret and the reasons why.

Finally, attention to the cohesion of patent applications will identify where preferred operating points are inadvertently being disclosed, particularly points which are not particularly important to the invention. While disclosure of the best mode is required by some countries, the inventor needs to question ancillary disclosures on operating parameters such as temperatures, pressures, and concentrations which may not be required to be disclosed to obtain a valid patent.

The best way to develop cohesion is to find a good patent agent and use this person for all patent applications as well as utilizing the services of a patent liaison or intellectual property manager if one is available. There is a benefit to be had by using the same people to process patent applications. However, even if the same agent cannot be used for all of the cases, most good agents will consider cohesion with older patent applications when they draft new patent applications.

ISSUANCE AND MAINTENANCE OF PATENTS

If a patent application is filed in many different countries, the speed at which it is examined will differ from country to country. Therefore, if the invention is patentable, the actual time required for all of the patents to issue could be as much as 10 years or more. During the whole of this time the patent agent will be responding to patent examiners and prosecuting the application with an aim toward issuance of the patent in all countries. Also during this time the agent may need the researcher to provide technical advice for the responses to the patent examiners.

If the invention becomes of no use, or the value of any patents obtained on the invention becomes questionable, the researcher should inform the agent so that the money spent on this unwanted or unneeded invention can be limited or stopped. The agent can abandon the remaining patent applications, which will in turn stop the ongoing expense of the prosecution of the applications. The agent can also abandon issued patents by not paying the maintenance fees to keep the patents in force. Of course, as the applications and patents are abandoned, the original patent holder forfeits his rights to the invention; the abandonment means the invention will be in the public domain of those countries where the application has been abandoned.

If a company has a patent liaison, one function he may provide is a regular analysis of the patent portfolio to identify cases which may be safely abandoned to save maintenance costs without jeopardizing the business. The researcher should help in this process; he should evaluate the patents proposed for abandonment and provide comments to the patent liaison about the value of the inventions.

As mentioned earlier in the book, maintenance fees in most countries start at a relatively low amount and increase, sometimes dramatically, over the life of the patent. For this reason, many patent professionals argue that many patents should be abandoned late in their life to save the payment of these excessive late-term maintenance fees. The logic behind abandoning a patent with a few years left until expiration is that the probability that infringement of the patent could be detected and acted upon decreases as the expiration date for the patent approaches. In short, the effort to try to protect an expiring patent may not be worth much because the invention will be in the public domain shortly anyway. A competitor who starts practicing a patented invention near its expiration date would have a limited liability, which would typically not justify the cost of the legal effort which would be needed to prove infringement. The researcher can help identify those patents which really provide a competitive advantage and which should be kept to the expiration date; conversely, this same researcher can be an indispensable part of the analysis team which decides which patents are no longer valuable.

9 The Future of Intellectual Property Efforts

Many patent issues deal with the future. A patent is hoped to be enforceable for many years into the future. Selection of countries in which to file a patent application relies on an understanding of future markets. The filing of an application in many countries imparts a large future maintenance bill should the patent issue in all those countries. In this final chapter we will attempt to gaze into our crystal ball and speculate on how things might be in the future of intellectual property.

Some issues are easy to predict. For example, patent offices around the world have been working for some time to fully utilize the internet in the filing and handling of patent applications. Clearly, this has already come a long way and will become a more common and ordinary experience as systems are refined and a comfort level is attained. The internet will provide more information than ever before and therefore exceedingly good prior art search techniques and complete search summaries will be required. The challenge will not only be in searching for the references; in many cases much of the challenge will be in reviewing the details of a large number of references found by the search. Therefore, as the world becomes linked electronically, and the world becomes a seemingly smaller place, the challenge to review quickly all this easily attainable information will become greater and greater.

Over the past 10 years, new patent laws, regulations, and guidelines have issued which have dramatically changed the patenting landscape. In the United States, the patent term has changed and patent applications will be published. The ability to manipulate the system and obtain additional patent term by delaying or continuing patent applications is no longer a benefit to an applicant. With new laws and new rules will come unforeseen problems. There is no doubt that there will be additional laws and rules to repair these unforeseen problems. Since there are so many changes, one would have to expect the rules, regulations, and laws to continue to be in flux for many years to come as the systems become harmonized and optimized and as court challenges resolve the various issues which will be generated. One job of the patent attorney and agent will be to stay on top of these changes.

Independent inventors could be especially affected by these new changes. If the independent inventor has good patent professionals working with him, many potentially negative effects from these changes should be minimized. However, it is likely that future increases in the cost of filing and prosecuting patent applications will have more effect on an independent inventor than on corporate organizations. Independent inventors will have to get more monetary support for their inventions prior to filing patent applications. They will need to learn better how to sell their inventions while remembering the various rules and bars to obtaining a valid patent. Clearly the future belongs to the inventor that is able to learn continuously about the patent law changes and is also able to find professional patent help to use those changes to his advantage.

Corporate organizations will also feel the pressure to obtain more intellectual property and to make sure that property generates or protects revenue. In many cases, corporations will have to make major mind set changes. Management of intellectual property in the future will require more resources. The primary reasons are as follows:

1. *More types of available patents.* As discussed in previous chapters, more things are now patentable than ever before. Specifically, methods of conducting business, software, internet, and biotechnology are all new types of patentable subject matter. Inventors in some of these areas, like biotechnology, can generate large numbers of applications on very closely related technology. All of these areas have experienced tremendous growth which will continue for some time to come. Most corporate organizations will have the opportunity to develop technology in at least one of these areas.

2. *More legal opinions.* As the amount of intellectual property increases worldwide, the possibility that a new invention may infringe another's patent increases also. This will increase the demand for legal opinions from attorneys on whether or not one has freedom to operate. In addition, the need for legal opinions on the validity of adverse patents will also increase. These opinions are not simple exercises, they can require extensive prior art searches and intensive study by attorneys. Therefore, they can take up a tremendous amount of an attorney's time that could have been spent writing and filing patent applications.

3. *More oppositions.* Along with the need for more opinions, there will be a need for more oppositions of potentially adverse patents after they issue in Europe, Japan, and other places where opposition is possible. An opposition takes a long time to resolve. This means many oppositions important to a business can be ongoing at any one time. One's attorney will need to both prepare and file oppositions of others' patents and also defend one's own patents when they are opposed. Oppositions will also become more important as the cost of patent litigation continues to rise. Those adversely affected by the issuance of a patent will want to

take the relatively inexpensive route of trying to modify the claims of an adverse patent during opposition, hoping they will be able to restrict the invention so they have freedom to operate. They can then potentially avoid more costly patent litigation.

4. *More licenses.* Many of the potential patent conflicts mentioned above will end in a license. Therefore, more resources will be needed to generate these licenses. In addition, businesses will be more anxious to obtain revenue from their patents, and therefore patent professionals will be needed to help identify potential licensees and negotiate licenses.

5. *Increased efficiency.* Patent offices around the world are working to shorten the time required to examine and otherwise process patent applications. In many cases, it will be to the benefit of the applicant to get a patent issued as quickly as possible. Therefore, the applicant's patent agent will need to respond to the patent offices promptly without paying fees for extensions of time.

All of these reasons point to the need for increased staffing of intellectual property professionals to handle the increased involvement of intellectual property in the bottom line of a business. Businesses have traditionally considered such functions as support or staff functions; however, they need to consider their intellectual property as a business staffed to perform revenue generating or protecting activities. Those businesses that provide adequate resources will be better able to take advantage of the new world of intellectual property. Those that do not will miss opportunities to proactively affect the profitability of the business.

One thing that can be predicted accurately is that patents issued in many of the technology areas that only recently became patentable will be tested in the courts. Already, some biotech patents have been revoked, and some of the patents in other areas will fall also. However, it is very likely that much of what is now newly patentable will remain. These items will survive because the key to success in these new areas is not too terribly different from what has been established in the past. The key is the invention itself. The pace and number of filings may increase, as will the need for better and better patent applications, but in the final analysis success will depend on the ability of a patent application to illustrate that an inventor was truly in possession of an invention at the time of filing. This has always been a basic premise but remains the key challenge for everyone involved with obtaining patents on inventions. It is a simple but powerful idea that will be key in many patent issues to come.

References

Alter, Scott M., 'The Rest Of The Wall Comes Down: Federal Circuit Holds Software Is Freely Patentable', *Intellectual Property Today*, September 1998, pp 32–35.

Amernick, Burton, *Patent Law for the Nonlawyer: A Guide for the Engineer, Technologist and Manager*, New York: Van Nostrand Reinhold, 1986.

Ashton, W. Bradford, and Rajat K. Sen, 'Using Patent Information in Technology Business Planning – I,' *Research Technology Management*, November–December 1988, pp 42–46.

— 'Using Patent Information in Technology Business Planning – II.' *Research Technology Management*, January–February 1989, pp 36–42.

Berkowitz, Leonard, 'Dust Settling (For Now) on Patent Harmonization'. *Research Technology Management*, May–June 1994, pp 5–6.

— 'Getting The Most From Your Patents,' *Research Technology Management*, March–April 1993, pp 26–31.

Brown, Kenneth A., *Inventors At Work*, Redmond, Washington: Tempus Books of Microsoft Press, 1988.

Chatterji, Deb, and Thomas A. Manuel. 'Benefiting From External Sources of Technology.' *Research Technology Management*, November–December 1993, pp 21–26.

de Bono, Edward, *Tactics: The Art and Science of Success*. Boston: Little, Brown and Company, 1984.

Diebold, John, *The Innovators: The Discoveries, Inventions, and Breakthroughs of Our Time*, 1990; rpt. New York: Truman Talley Books/Plume, 1991.

Dunning, Edward, Burton A. Amernick, and T. Gene Dillahunty, *Patent Law for Scientists and Engineers* (Course Notes), Brunswick, New Jersey: The Center for Professional Advancement, 1990.

Erlich, Jacob N. 'Understanding Intellectual Property,' *Cooperative Technology RD&D Report*, July 1992, pp 24–31.

Faber, Robert C., *Landis on Mechanics of Patent Claim Drafting*, 3rd edn. New York: Practising Law Institute, 1990.

Farrell, Chris, 'Survival Of The Fittest Technologies,' *New Scientist*, February 6, 1993, pp 35–39.

Ferris, Timothy, ed., *The World Treasury of Physics, Astronomy & Mathematics*, Boston: Little, Brown and Company, 1991.

Flatow, Ira, *They All Laughed … From Light Bulbs to Lasers: The Fascinating Stories Behind the Great Inventions That Have Changed Our Lives*, New York: Harper Collins Publishers, 1992.

Fleming, Samual C., 'Using Technology For Competitive Advantage,' *Research Technology Management*, September–October 1991, pp 38–41.

'Former Soviet Republics Initial Pact To Create Eurasian Patent Convention,' *BNA Patent, Trademark & Copyright Law Daily*, March 11, 1994.

Friedel, Robert. 'New Light on Edison's Light,' *American Heritage of Invention & Technology*, Summer 1985, pp 23–27.

Garrett, Alfred B., *The Flash of Genius*, Princeton, New Jersey: D Van Nostrand Company, Inc., 1963.

Gilman, John J., 'Research Management Today,' *Physics Today*, March 1991, pp 42–48.

Goodman, Davis P., '30 Top Countries for Trade & Expansion,' *World Trade Magazine*, June 1999, pp 32–38.

Griffin, Gordon D., *How To Be A Successful Inventor: Turn Your Ideas Into Profit*, New York: John Wiley & Sons, 1991.

Hamermesh, Richard G., *Making Strategy Work*, New York: John Wiley & Sons, 1986.

Japanese Patent Office, *Examination Guidelines for Patent and Utility Model in Japan*, Tokyo: AIPPI JAPAN, 1994.

Kleiner, Kurt, 'Stop: Software Speed Trap Ahead,' *New Scientist*, April 24, 1994, pp 14–15.

Klimstra, Paul D., and Ann T. Raphael, 'Integrating R&D and Business Strategy,' *Research Technology Management*, January–February 1992, pp 22–28.

Maier, Gregory J., 'StateStreet Bank: Are Useful Algorithms Patentable?', *Intellectual Property Today*, March 1999, pp 18–20.

Marcy, Willard, ed., *Patent Policy: Government, Academic, and Industrial Concepts*, Washington DC: American Chemical Society, 1978.

Marino, Fabio Elia, and Michael Joel Schallop, 'A Strategic Approach to Intellectual Property Protection for Software,' *Intellectual Property Today*, February 1999, pp 8–10.

Mestel, Rosie, 'Rich Pickings for Cotton's Pioneers,' *New Scientist*, February 19, 1994, pp 13–14.

Miller, Michael W., 'Microsoft To Pay A Patent Fee In IBM Accord,' *The Wall Street Journal*, June 29, 1992, p. B1.

Morone, Joseph G., 'Technology and Competitive Advantage – The Role of General Management,' *Research Technology Management*, March–April 1993, pp 16–25.

Mulconrey, Brian G., 'Edison's Greatest Invention,' *Research Technology Management*, March–April 1993, pp 6–7.

Narin, Francis, Vincent M. Smith, Jr., and Michael B. Albert, 'What Patents Tell You About Your Competition,' *Chemtech*, February 1993, pp 52–59.

Ohmae, Kenichi, *The Mind of the Strategist*, New York: McGraw-Hill, 1982.

Pachman, Ludek, *Modern Chess Strategy* (Trans. Alan S. Russell), 1963, rpt New York: Dover Publications, 1971.

'Patent Protection in Japan: II – Causes of US Firms' Patent Problems, Effect of Firms' Patent Practices, Recent JPO Changes,' *East Asian Executive Reports*, Vol 15, No. 11, November 15, 1993, pp 6–14.

Petroski, Henry, *The Evolution of Useful Things*, New York: Alfred A. Knopf, 1993.

Pfeffer, Martin, ed., *The 54th Patent Bar Review Course* (notes), New York: Practising Law Institute, 1993.

Ransley, Derek L., and Jay L. Rogers, 'A Concensus on Best R&D Practices,' *Research Technology Management*, March–April 1994, pp. 19–26.

Rensberger, Boyce, 'As Birthrates Fall, Population Rises' (With Maps & Tables by Richard Furno), *The Washington Post*, September 4, 1994, Sec. A, pp 1, 40–41.

Robertson, Nat C., 'Technology Acquisition for Corporate Growth,' *Research Technology Management*, March–April 1992, pp 26–30.

Root-Bernstein, Robert S., 'The Discovery Process,' *Chemtech*, May 1994, pp 15–20.

Rosenberg, Peter D., *Patent Law Fundamentals*, New York: Clark Boardman Company, 1975.

Tani, Yoshikazu, 'How to Utilize the New Patent Law in Japan from Viewpoint of Applicant,' Tani & Abe (Version 1.1), 1994.

Teich, Albert H., ed., *Technology and Man's Future*, New York: St. Martin's Press, 1981.

Unkovic, Dennis, *The Trade Secrets Handbook: Strategies and Techniques for Safeguarding Corporate Information*, Englewood Cliffs, New Jersey: Prentice-Hall, 1985.

United States Department of the Army, *American Military History 1607–1958*, (ROTC Manual No. 145–20) Washington DC: U.S. Government Printing Office, 1959.

United States General Accounting Office, *Intellectual Property Rights: U.S. Companies' Patent Experiences in Japan*, GGD-93-126, July 1993.

United States Patent and Trademark Office, 'Patentable Subject Matter: Mathematical Algorithms and Computer Programs,' June 1989.

Webster's Ninth New Collegiate Dictionary, Springfield, Massachusetts: Merriam-Webster, 1989.

Wyatt, Geoffrey, *The Economics of Invention. A Study of the Determinants of Inventive Activity*, Great Britain: Wheatsheaf Books, 1986.

Further Reading

Alpert, Frank H., 'An Analysis of Patent Length: Encouraging Innovation By Shortening Patent Protection,' *Journal of Macromarketing*, Spring 1991, pp 40–45.

Amernick, Burton, 'Essentials of Patent Law,' *Journal of the National Cancer Institute*, Vol 81, No. 19, October 4, 1989, Commentary.

Arnold, Robin H., 'Pitfalls of Decentralization, or Setting the Fox to Guard the Chicken Coup,' *Research Technology Management*, May–June 1992, pp 9–11.

Arthur, Charles, 'Winners and Losers in the Invention Game,' *New Scientist*, October 5, 1991, pp 25–30.

Baird, Inga S., Marjorie A. Lyles, and J. B. Orris, 'The Choice of International Strategies By Small Businesses,' *Journal of Small Business Management*, January 1994, pp 48–59.

Breyer, Wayne S., 'Know The Basics to Protect Your Inventions,' *Chemical Engineering*, September 1993, pp 120–124.

Chaudhari, Praveen, 'Corporate R&D in the United States,' *Physics Today*, December 1993, pp 39–40.

Chester, Arthur N., 'Aligning Technology with Business Strategy,' *Research Technology Management*, January–February 1994, pp 25–32.

Coghlan, Andy, 'Truce Declared in Gene Patent War,' *New Scientist*, November 6, 1993, p 10.

Collen, Jess M., 'A ChE's Guide to Copyright Law,' *Chemical Engineering Progress*, October 1994, pp 74–78.

Coy, Peter, John Carey, and Neil Gross, 'The Global Patent Race Picks Up Speed,' *Business Week*, August 9, 1993, pp 57–62.

Das, T. K., 'Time: The Hidden Dimension in Strategic Planning,' *Long Range Planning*, Vol 24, No. 3, pp 49–57, 1991.

Dwyer, Paula, Laure Jereski, Zachary Schiller, and Dinah Lee, 'The Battle Raging Over "Intellectual Property",' *Business Week*, May 22, 1989, pp 78–89.

European Patent Office Branch At the Hague, 'Search and Documentation in the EPO,' undated.

Fox, Barry, 'Inventions That Almost Were,' *New Scientist*, November 20, 1993, pp 24–27.

Hayes, David L., and Albert C. Smith, 'What is That Patent, Trademark, of Copyright Worth?' *Chemtech*, November 1994, pp 16–20.

Heines, M. Henry, and Karen Babyak Dow, 'Proprietary Information: What Are Your Rights and Responsibilities?' *Chemical Engineering Progress*, July 1994, pp 78–84.

Helfgott, Samson, and Charles Berman, ed., *Global Intellectual Property Series 1992: Practical Strategies – Patent*, New York: Practising Law Institute, 1992.

Heyn, Ernest V., *Fire of Genius: Inventors of the Past Century*, Garden City, New York: Anchor Press/Doubleday, 1976.

Kane, Siegrun D., and Bruce W. Schwab, ed., *Global Trademark and Copyright*, New York: Practising Law Institute, 1994.

Konold, William G., Bruce Tittel, Donald F. Frei, and David S. Stallard, *What Every Engineer Should Know About Patents*, New York: Marcel Dekker, 1979.

Lee, Lim Heng, 'Scare The Competition?' *Managing Intellectual Property*, July–August 1994, pp 35–40.

Macdonald, Anne L., *Feminine Ingenuity: Women and Invention in America*, New York: Ballatine Books, 1992.

Mathis, James F., 'Turning R&D Managers Into Technology Managers,' *Research Technology Management*, January–February 1992, pp 35–38.

Maynard, John T., and Howard M. Peters, *Understanding Chemical Patents: A Guide for the Inventor*, 2nd edn, Washington DC: American Chemical Society, 1991.

Mestel, Rosie, 'Bean Patent Sweets the Field,' *New Scientist*, April 30, 1994, p 7.

Petty, Scott, 'Do Business Model Patents Provide an Unfair Competitive Advantage?', *Intellectual Property Today*, April 2000, p 28.

Petty, Scott, 'State Street Bank Fuels Boom in Business Model Patents,' *Intellectual Property Today*, April 1999, p 30.

Pous, Robert T., and Charles L. Gholz, 'Will Inter Partes Reexamination Be Embraced By Third Parties As an Alternative To Litigation?' *Intellectual Property Today*, March 1999, pp 37–41.

Prahalad, C. K., and Gary Hamel, 'The Core Competence of the Corporation,' *Harvard Business Review*, May–June 1990, pp 79–91.

Pursell, Carroll W., ed., *Technology in America*, Cambridge, Massachusetts: The MIT Press, 1981.

Racine, Richard B., Kenneth J. Nunnenkamp, and Thomas W. Banks, 'To Sue or Not to Sue?' *Chemtech*, March 1994, pp 53–57.

Richardson, Robert O., *The Weird & Wondrous World of Patents*, New York: Sterling Publishing Co, 1990.

Rose, Alan C., 'Cost Effective Protection of Intellectual Property,' *Intellectual Property Today*, January 2000, pp 15–17.

Seltzer, Richard, 'Intellectual Property Rights: Risk Cuts Flow of Investment, Technology.' *Chemical and Engineering News*, March 14, 1994, pp 6–7.

Stobbs, Gregory A., 'In Search of the First Software Patent,' *Intellectual Property Today*, November 1998, p 11.

United States Department of Commerce Patent and Trademark Office, 'Basic Facts About Patents,' Washington DC: U.S. Government Printing Office, undated.

— 'Basic Facts About Trademarks,' Washington DC: U.S. Government Printing Office, 1992.

— 'Helpful Hints from the PTO,' November 1990.

Usher, Abbott Payson, *A History of Mechanical Inventions*. Revised edn 1954; rpt New York: Dover Publications, 1988.

Vare, Ethlie Ann and Greg Ptacek, *Mothers of Invention*, New York: William Morrow and Company, Inc., 1988.

Via, Francis A., 'Hatching Good Ideas,' *Chemtech*, March 1994, pp 10–18.

Walton, Kenneth R., John P. Dismukes, and Jon E. Browning, 'An Information Specialist Joins the R&D Team,' *Research Technology Management*, September–October 1989, pp 32–37.

Williams, Jeffrey R., 'How Sustainable is Your Competitive Advantage?' *California Management Review*, Spring 1992, pp 29–51.

Wills, Stefan, and Kevin Barham, 'Being an International Manager,' *European Management Journal*, Vol 12, No. 1, March 1994, pp 49–58.

Wolff, Michael F., 'Scouting For Technology,' *Research Technology Management*, March–April 1992, pp 10–12.

Index